Reform Judaism for the Rest of Us

Alexander Maller

Reform Judaism for the Rest of Us

Faith versus Political Activism

iUniverse, Inc.
Bloomington

Reform Judaism for the Rest of Us
Faith versus Political Activism

iUniverse books may be ordered through booksellers or by contacting:

iUniverse
1663 Liberty Drive
Bloomington, IN 47403
www.iuniverse.com
1-800-Authors (1-800-288-4677)

Because of the dynamic nature of the Internet, any web addresses or links contained in this book may have changed since publication and may no longer be valid. The views expressed in this work are solely those of the author and do not necessarily reflect the views of the publisher, and the publisher hereby disclaims any responsibility for them.

ISBN: 978-1-4759-3584-4 (sc)
ISBN: 978-1-4759-3583-7 (hc)
ISBN: 978-1-4759-3582-0 (e)

Library of Congress Control Number: 2012912187

Printed in the United States of America

iUniverse rev. date: 08/13/2012

To my sons.

Contents

Preface

When inclusion is accomplished, it is done so continuously, or includes the sense of a finished act that is neither the site, the place, nor the point of view, but what remains in point of view, what occupies point of view, and without which point of view would not be. It is necessarily a soul, a subject. A soul always includes what it apprehends from *its* point of view, in other words, inflection. *Inflection is an ideal condition or a virtuality that currently exists only in the soul that envelops it.* Thus the soul is what has folds and is full of folds. [22, emphasis in the original] ... Thus God creates expressive souls only because he creates the world that they express by including it: from inflection to inclusion. 26

Gilles Deleuze, *The Fold: Leibniz and the Baroque*

I am a new "convert" to Reform Judaism. Becoming involved in the American Jewish experience led me to discover American Reform Judaism. *Reform Judaism for the Rest of Us* brings forward my personal experience in the process of understanding and becoming part of my newly found Jewish faith.

The misleading ideological vagaries that have haunted the spirit of many intellectuals in the twentieth century—Jews in particular—have left many of us confused and frustrated. As a reaction to the tragic events of the last century, many Jews regained their Jewish awareness, and like me, are trying to revive their spiritual confidence by finding inspiration in the Jewish faith. Contemporary

Judaism has a rich religious spectrum with many folds. The fold I discovered in America is Reform Judaism: an offspring of the Jewish Enlightenment, a faith that praises an open mind and an entrepreneurial and constructive approach to Judaism, recognizes the need to update religious practices, and promotes the separation between church and state.

While studying the history and opinions of my newfound religion, I became aware that radical individuals and groups that failed to fulfill their secular social agenda in the political arena have high jacked the leadership of the faith. Through convoluted interpretations of scriptures and an emphasis on the "guilt" of personal success, congregants are persuaded to support radical political causes packaged as religious messages. Much of this political agenda is dominated by failed nineteenth-century European ideologies centered on authoritarian governmental control and intervention. *Reform Judaism for the Rest of Us* exposes the fallacy of these ideologies and disputes the merit of their inclusion as part of the Reform Judaic faith.

In many ways my life experience is representative of the challenges faced by millions of European Jews in their struggle to survive and find a new spiritual life.

My parents, physicians by profession, resided in Eastern Europe. They lived their life as secular Jews and raised me as a secular Jew. To be a secular Jew appears to be a contradiction in terms, or at least a double affiliation. Being a secular Jew was neither unique nor exceptional in Eastern Europe. Conducting a secular life was the way to be accepted, to participate in the civic life, practice a profession, and build a career. Yet, a secular life did not mean assimilation or conversion to a local state religion. Essentially, the spirit that dominated twentieth-century Europe rejected Jews even when they had assimilated or converted. The militant beliefs of the first half of the century—Soviet socialism and German National Socialism—continued to use Jews, or people of Jewish origin, as subjects for hate and as scapegoats for the failures of those belief systems. By the end of the century and now into the twenty-first century, long after mass extermination and systematic persecution forced the surviving Jews to leave most European countries, the continent, virtually *Judenrein* (cleansed of Jews), is still showing perverse expressions of anti-Semitism.

Thanks to my mother's courage and wits, my parents survived the Holocaust. I was born toward the end of the Second World War and grew up in Romania in the 1950s. For us to survive in the Socialist "paradise," we had to act as loyal followers of the state-imposed Marxist-Stalinist idolatry. Still, we went to synagogue twice a year, on Passover and on Yom Kippur, and we fasted on Yom Kippur. As a child, I did not understand much of the meaning of the rituals except for the fact that they established my identity. This identity instilled in me the hope that one day we might immigrate to Israel. In their youth, my parents did not have a Zionist orientation. Some of our relatives, however, did have a Zionist inclination and managed to move early on to Israel.

Like millions in Eastern Europe at the time, we loathed the Communist spiritual and physical oppression, its incompetence and corruption, its arbitrary control of our life through various regulations applied at the discretion of the party's bureaucracy. The government's vast propaganda machine expected us to believe in an ever-receding utopian future, while imposing, in the name of "progress" and our "own good," more and more restrictions on our current life. The ultimate hypocrisy was that both the party and the public were fully aware of this big lie. To ensure their control of the population, the agents of the regime provoked attempts to criticize the regime and then immediately isolated critics and accused them of treason and other crimes. This simple method enabled the regime to impose deep mass fear and terror to which even children adapted at an early age.

In the late 1950s, through a fortunate congruence of circumstances—and once again, my mother's courage—we were able to narrowly escape Romania for Israel. We could not believe our luck until we actually landed in Vienna, Austria.

Being a secular Jew in Israel meant being part of the majority of the public and being a free person. My Judaism was enhanced by learning about the Jewish heritage and its connection to the land. The noticeable Jewish contribution to world culture made me proud to be a Jew. My newly gained Jewish identity did not require me to enhance my religiosity. I had the privilege throughout my career to meet some distinguished *Haredi* and *Masorti* rabbis and intellectuals for whom I have great respect and appreciation to this day. Still, I did not feel that I was well suited to their strict observant life. My childhood history of aversion to an obedience imposed by a top-down leadership, whose authority appeared to be indisputable, was probably one inherent reason for distancing myself instinctively from the Orthodox religious establishment. Also, my secular upbringing made me skeptical about traditional prescripts that may have made sense in the past but were irrelevant in the present. Following these many rules according to a ritual and mandatory conformity offered little spiritual or practical meaning for me.

My new life in the United States gave me the opportunity to discover new interpretations of the Jewish identity. My identity as a secular Jew served me well as long as I did not concern myself with my spiritual identity. When my sons showed interest in their Jewish identity as they were growing up, I realized that I had reached a stage in life where I could guide all three of us through a journey of self-discovery with regard to our Judaic affiliation.

For the first time, living in America, I could find faith-oriented Jewish denominations whose religious orientations were close to my beliefs. I joined a Conservative temple in Lincoln, Nebraska, which offered a welcoming approach and seemed well suited to lead my older son into his bar mitzvah. Yet, as a divorced father of two boys, preoccupied with my academic career, I had little energy to become involved in the essence of the faith.

Years later, in St. Petersburg, Florida, I met my future wife, Carol. She had been born and raised in midtown Manhattan. Her father was a distinguished physician and medical researcher and her mother a gifted musician and inveterate New Yorker. Carol's history struck me as a very American version of my own background. Her parents lived a secular life and did not introduce their children to any Jewish tradition, though they never denied their Jewish origin. Carol was enrolled in a private girls' school in Manhattan, where she was admitted because of special connections and as part of a Jewish quota. She attended prestigious colleges and developed a remarkable business career. She was a product of the 1960s, a secular Jew who knew very little about her Jewish heritage but was very aware of the ethos of mid-twentieth-century America.

It was probably on our second date that I took Carol to Kol Nidre services at a Reform temple in St. Petersburg on Erev Yom Kippur. It was a complete and quite shocking surprise for her, since she had never attended any Jewish service, much less those on High Holy Days in a synagogue.

A few years later, we moved to Easton, Massachusetts. As newcomers to a new town, we applied the common American approach and looked for a suitable local congregation. We found Temple Chayai Shalom and its friendly congregation. The temple had a small choir. Carol loved choral singing and here was her great opportunity. She had no clue about the ritual and did not know

Hebrew at all, but the music and the singing connected her to the liturgy and heritage she had been denied as a child. The temple was contemplating building an addition, so I found that being an architect, I could become useful on the building committee. Soon we made friends in the congregation and became active members.

In addition to our activity in the temple, I became involved in the civic life of Easton. As an architect and urbanist, I was delighted to discover the beauty of this amazing New England town, an outstanding example of country living. Easton has a few remarkable buildings designed by the great American architect H. H. Richardson and gardens designed by the noted landscape architect F. L. Olmsted. Its townscape follows the configurations of the land and history, all immersed in a rich leafy vegetation. Its physical features were matched only by the excitement of its quintessential New England town hall meetings, with their long deliberations and the tenacity of the participants. I was quite amazed that, as a newcomer, a stranger to the area in many ways, I was well accepted and encouraged to participate in the town's affairs and social life. It appeared to me that our adjustment to our new community took a natural turn, reminding me of a smooth ride in a good old American car. Gone were the convolutions and drama of the Old Continent, with its little funky Fiats or quirky Beetles.

Prior to our arrival in Easton, the congregation had hired a new rabbi. The new rabbi was a recently ordained young woman, attractive, personable, and dedicated to her service. I believe that she had the ability to choose from a wide range of careers, yet she chose to be a rabbi. She quickly demonstrated strong spiritual leadership and a noticeable savvy in the politics of the congregation and the community. The year was 2008 and the frenzy of the national political battles did not bypass Easton. As a follower of politics all my life, I admired her ability to balance the political debate without taking sides. She managed to keep the temple above the political strife, while effectively cooperating with a quite assertive lay leadership. Her spirit and leadership were a revelation that I had not previously witnessed in my Jewish experience.

In my youth, my spiritual struggle against the Socialist evil had been symbolized by Delacroix's portrait of young Marianne, storming the barricades while waving the French flag and holding a rifle. Now my spiritual faith was epitomized by the young Reform rabbi from Temple Chayai Shalom in Easton, who inspired us from the pulpit. This is how I became interested in Reform Judaism.

Acknowledgments

The inspiration for this book came initially from the sermons and teachings of Rabbi Jodi Seewald Smith at Temple Chayai Shalom in Easton, Massachusetts, and extensively from Rabbi Emeritus Raymond Zwerin, Rabbi Rick Rheins, and Rabbi Jay TelRav at Temple Sinai in Denver, Colorado. The open-minded discussions and debates during the adult education sessions at Temple Sinai exposed me to the rich thinking of Reform Judaism. I also must express my gratitude to the members of our congregation who participated in the discussions, provided informative insight on the thinking of our rank and file, and stimulated me to write this book.

Special thanks to Rabbi Rheins for introducing me to the writings of Eugene B. Borowitz and Michael A. Meyer, which provided me an initial in-depth understanding of the tenets and heritage of Reform Judaism.

I owe special gratitude to Rabbi Emeritus Raymond Zwerin for taking the time and having the patience to review the draft manuscript. His comments and challenging questions helped me clarify my thoughts and significantly improved the content of this book.

And a final "thank-you" to my wife Carol, who has provided steady encouragement and support in the research and writing of this book and has brought excitement and joy to our newfound faith.

Introduction

"The Jews" are exiled, scattered, oppressed, and assimilated on this scene, but they don't belong to it. They belong to the Covenant with the Other that is promised and registered in the Book. This is the resistance that has to be annihilated, that must not stop being forgotten because it has never stopped being "present" to metaphysical Europe as what it hasn't been and will not be able to say, as the impotency of its potency. This resistance simply mumbles: the Other is prior to the Self.

Jean-Francois Lyotard, *Postmodern Fables*[1]

Is Reform Judaism in a crisis?[2] What is the nature of the crisis? Modern Jewish denominations seem to have been confronted with various crises since emerging from the eighteenth-century Jewish Enlightenment.[3] It is worth noticing that reform, as a notion, is the result of a crisis; hence our denomination reflects well the innovative and competitive spirit of modern times. We are living now in a new era with new and challenging agendas. Is Reform Judaism prepared for and equipped to answer these challenges?

By sharing the Jewish heritage with an increasingly educated public, reformation offered to replace obedience to tradition with an open discourse about the Jewish heritage and a voluntary affiliation to Judaism. This process evolved over two centuries, resulting in a vibrant involvement of Jewish individuals and groups in the modern discourse that shaped Reform Judaism, the foundation and

1

realization of the Zionist dream, and more recently, a constructive reconsideration of the relations between Christianity and Judaism. Can these achievements continue to inspire us to reach future suitable venues of faith for Reform Judaism?

Initially I thought to title this book *In Defense of Reform Judaism*. Research on the topic convinced me that Reform Judaism does not need to be either defended or defensive. Reform Judaism is a unique, original, and resourceful Jewish denomination whose real power and depth has yet to be revealed.

Reform Judaism has evolved into an authentic American religious denomination that can distinguish itself from its Judaic origins and other Jewish religious denominations in three ways:

1. It incorporates the American interpretation of the Enlightenment in its Jewish divine faith-based spiritual culture.
2. It is a grassroots denomination that encourages individual initiative and nurtures a diversity of Jewish faith-based ideas.
3. It promises to provide a Judaic vision responsive to the emerging culture of the twenty-first century, a vision that redefines in modern terms being Jewish and Judaism.

Reform Judaism proposed the most ambitious and radical platforms for the revision of Judaism and played a major role in shaping events and opinions in the non-Orthodox Jewish world, in particular in the United States. Like most revolutionary movements, Reform Judaism has had its share of failures and mistakes, but it has also opened new spiritual horizons in Judaism. It is for these reasons that I have chosen to focus, from the perspective of a lay person, on Reform concepts and promises and consider their implications for the future.

Reform Judaism for the Rest of Us is not an elaborate historical analysis of the events and opinions that have shaped Reform Judaism, nor is it an attempt to challenge theological doctrines. The main focus of this work is to clarify positions, elucidate contradictions, and invite answers for the future. Any opinions expressed in this publication are personal reflections on developments in Reform Judaism and most definitely open for discussion.

Traditional *Tanachic* Judaism emerged, by design, as a nation-building religion that evolved and adjusted itself over centuries through dialogue and interpretation. European Reform Judaism expanded the inherited discursive tools, commentary, and interpretation of the Jewish heritage into aggressive, transformative means of reflection and expression, while incorporating ideas of the Enlightenment, the French Revolution, the Industrial Revolution, and some revolutionary social ideas of the nineteenth century.

The transformation of the Jewish Reform movement from its European religious roots into an American phenomenon is traceable to the unique and exceptional historic and constitutional conditions provided by the United States. These conditions included the following: freedoms, such as freedom of speech and freedom of religion; American public practices based on grassroots popular organizations governed according to checks and balances and intended to express and safeguard the interest "of the people, by the people, for the people"; and the conscientious and voluntary adoption of the separation between church and state authorities. Reform Judaism emerged and evolved as a genuine response to these conditions.

The first two chapters of this work are dedicated to a brief discussion of the sources and history of Reform Judaism in the last two centuries, initially in Europe and later in the United States. It is my belief that the historic context provides a useful source for the understanding of factors and events that shaped current Reform Judaism. Chapters 3 through 6 address tenets of Reform Judaism such as faith in the Almighty, pride in the Jewish heritage, separation of church and state, and grassroots governance in reference to current circumstances in the United States. Chapters 7, 8, and 9 debate political platforms included in the official agenda of the national movement, with a specific focus on notions such as "repairing the world," "social action," and "social justice." Chapters 10 through 13 reflect on the family spirit of Reform Judaism, its views on education, its rituals and practices, and the Reform sense of belonging and the pursuit of happiness. Chapter 14, entitled "The Fraternal Dispute," details some aspects of the historical divisions between Reform Judaism and Zionism and offers options to bridge the differences. The last two chapters provide a personal vision of the opportunities Reform Judaism can offer—now and into the foreseeable future—to individuals and congregations.

Members of our congregations expect to find in Reform Judaism rewarding religious activities, inspired rituals, practices and studies, educational enrichment, charitable activities, and a dignified active interfaith dialogue. These are core activities that sustain the grassroots nature of our movement. There is past and present evidence of attempts made by individual leaders, think tanks, and self-appointed national bureaucracies to advocate and impose agendas that have been and are disputed by grassroots constituencies. The current intense advocacy of politically loaded platforms, such as *Tikkun Olam* (repairing the world), social action, social justice, the "green" agenda, and socialized health care, promoted by the national leadership and some of its affiliated organizations, such as the Religious Action Center, are increasingly controversial. Upon careful consideration, these assertions, proclaimed as national agendas, which some consider lacking religious content, may contradict the tenets of Reform Judaism and endanger the faith-based status of our congregations. Assertive, uncompromising positions can become sources of conflict and have and will undermine the integrity of the movement, its open-minded spirit, and its grassroots orientation. A division between the national leadership and the rank-and-file membership and their congregations harms the vitality, the credibility, and ultimately the promises of the Reform movement. In my opinion, the current situation mandates an urgent need for an improved, enlightened, open-minded, and inclusive American Reform Judaism, unencumbered by the defunct ideologies of the nineteenth and twentieth centuries.

It is my belief that the historic goal of Reform Judaism remains the reformation of our faith to effectively address the issues of the modern era. This book is directed to active members of congregations, rabbis, and potential new members in search of a religious experience suitable to our time.

In the course of developing this book, I was inspired by a diverse range of sources, many of which I cite. Shmuel Feiner's book, *The Jewish Enlightenment*, was a valuable source for understanding the roots of Reform Judaism in the Jewish Enlightenment. Michael A. Meyer's seminal history of the Reform movement, *Response to Modernity*, provided a critical orientation to the intricate evolution of the movement, especially in the United States. Eugene B. Borowitz's extensive commentary on the 1976 "Centenary Perspective" of the Central Conference of American Rabbis, developed in his book *Reform Judaism Today*, was a comforting and inspirational source for the writing of this book. A variety of additional sources, directly or indirectly related to the topic, helped me analyze and understand the complexities of Reform Judaism and the Jewish reformation. I found this eclectic approach useful, as it provided me with multiple tools for understanding the intricacies of the material under discussion.

My research also included an array of publications disseminated by various organizations affiliated with the Reform movement and the Jewish press.

A glossary is provided at the end of the book and is intended to clarify my understanding of terms used in the text and to reduce common confusions in the public's interpretation of these terms.

Finally, I believe that the passion and urgency that drove me to research and write *Reform Judaism for the Rest of Us* is shared by many of my colleagues in faith. The dramatic events that engulfed Jews in the last century make me believe that we can and must shape our fate, survival, and strength. Reform Judaism can be an inspiring vehicle in our survival and success. The intrinsic tenets of Reform Judaism have placed the spirit of the individual member and the commitments of congregations at the center of our faith, a faith which is an integral part of the American culture and civilization.

Notes

1. "The Earth Had No Roads to Begin With," in Jean-Francois Lyotard, *Postmodern Fables* (Minneapolis, MN: Univ. of Minnesota Press, 1997), 110.

2. Concerns about the vitality and survival of the movement have been the topic of recent publications such as these: David Ellenson, "Reform Judaism Isn't an Island," Opinion, *Jewish Daily Forward*, March 25, 2011, posted March 16, 2011, at http://forward.com/articles/136236/reform-judaism-isn-t-an-island/; Josh Nathan-Kazis, "Liberal Denominations Face Crisis as Rabbis Rebel, Numbers Shrink," *Jewish Daily Forward*, February 18, 2011. Peter Weidhorn reflected on the sense of crisis in the movement in his "Chairman's Perspective" in the 2011 Spring issue of *Reform Judaism*.

3. A historic perspective of the crisis mode in which our movement performs was provided by Michael A. Meyer in his article, "History: Confronting Crisis," *Reform Judaism*, Fall 2009.

Chapter 1: Jewish Reformation—The European Experience:

Enlightenment, Extremism, and Exhaustion

Be a Jew in your home and a man outside it.

J. L. Gordon

The collapse of Israel's political independence was once regarded as a misfortune, but it really represented progress, not atrophy but an elevation of religion. Henceforth Israel came closer to its destiny. Holy devotion replaced sacrifices. Israel was to bear the word of God to all corners of the earth.

David Einhorn[1]

European Reform Judaism emerged as a result of major cultural developments that occurred in Europe in the seventeenth and eighteenth centuries, a period recognized as the late Renaissance and the Age of Enlightenment. Elites in European states recaptured the Classical heritage and embarked on a reconstruction of Classical values in the political and social context of the time. It was in the same period that major Christian denominations reached a considerable consolidation in their relations to the sovereign monarchies that divided Europe.

Jews were discriminated against or tolerated in different states following a tradition whose roots were in the Middle Ages. In

7

Western Europe, if tolerated, Jews were confined to separate urban enclaves, ghettos. In parts of Eastern Europe, Jews were allowed to live in rural communities, with reduced access to land ownership and economic opportunities. In spite of their isolation and limited resources, Jewish communities survived and were able to preserve their identity and develop distinct cultural values.

Inspired by the Classical revival, the intellectual Enlightenment of the eighteenth century became interested in the situation of the Jewish communities, an interest that opened opportunities for educated Jews to become involved in dialogues with Christian thinkers. For us to understand the evolution of the changes that occurred in the Jewish thinking, we need to take a closer look at the living conditions of Jewish communities in Europe in the Renaissance period and beyond.

The Renaissance was the age that witnessed an extensive flourishing of urban living. In many parts of Europe, cities were the most active and prosperous communities and were emerging as power brokers in the regional political struggles. The city's driving force was a combination of commerce, crafts (later industry), and to a certain extent, finance. The city was a hub for regional services, with some cities developing a regional and international outreach through services and alliances. City-dwellers, otherwise known as burgers or the bourgeoisie, managed to evolve from the Middle Ages as a distinct civilization that competed with the two other powerful communities: the landed aristocracy and the Christian religious establishment.[2]

The bourgeoisie was not homogeneous; it included a diverse population with a wide range of economic, cultural, and even ethnic groups. Poor and rich, merchants and craftsman, educated and illiterate, homeowners and homeless, residents and transients all mixed together within the confinements of the city's walls. In general terms, urban living was characterized by its dynamic need to negotiate improvement and change. Western European Jews, who as a group were prevented from being accepted into the established classes, found refuge in cities where the bourgeoisie was occasionally more open to diversity.[3]

Aristocracy and clergy could be defined as "classes" due to their "sanctified" entitled status, rigid structure, and inherited privileges. The aristocracy depended on inherited land ownership, while the clergy relied on its sanctified status, income from land rents, and charitable donations. The well-being of the bourgeoisie was conditioned on the results of the work performed by its members and the success of the transactions between individuals and organized groups. Because of its diversity and mobility, to define the bourgeoisie as a class—middle or otherwise—is wrong. Rather, it is a distinct civilization: the living element of cities, from ancient cities lost in the fog of history to contemporary cities, a complex and often misunderstood civilization. Different from aristocracy and clergy, the bourgeoisie can be defined as a human congregation of "city dwellers practicing an honored profession or owning a business or functioning at a managerial level in someone else's enterprise, including governmental and nonprofit enterprises."[4] For ruling elites, confident in their established order, the chaotic urban living appeared strange, unreliable, and threatening.

The continuing and complex competitions for regional power between factions of the aristocracy, between monarchy and church, and between the Catholic Church and the Lutheran Reformation, offered cities and alliances of cities the opportunity to become partners in this agitated political arena. Well-established cities could provide financial resources, armies, and physical presence as fortified bastions of power. In parts of Europe, such as the Low Countries, the Italian peninsula, and Central Europe, alliances of cities became strong enough to assert their independence and establish distinct states, able to defend themselves from kings and church.

At the same time, absolute monarchies attempted to unify their different power components into one political entity controlled by the royal authority. The absolute kingdom strove to control every aspect of the state, including its religious life. Even successful absolute monarchs such as France's Louis XIV had to be on constant alert to internal and external competing powers. As part of the absolute state, cities still had a considerable degree of autonomy. So long as cities paid their dues and did not rebel, their populations were left to govern themselves.[5]

In the late Renaissance period, Jews were gradually allowed to return to parts of Western Europe. The shelter granted to Jews in medieval cities conditioned Jews in exile to develop their own bourgeois civilization. As a tolerated minority, often reduced to practice very limited activities in segregated parts of town, Jews were the subject of abuse and discrimination. Monarchy and aristocracy, in their power struggle, used Jews for financial purposes and forced them into usury, positioning Jews in precarious situations that exacerbated the competitive relations between Gentile and Jewish bourgeoisies.[6]

In Western Europe, Jews were prohibited from owning land or making a living out of agriculture or industry. They were excluded from any political debates or governance of cities and were prohibited to bear arms or organize in any form of power grouping. Initially, Jews were confined to providing financial services and some professional services, such as medicine and commerce. Jewish rituals and celebrations were restricted to the indoors only, and places of worship, if permitted, were not allowed to exhibit religious distinction in their architecture or messaging.

In Eastern Europe, particularly in Poland, the situation was somehow different. Because of the predominance of the feudal system, starting in the fourteenth century Jews were able to gain a degree of business autonomy, as tax collectors and land managers, and later to gain the right to own land. As a result they developed certain political self-governance.[7]

In spite of their dire conditions, Jewish communities in Western Europe managed to consolidate and to a certain extent even thrive economically and culturally. Paradoxically, the isolation of the Jewish population into ghettos facilitated their survival in two ways.

The Jewish ghetto, separated from the surrounding communities, operated as a "state in state" or "city in the city" autonomous authority. Essentially, it provided a physical enclave that allowed the Jewish population to develop and maintain a distinct and cohesive community based on Jewish laws and traditions. Its activities were regulated by *Torah* and *Talmud*—inspired regulation, led and implemented by rabbis. In principle, the rabbinic authority was based on erudition in Jewish jurisprudence and community leadership. It was a theocratic society sustained by the public respect for the rabbi's wisdom, knowledge, and teaching. The rabbinic authority was absolute, including the assignment of penalties and even excommunications.

On the other hand, as part of the overall urban fabric, ghetto residents could take advantage of transportation and information services as well as commercial and manufacturing amenities a city provided to all its residents. By congregating voluntarily into Jewish quarters or by being confined to ghettos, Jews became city dwellers par excellence and developed urban skills and community characteristics of urban living. The Jewish bourgeoisie was not much different in its profile from the Gentile bourgeoisie: there were rich and poor groups, merchants and craftsmen, educated and illiterate, homeowners and tenants. The household was patriarchic and included an extended family and helpers. In most cases the ghetto life, by following the *mitzvoth* (rules) of the *Halacha* (the Jewish law) and rabbinical leadership, was more regulated and disciplined than the life in the adjacent city, inspiring certain admiration, respect, and possible envy from their Gentile neighbors.

In one significant sense, Jewish urban living was different from that of its Gentile neighbors: Jewish life and property were under constant threat from the capricious interests of rulers and the greed of urban mobs. At any time, Jews could be deprived of their property, expelled, or killed with little defense, judicial or otherwise.

Because of their limited civic rights and vulnerable existence, Jews survived by becoming a mobile community with an international network based on the Jewish Diaspora. In other words, the living conditions of the Jewish communities created a separate transcontinental culture. The Jewish Diaspora shared a basic international common denominator: a constitutional allegiance (the *Tanach*), a judicial tradition (the Halacha), and a cultural base, the Jewish heritage. This shared heritage, in its continental and global spread, provided a bond between all Jewish communities, which did not have a parallel in the Christian communities. In good times this bond helped to conduct long-distance transactions. In bad times, it provided venues and destinations to escape persecution. The dependency on shared heritage determined that the most respected individual in the Jewish community was the scholar, and most often, in particular, the rabbi.

Already in the fourteenth century and to a greater extent as the Renaissance progressed, the wealthy bourgeoisie, as an expression of their autonomy, supported education and research separate from the knowledge and teachings provided by the religious establishments. New universities were established in Italian and German cities as well as in England and Poland. Jewish rabbis and scholars became well aware of this intellectual and academic development. Initially, the Jewish establishment was ambivalent and suspicious of this lay education. Strong urbanization and a more liberal attitude toward Judaism allowed Italian Jewish communities to engage earlier in adopting the new education.[8] Some Central European rabbis encouraged gifted young followers to attend universities. Other rabbis remained doubtful of the benefit such education could provide to the Jewish community at large.

The establishment of the Christian Reformation and more efficient and cost-effective mass communications—the printing process—already had popularized the Old and New Testaments in native languages. Christian popular opinion, while gaining a better understanding of Judaism, asserted that since a considerable amount of biblical content was perceived as being common with Christianity, Jews should convert and join the mainstream of Christian beliefs. Such a conversion would supposedly eliminate the exclusion and oppression of the Jews.

By the end of the seventeenth century and mostly in the eighteenth century, a new kind of Jewish intellectual emerged, the *maskilim*, meaning in Hebrew, the educated people. The maskilim were educated in both academia and Jewish institutions. The maskilim emerged not only because of improved living conditions but also because of a more open access for Jews to academic institutions. Inspired by the most representative and well-known Jewish personality of that period, the brilliant rabbi and German philosopher Moses Mendelssohn, and encouraged by some notes of tolerance toward the Jewish population from the state establishments, the maskilim attempted to merge the Jewish heritage with the emerging knowledge. They also were active in reviving the public use of the Hebrew language, its aesthetic and its subtle meanings, its imagery and poetry, its mysticism and humanity.

Mendelssohn was able to initiate and inspire the perception that Jews could be loyal and effective subjects of king and state while proudly practicing their Jewish faith. He wrote in *Jerusalem*:

13

Let everybody be permitted to speak as he thinks, to invoke God after his own manner or that of his fathers, and to seek eternal salvation where he thinks he may find it, as long as he does not disturb public felicity and acts honestly toward the civil laws, toward you and his fellow citizens.[9]

The enlightened spirit of the eighteenth century presented and brought into public debate a more tolerant approach toward Jews, especially those who accepted the modernization of the Jewish education and lifestyle.[10] This new spirit was not devoid of criticism and controversy. Voltaire made famous his criticism of Judaism using secular and rationalist arguments.[11] Challenges to Moses Mendelssohn to justify his Jewish faith, brought by the pastor J. C. Lavater and later by the writer and satirist A. Cranz in an effort to convert Mendelssohn, are vivid examples of the intensity of the debate.[12]

The Jewish Enlightenment expanded mostly within the Jewish communities of Central Europe. Central Europe covered a significant part of the continent, from the shores of the Nordic and Baltic seas to the Alps and the Carpathian mountains. This territory was divided into many states but shared a common cultural component, the German language. The political and religious diversity of the region offered opportunities for Jews to be accepted and set roots in many cities and states in the region, with various degrees of civil rights. The emancipation granted to Jews by the new European spirit enabled Jews to fully assimilate in the surrounding society and later convert. Gradually, emancipated Jewish intellectuals, professional practitioners, and merchants were accepted into the elite circles of Berlin, Hamburg, or Vienna.[13]

Jewish opposition to the Jewish Enlightenment was located mostly in the periphery of the German area of influence and was prevalent in Eastern European communities where the Western Enlightenment was out of reach. A prolonged *Kulturkampf* (culture war) emerged between Jewish traditionalists, who defended the intact preservation of the Jewish heritage, and scholars of the Jewish Enlightenment, who advocated modern interpretations. The new knowledge appeared to contradict and refute parts of the accepted Jewish norms. The hidden agenda steering the dispute was the fear that the new knowledge and its promoters might undermine rabbinical authority and the Jewish establishment. Such subversion was viewed as encouraging assimilation and conversion to Christianity, hence endangering the very existence of the Jewish faith and the Jewish people.[14]

The political and cultural events that emerged in the eighteenth century brought rapid and significant changes to the overall European situation. The European Enlightenment became increasingly critical of the role played by religion in public and private life. Many intellectual leaders started to advocate a separation between church and state. This was an explosive concept. By the end of the eighteenth century, freedom *from* religion was one of the key messages of the French and European revolutionary aristocracy and bourgeoisie. The changes brought by the French Revolution and the Napoleonic conquests were broad and comprehensive, including constitutional, political, and socioeconomic issues that conditioned new ways of life not only in Europe but also globally.

The period generally defined as the nineteenth century can be framed, in Europe, by two historic events: the French Revolution and the First World War. The period included between these two events was characterized by an extraordinary explosion of major achievements in every human domain: cultural, political, economic, industrial, and more. Literacy and academic education drastically expanded, especially in urban areas, with the greatest increase in the German-speaking states. During this time, empires were built, industry and commerce boomed, and transport leaped into mechanization with major continental consequences. Liberal laissez-faire capitalism pushed industrial development into unprecedented achievements, commerce expanded considerably in its volumes of exchange and revenues, and new financial instruments were developed to address the expanding economy. While branching out globally, the European players continued their political struggle on the Old Continent. It was a period of high turmoil, with vigorous and extreme controversies that often became violent on local and international levels. The century was marred by rebellions, revolutions, and wars.

The French Revolution propagated the principle of freedom *from* religion and secular affiliation. This concept of freedom from religion intended to remove religion from the civic debate. In reality, it had an opposite effect. The humanism and enlightenment of the eighteenth century receded and was replaced by the Jacobin revolutionary extremism and anti-revolutionary reactions. Traditional religions were pushed into opposition to secular society, while secular groups defended their positions with zeal and often transformed their opinions into beliefs of religious posture and intensity. In the nineteenth century, Romantic hope—well symbolized by Byron and Beethoven—as well as Hegel's nationalistic philosophy on one hand and anarchist and Socialist groups on the other hand, became the political forces of the century. In retrospect we can view the convolutions of the nineteenth century as the last struggle between the emerging power of the urban, industrial capitalistic civilization and the "old regime" of aristocratic land owners, with its basis in the agricultural economy.

Prominent nineteenth-century thinkers proclaimed the "death of God" (F. Nietzsche) or disqualified religion, labeling it "the opium of the people" (K. Marx). The demise of Divinity did not diminish the conflicts dividing Europe; in many cases it exacerbated them. In the nineteenth century, the European continent restructured into nation states according to national heritages, most often based on religious foundation. The bourgeoisie splintered into various intellectual advocacies favoring civil life, while at the same time it adhered to traditional local religious affiliations. Religious discrimination was not eliminated but rather was redefined with new and more complex priorities.

In Western Europe, Jews gradually gained emancipation and civil rights, and ghetto walls started to be removed. The first German ghetto walls were removed in Bonn as early as 1798. In the early nineteenth century, Jews in France received civic rights as part of the Napoleonic legislation separating church from state.[15]

In the second half of the century, politicians of Jewish origin began to gain recognition and prominence. Jews enrolled in the armies fighting Napoleon and fought in liberation armies and revolutions in Italy and in provinces of the Austrian Empire. The Baron Rothschild helped Prince Metternich escape the wrath of revolutionaries. Jews helped Bismarck in the unification of Germany and participated enthusiastically in the war against Napoleon III. In the latter part of the century, individuals of Jewish origin reached positions of high distinction in both Britain (Disraeli, Montefiori, Isaacs) and Italy (Luzzatti, Ottolenghi, Sonnino).

On the other hand, Jewish success raised envy among Christians and caused them to question the impact these Jewish circles had on their Christian society. One consequence of Jewish visibility and leadership in national affairs was the emergence of anti-Semitism all over Europe.[17] One source of state-originated anti-Semitism was in Russia, which vacillated between liberalization and absolute power; between Czar Alexander II's attempts for modernization, which included a liberal policy toward Jews, and the resistance of the aristocracy to accept that process. Again, as part of the nationalistic sentiment emerging in many countries, Jews became scapegoats and targets for defamation based on prejudice and fabrications, such as the *Protocols of the Elders of Zion* in Russia and the Dreyfus Affair in France.

Germany presented a complex and diverse situation. The general tendency of the authorities was to assimilate their Jewish communities and ultimately convert them. The policies intended to achieve this goal varied from state to state. In some states, such as Prussia and Bavaria, restrictions were imposed on reformative initiatives. In other states, such as Baden or Saxe-Weimar, reforms were encouraged and even forced.[17] Many anticipated that Judaism would follow one of the two directions, either Orthodox seclusion or complete disintegration and assimilation into either the Christian faith or the secular movement. This anticipation was wrong. The most significant result was the emergence of the Reform movement, with its center of gravity in the German-speaking states.

On July 17, 1810, the first official Reform temple was inaugurated in Seesen, in the Kingdom of Hannover (today Lower Saxony, Germany) by Israel Jacobson, a local lay leader and businessman. In Berlin and in Hamburg, new Reform congregations emerged. A new generation of preachers and Reform rabbis educated in Jewish studies and lay universities found opportunities to express themselves and envision careers from the pulpit. It is worth noticing that the notion of "Reform" Judaism was not enunciated until the middle of the century by Ignaz Einhorn (1825–1875), the radical rabbi of the Pest Reform Association in Hungary.[18] The significance of the emergence of the Reform movement was not so much in its size, which remained quite limited, but in its concept: to expand Judaism, beyond its Medieval traditions and the compliance of the Jewish Enlightenment to king and country, into a distinct Jewish denomination relevant to the emerging revolutionary thinking of the time.

Reformist thinkers covered a wide range of ideas and considerations that had to mitigate between the tenets of traditional Judaism, state regulations and Christian sensitivities, the impact of new philosophical schools of thought, and economic survival. For many, these ideas seemed to provide the justification for the reformation and its distinction from traditional Judaism. Lay thinkers such as L. Zunz (1794–1886), S. L. Steinheim (1789–1866), and S. Fromstecher (1808–1889) and rabbis with an education in non-Jewish studies such as S. R. Hirsh (1808–1888) and Z. Frankel (1801–1875), along with maskilim such as I. B. Levinsohn (1788–1860) and J. Perle (1773–1839), started to address the emerging thinking of the nineteenth century and its implication for Judaism. In order to address the suspicions of local rulers and obtain permission for their activities, lay and religious Reform leaders initially formulated their practices in cautious terms such as "improvements" rather than radical changes.[19] In addition to changes in content, Reform congregations also emphasized the importance of decorum in the performance of religious rituals. In time, encouraged and influenced by the radicalization of thinking in the non-Jewish world, some rabbis and preachers, most notably I. N. Manheimer and D. Einhorn, became involved in supporting extreme political causes, adopted radical activism, and participated in the revolutions that swept Europe.[20]

Much of the success of the new Reform leaders, preachers, and rabbis was due to their rhetorical ability and the level of excitement they could raise in their audience. This phenomenon was nurtured by an increasing number of Jewish intellectuals educated in modern universities, who were prevented by discriminatory regulations to pursue academic careers or join the civil service. The remaining alternatives were in Jewish communities interested in modern spiritual leadership. The frustration of these intellectuals with the establishments that dominated Central Europe may have been an additional impetus for Jewish Reform preachers to advocate radical social action and political revolution.

Nothing better represents the struggle of Jewish Reform intellectuals in the nineteenth century than the personality and career of Abraham Geiger (1801–1875), one of the most influential spiritual Reform leaders.[21] Geiger grew up in an observant family in Frankfurt am Main, which provided him with an intensive Jewish education. He later moved to study Classical and Oriental languages in the highly regarded University of Heidelberg. From there he moved to the University of Bonn to study philosophy and history. Historian Michael A. Meyer emphasizes that

> Geiger would have preferred to become a university professor rather than to be split, internally and externally, between the conflicting feelings and roles of the writer of critical essays, that could undermine accepted beliefs and practices, and the practicing rabbi who spoke of preservation and unity in his weekly sermons and apologetic writings. He argued for the establishment of a Jewish theological faculty at a leading university. But in the anti-Jewish atmosphere of nineteenth-century Germany his efforts and those of others met no success.[22]

The resistance of the German establishment to accept outstanding intellectuals such as Geiger is reminiscent of the King of Prussia's humiliating rejection of Moses Mendelssohn's admission to the Royal Academy. The difference here was that while Mendelssohn was stopped only as a last resort, the nineteenth-century German intellectual milieu generally was not receptive of Jewish intellectuals on most levels of employment, in particular in the civil service and academia.

The diversity of ideas and opinions gathering at the intersection between Judaism and modern thinking became one hallmark of Reform Judaism. The fact that these debates somehow bypassed states' control provided Reform Judaism with a sense of intrinsic autonomy that would become a fundamental factor in the development of the movement. The dependence of the spiritual leaders on the support of lay benefactors—and the occasional intervention of these lay leaders in determining the preferred direction of a congregation—established another characteristic pattern of the Reform practice: dual leadership.

Arduous debates between spiritual leaders, the significant role played by local lay leaders, and the interference of state authorities prevented the establishment of formal Reform regional networks among congregations. The factual separation between congregations and their geographic dispersion ultimately enhanced the sense of autonomy and diversity adopted by the Reform congregations.

In Eastern Europe (Poland, Russia), Reform made little progress. Entrenched Orthodox leadership and strong suspicion from local and regional lay and Christian authorities limited the expansion of Reform Judaism in its Western—German—format.

Viewing Judaism at the end of the nineteenth century, one sees it did not escape the convoluted intellectual spirit of that century. Emancipation was imposed from the top down on the Jewish public, in the name of freedom from religion, support of secularism, and disdain to Divinity. Ideas advocated by French intellectual elites, initiated by Jacobin revolutionary leaders, and implemented by Napoleonic policies, were adopted by rulers who were supportive of Napoleonic ruling and later by rulers who were its opponents. The expectation was that Jewish communities would conform to the edicts. Some rulers adopted tolerance, others adopted force.

In true European tradition, elitism dominated the intellectual and political environment. The reaction of the public remained unacknowledged or was manipulated to follow top-down policies. Some segments of the public were receptive to the assimilation of Jews with the expectation that this would bring ultimate conversion.

In states where Jewish assimilation and conversion were high, some nationalistic and Christian religious establishments seemed more comfortable with traditional Jewish communities, which were known and controllable entities, rather than the new, emerging, competitive, and unchartered Jewish enlightened elite.[23] This resistance to assimilation was also nurtured by continuous and vehement opposition to Reform from Orthodox and traditional Jewish rabbinic elites and establishments. Some of the Jewish opponents to Reform did not hesitate to solicit local state or city authorities to interfere and restrict reformative Jewish religious activities.[24]

In spite of all the energy invested by Reform rabbis and intellectuals in promoting their views on Reform Judaism, by the end of the nineteenth century, European Reform Judaism was in decline. The innovative thinking exposed with pathos by some preachers and rabbis such as Samuel Hirsh, Isaac Noah Mannheimer, Samuel Holdheim, and David Einhorn reached extremes in their religious and social positions that often estranged them from the Reform Jewish public. This public either did not agree with the content of the sermons or was afraid of the repercussions that inflammatory rhetoric might bring upon them from state authorities. As a consequence of this disconnect and fear, quite a few religious leaders were reduced to leading marginal communities or were forced to leave Europe, mostly for the United States. By the end of the nineteenth century, in Western and Central Europe secularization and assimilation characterized the majority of the non-Orthodox Jewish public.

Exhausted by its defeat in the First World War and humiliated by the Versailles Pact, Germany was the theater of a complicated political scene. Immediately after the war, an extremist Marxist group, the *Spartakusbund* (Spartacus League), tried to imitate the Bolshevik putsch in Russia and take down the Social Democrat government led by Prime Minister Friedrich Ebert. The attempted putsch failed. One of the most outspoken and visible leaders of the group was of Jewish origin: Rosa Luxemburg. Under her leadership, together with Karl Liebknecht, the Spartakusbund became, in the year 1919, the German Communist Party.

The young Weimar Republic, established as part of the peace agreements, was structurally weak and had poor leadership. The republic lacked active Western support, since the victorious allies, in particular Great Britain and France, could not overcome their hate and sense of revenge for their suffering in the war. At the same time, the Weimar regime was under active attack from the Communist Party and the Communist international movement, which considered Germany ripe for a Marxist takeover. The apparent success of the communists in Russia and the massive propaganda the Soviet regime deployed in Western Europe, especially in Germany, created a tense confrontational political atmosphere in Germany.

The Weimar Republic officially attempted to eliminate discrimination, and Jews had the opportunity to become noticeably successful in political, economic, and cultural areas. The participation of many secular and assimilated Jews in Communist and Socialist organizations was well noticed by the local public together with the fact that many of the leaders of the Soviet Communist Party were of Jewish origin. The open solidarity and connection between local left organizations and Soviet international agencies raised serious concerns in the German and other European center-right constituencies. It is no wonder that just a few years after the putsch attempt conducted by the Spartacists, a similar attempt by the National Socialists took place in Bavaria led by Ludendorff and Hitler. It also failed.

In the context of the poor political performance of the center-left coalitions in Germany and the success in Italy of the Fascist movement, which rose to power soon after the end of the war, many in Germany viewed the National Socialist autocratic approach as a valid alternative to democracy. It is worth mentioning here that the Left offered a similar autocratic approach, which the public suspected to be an extension of Soviet imperialism.

In Germany, the volatile and inflammatory political situation enabled the National Socialists to win the elections in 1933. Hitler's virulent anti-Semitic rhetoric was dismissed as demagogical and politically irrelevant. The early suppression of Jewish communities was accepted by the public as part of a safeguard against enemies of the nation. The spirit of appeasement toward tyranny prevailed.

In spite of their expressed concerns, the mainstream public in the Western democracies had no significant reaction to the mass oppression, brutal purges, and consolidation of a vast concentration camps network established by Stalin in the Soviet Union in the 1930s. Most of the focus at the time was on the economic devastation of the Great Depression and its astronomic inflation. The passive reaction of the democratic powers toward totalitarian regimes encouraged tyrants to adopt more extreme policies. Following the Soviet example, Germany established its concentration camp system. There was little international attention or reaction to this development, nor were the Western powers worried by the increasing cooperation emerging between Germany and the Soviet Union. It is important to note that the alliance between the two leading totalitarian regimes in Europe was able to silence most of the opposition to their policies that could have been expected from their respective supporters.[25] In *The Opium and the Intellectuals*, the distinguished mid-century French political theorist, Raymond Aron, describes this phenomenon as follows:

> The faithful, accustomed to following the twists in the line, in repeating parrot-wise the successive and contradictory interpretations of the Nazi-Soviet pact, for example, or of the "Doctors' Plot," became in a certain sense "new men." According to the materialistic conception, men trained after certain methods are docile to authority and completely satisfied with their lot. The engineers of the soul have no doubt about the plastic nature of the psychic material at their disposal.[26]

Local and international Jewish organizations followed the general trend of the European governments. Michael A. Meyer includes in *Response to Modernity* a brief description of the organizational efforts conducted by the European Reform movement in the first half of the twentieth century.[27] What is missing from the reporting is an explanation of how was it possible that the Reform movement did not identify or actively address the dangers to Judaism—liberal Judaism in particular—raised by Soviet socialism and National Socialism. It is important to highlight that in the period between the two world wars in Germany and Poland, Zionist leaders, in particular Ze'ev Jabotinsky, were very outspoken about the dangers facing the Jewish population in Eastern Europe.

Initially, in particular in Germany and Austria, the majority of the secular Jewish liberal public refused to believe that the official state establishment could doubt the patriotic commitment of the Jewish citizens. As believers in the integrity of the existing political system, many Reform and secular Jews dismissed the calls for preventive defensive acts or alternative solutions (Zionism) and instead joined forces with the left-leaning parties in local political activism. This alliance was exploited by the National Socialists to incite anti-Semitic feelings. After Hitler's rise to power, a portion of the German Jewish population immigrated to the United States, Palestine, and other parts of the world. Another portion, which could not escape or buy its way out, was held captive and used as slave labor by the Nazi regime.

The consequences of the West's political blindness after the First World War were the Second World War, the Holocaust, and the Cold War. In Jewish terms, the result was the mass murder of most of the European Jewish population and the decimation of its heritage. European Reform Judaism, according to its divine faith and its social awareness, was supposed to actively oppose the radical secularism as well as the despotism that dominated Europe in the first half of the century. As a modern religious denomination, Reform Judaism could have easily identified the damaging nature of the two secular tyrannies and their perverse cooperation. Instead, the leadership of the Reform movement joined those socially oriented intellectuals who were mystified and "infected" by the Marxist "opium," to use Raymond Aron's characterization of the left-oriented European intellectual world of the twentieth century. Aron explains this development as follows:

> Socialism appeared not so much a technique applicable to the management of enterprises or to the functioning of the economy, as a means of curing once and for all the age-old misery of mankind … In this vague sense, every political movement which has agitated modern Europe has had a religious character. Yet one does not find in them the

framework or the essence of a religious philosophy. In this respect Communism is unique ... It is an easy transition from Marxist prophetism to "the great hope of the twentieth century," from revolutionary faith to the theory of economic progress.[28]

I believe that this socioeconomic mystification, which influenced many in the Reform movement, blinded them to the Jewish divine essence and also, tragically, to the imminent spiritual and brutal physical disaster that was brewing around them.[29]

The European Jewish reformation, through its intellectual effort to modernize Judaism and the origination of new types of congregations and synagogues with revised and experimental rituals, provided inspiration and the spiritual seed for the emergence of two new dynamic reformative developments; one was the Jewish Reform movement, the other was the Eastern European humanism and nationalism, the roots of the Zionist project. In the twentieth century, the radicalization of the Reform leadership along Socialist lines of thought, and the extreme political and economic circumstances that dominated Europe in the first half of the century, almost brought to extinction Reform Judaism in Europe. The future of Reform Judaism moved to North America.

Notes

1. David Einhorn, "Protocolle der ersten Rabbiner-Verswamlung, 61," in Michael A. Meyer, *Response to Modernity* (Detroit, MI: Wayne State Univ. Press, 1995), 138.

2. It is important to understand well the unfairly maligned notion of "bourgeoisie." Deirdre N. McCloskey in *The Bourgeois Virtues* (Chicago:

Univ. of Chicago Press, 2006), 68–78, undertakes an extensive discussion on the meaning of the notion and its social and ethical implications while emphasizing the constructive role the bourgeoisie fulfilled in developing Western civilization.

3. The evolution of the Jewish communities prior to the fifteenth century is complex and reflects conflicting and contradictory positions the dignitaries of the Christian Church and the landed aristocracy had on the usefulness of Jews. Barbara W. Tuchman describes some of the gruesome persecutions of Jews that took place in Western Europe on religious background. (See Barbara W. Tuchman, *A Distant Mirror: The Calamitous 14th Century* [New York: Knopf, 1978], 113–19.) Other sources, in providing a more detailed picture of Jewish life in the Middle Ages, reveal a more complex relationship between Jews and Christians. In many cities, when left alone from church or aristocratic interference, Jews and Christians could live together peacefully and mingle together. Jews often received a degree of respect from their gentile neighbors for their compliance to behavioral rules, learning interest, and solidarity. In this context, the discrimination and explanation for the expulsion of the Jews can be found in the increased financial ability of Christian bankers and the improved education of the Christian bourgeoisie, which did not tolerate competition. (See "The Yellow Badge of Courage" in Max. I. Dimont, *Jews, God and History* [Simon & Schuster/Signet, 1962], 245–55.) The tense relations between the Christian communities and the Jewish people seeded in the Middle Age by interested parties will remain an inbred obstacle for tolerance in European culture for many centuries.

4. See McCloskey, *The Bourgeois Virtues*, 85.

5. In spite of many attempts to control and regulate European cities, cities continued to grow and assert their power. Even capital cities such as Paris continued to grow, in spite of continuous attempts by the kings of France to control it. The urban masses and their economic power could be influenced but hardly controlled. Cities changed history through their economic power and through their explosive revolutionary energy when suppressed. For the interested reader I suggest three sources: L. Mumford, *The City in History* (London: Penguin, 1966), 282–323; Wolfgang Braunfels, *Urban Design*

in Western Europe: Regime and Architecture, 900–1900, trans. Kenneth J. Northcutt (Chicago: Univ. of Chicago Press, 1988), 307–39; C. E. Schorske, "The Idea of the City in European Thought: Voltaire to Spengler," in *The Historian and the City*, eds. O. Handlin and J. Burchard (Cambridge, MA: MIT Press, 1970), 95–114.

6. See "The Ghetto Capitalist" in Dimont, *Jews, God and History*, 255–67.

7. Informative data on the position of Jews in Eastern Europe before the nineteenth century is included in Abram Leon's essay, *The Jewish Question*, chap. 4, "The Jews in Europe after the Renaissance," http://www.marxists. org/subject/jewish/leon/ch4.htm.

8. At the time that the culture war in Central Europe between maskilim and traditionalists was raging, reformation was quite well established in Italian communities. Shmuel Feiner indicates that "in the Italian communities, where Jewish acculturation was already a natural, enduring process that had encounter no rabbinical opposition, there was no need for the emergence of the militant maskil or for the development of a maskilic ideology aimed at changing the nature of society and culture." Shmuel Feiner, *The Jewish Enlightenment*, trans. Chaya Naor, Jewish Culture and Contexts (Philadelphia: Univ. of Pennsylvania Press, 2003), 179.

9. As quoted by Feiner in Shmuel Feiner, *Moses Mendelssohn* (New Haven, CT: Yale Univ. Press, 2010), 178.

10. Plans for the "amelioration of the civil status of the Jews" published in Prussia by Christian Wilhelm von Dohm entitled *On the Civil Improvements of the Jews* and *Edicts of Tolerance* issued by the Austrian Empire (Emperor Josef II) were considered important policy documents intended to improve the status of the Jews. Feiner, *Jewish Enlightenment*, 119–25.

11. See Feiner, *Moses Mendelssohn*, 13–14.

12. Shmuel Feiner, in his biography of Moses Mendelssohn, details the exhausting debates sustained by Mendelssohn in defending his position that loyal, enlightened Jews should be accepted by the state as a legitimate identity. See Feiner, *Moses Mendelssohn*.

13. "Paintings and sculptures depict the men and women of Berlin's Jewish elite in fashionable dress, the men clean shaved and bareheaded. In the literature and the press, we find images of the nouveaux riches, of young women swept up by the cult of Kant and Goethe, women pushing their way into front rows at the theater, and others involved in tempestuous liaisons with Christians." Feiner, *Jewish Enlightenment*, 305.

14. Feiner, in the chapter entitled "The Rabbinical Elite on the Defensive" in *Jewish Enlightenment*, 139–62, describes aspects of this controversy, in particular the so-called Wessley Affair and the dilemma it created. The drastic rabbinical resistance to Wessley's reformative ideas exposed Enlightened Judaism to Christian criticism that attempted to draw a parallel between Christian discrimination of Jews and Jewish religious intransigency.

15. See Dimont, *Jews, God and History*, 302–03.

16. Max I. Dimont explains the difference between anti-Jewish and anti-Semitic acts. Anti-Jewish positions express a dislike of Jews and an antagonism to Judaism similar to the historic adversity between, for instance, French and Germans. Anti-Semitism is a hate belief that considers being Jewish as an irrevocable crime and for some anti-Semites conversion does not expel the inherent crime. Ibid., 312–13. (See also Meyer, *Response to Modernity*, 201–02.)

17. See Meyer, *Response to Modernity*, 100–42.

18. See ibid., 162.

19. See ibid., 33, 107.

20. By the middle of the century, lay leaders and rabbis such as Sigismund Stern, Isaac Noah Mannheimer, and Ignaz Einhorn started to introduce radical reform ideas in their appeals to the public and sermons, speak out for general social issues and some participated in local revolutions. See ibid., 125, 150–51, 160–62.

21. See ibid., 89–99.

22. See ibid., 91.

23. See ibid., 182.

24. On numerous occasions, Orthodox leaders and communities attempted to stop Reform activities by opposing requests for building permits for new temples, see the Hamburg controversy (Ibid., 58), or complaining to authorities on rituals that deviated from proper religious tenets, as in the Geiger-Tiktin conflict in Breslau (Ibid., 110). In a political situation where the Jewish religious denominations were under state supervision, such requests became part of the political game playing used against Reform congregations.

25. In the eyes of the Communist or National Socialist ideological extremes and their dedicated activists, the "decadent" bourgeois capitalist democracies were doomed; hence an alliance between the forces of the "future," as formalized by the Molotov–von Ribbentrop agreement was a natural development. Under these circumstances, this union was considered in the minds of followers necessary and deserving of their support. The acquiescence of the French intellectual Left to the Vichy government collaboration with the German occupation is an additional sad illustration of the fusion between ideological extremes. "Everything we did was equivocal. We never quite knew whether we were doing right or wrong. A subtle poison corrupted our best action." This is J. P. Sartre's beautifully worded explanation for his own embarrassing position under German occupation (as quoted by Frederic Spotts in *The Shameful Peace: How French Artists and Intellectuals Survived the Nazi Occupation* [New Haven, CT: Yale Univ. Press, 2008], 4).

26. See R. Aron, *The Opium of the Intellectuals* (New Brunswick, NJ: Transaction Publ., 2003), 269–70.

27. See Meyer, *Response to Modernity*, 335–45

28. Aron, *Opium of the Intellectuals*, 266–68.

29. Over the years, especially after the dismantling of the Soviet Empire, much of the anti-Marxist criticism proved to be justified. Still, the dream of a global, pacifist, equalitarian Socialist "paradise on earth," devoid of poverty and conflict, often remains the core topic of political demagogues and continues to mystify uninformed minds.

Chapter 2:   **American Reform Judaism:**
Trends, Separation, and Hope

> It now seems self-evident to most Jews: that our tradition
> should interact with modern culture; that its forms ought
> to reflect a contemporary esthetic; that its scholarship needs
> to be conducted by modern, critical methods; and that
> change has been and must continue to be a fundamental
> reality in Jewish life.
>
> Eugene B. Borowitz, *Reform Judaism Today* [1]

Similar to Europe, the nineteenth century in North America was
framed by two historic events: the American Revolution and the First
World War. The American Revolution and the founding documents
of the republic can be considered the most important and substantive
products of the Enlightenment. They were the foundation for an
exceptional and unique political and human development, unmatched
before or since. The American nineteenth century was characterized
by the shaping of a nation as a constitutional republic with an original
democratic regime on a continental scale. The amazing aspect of the
American national creation was its emergence and evolution that
followed a consistent constitutional framework with little internal
turmoil, except for one major convolution: the Civil War.

The success of the American project, contrasted with the failure
of the French Revolutionary project, intrigued and puzzled the
European leadership. Initially, the tenets of the US Constitution were
criticized and rejected by the European republicans, in particular the

leaders of the French Revolution.[2] For them, the freedoms granted in the Constitution and the framers' intrinsic suspicion of control of governmental power were anathema. The European culture was deeply enshrined in elitist leadership. It was this elitist spirit that prevented European political and intellectual elites from grasping the essence and merit of the American constitutional republic.

One key aspect of this success was the freedom and opportunity of individuals to build their future independently of state or political patronage, including the freedom of practicing religions of their choice and design, a freedom that did not exist in Europe.

In nineteenth-century America, the explosion of new thinking, free-market enterprise, and the spirit of liberation enhanced individualism on the personal level. "Going west," acting, and taking initiatives were the means to reach success. The idea was that only after acquiring the security offered by wealth could people dedicate time to develop their spirit. In many ways, free individual enterprise liberated the person from the confinements of established mores such as religion or family. The praiseworthy attributes were individual initiative, imagination, and risk taking. Many succeeded in attaining a reasonable amount of wealth. The spiritual result was quite diverse: many found new interest in religion; others pursued secular intellectual endeavors.

Throughout the nineteenth century, many Jews managed to rise from poverty into wealth and establish themselves as a dynamic factor in the American capitalistic system. Despite the opportunities offered in America, however, there were no outstanding civic or cultural achievements, on the national scene, that can be attributed to Jews until the last decade of the century. The reasons for this weakness can be found in varying degrees of discrimination toward Jews in academia and in political establishments. Apparently, individual freedom and attaining economic success remained the predominant objectives of the majority of the Jewish public. In contrast, as mentioned in the previous chapter, during this same time, European Jews managed to produce an expanding number of leading professional, political, and cultural leaders, in spite of anti-Jewish and anti-Semitic policies and regulations. We can identify one exception in America: Judah Benjamin, the son of one of the founders of Congregation Beth Elohim in Charleston, South Carolina, who, among other significant achievements, served as secretary of state under Jefferson Davis in the Confederate government.

Initially, Reform Judaism in America adopted the independent spirit of the pioneers on an individual level and at the congregational level.

By the turn of the nineteenth century, the small Jewish population in the United States was essentially traditional and followed mostly Sephardic rituals. In their appearance they were undistinguishable from the rest of the population.[3] Early Reform Judaism in America searched for new religious options, a search that was rooted in the bourgeois nature and capitalist orientation of the new Jewish communities. Jewish Reform was perceived as a break from established traditions, as an inquirer looking for new horizons. Different from other religions and denominations with a long history of global commitments that were often contradictory to the tenets of the American republic, Reform Judaism offered an independent, new, and fresh approach to religion, centered on the individual congregant. On a popular and intuitive basis, Reform congregations took advantage of the American freedom. One could have expected that the Land of Promise, with its enlightened roots, would offer Reform Judaism new, meaningful religious concepts.

In the early 1820s an attempt was made to introduce changes in the ritual of the Beth Elohim congregation of Charleston, South

Carolina, one of the first well-established congregations in the United States.[4] The attempt failed, and the dissidents who left Beth Elohim established the independent Reformed Society of Israelites. The "Society," rather than congregation, was inspired by Tanachic Judaism and was critical of traditional practices and the Halacha. The Society considered its practices and services to be determined by the understanding of the membership and the needs of the Society and lived free from previous commitments or prescriptions. In many ways, the Society was a pioneering experiment in emancipation from traditional Judaism. The inability of the Society to sustain itself financially, and its dismantling by the early 1830s, should not diminish the importance of the experiment.[5]

A few years after the dissolution of the Reformed Society of Israelites, Beth Elohim gradually adopted Reform changes. Its members started with small changes in ritual (the introduction of an organ), and gradually evolved until finally declaring themselves, at the beginning of the forties of the century, "the only open and avowed reformers in the United States."[6] The Charleston experiments seem to have been rather exceptional; the development of Reform Judaism in the rest of the country took a different path.

In the absence of an educated religious leadership, Reform Judaism in America was practiced, until the 1840s, as a convenient simplification and beautification of Judaic rituals rather than a coherent theological re-envisioning. This trend reflected the individualistic spirit of America but diluted the Jewish faith to a level that made it almost meaningless.[7] Realizing this danger, some congregations looked for spiritual leadership from Europe.

The midcentury large German emigration brought to America more educated and affluent Jews who included the first religious leaders, such as Abraham Rice and Leo Merzbacher. Many preachers and rabbis who could not find positions in Europe because of poor employment opportunities or their own radical opinions started to find refuge and positions in the United States. Even in the later part of the century, when local leadership and regional organizations emerged, the influence of German Reform Judaism remained predominant. One feature that symbolized the distinction between the orientation of the faith and the realities of the country was that for a long time, many sermons and publications were written and delivered in German rather than English.[8] The fact that these emigrants were forced to leave the German states did not diminish their dependency on the German culture. Many German-trained preachers and rabbis were committed to the philosophical, political, and social issues debated in Europe and had little understanding of the Anglo-Saxon traditions and American conditions that were shaping the United States. Living as free citizens in the United States did little to affect the beliefs brought over from Europe and their interpretations of religious or sociopolitical issues.[9]

The congregations were highly autonomous because of both geographic distance and the independent spirit of the country. The highest concentration of congregations was on the East Coast but, in time, well-established and influential congregations developed all over the country. The congregational governance was a bilateral relationship between the lay leadership and the hired rabbis and preachers. Significantly, Reform congregations relinquished Jewish jurisprudence (the Halacha) to civic constitutional justice. In time this separation would become a hallmark of American Reform Judaism.

In this same period, Isaac Mayer Wise, considered the foremost American Reform leader of his time, stood out in his organizational abilities and his strong belief in the material opportunities America offered.[10] His major goal was to consolidate and unite the movement. The unification and standardization of rituals and practices Wise had in mind can be viewed as an American interpretation of the

European tradition for a controlling, centralized organization in charge and in command. This was the central theme of the 1855 Cleveland conference that he spearheaded. Wise's approach in realizing his vision was based on compromise between the different participating factions. Wise's tendency to compromise instigated immediate criticism and brought David Einhorn to preeminence. Einhorn successfully made his Universalist approach dominant in American rabbinic circles.[11] Most of the passionate debate at the conference focused on the unified movement's religious content and its interpretation of Reform tenets, practices, and rituals. One key debate was whether to continue to preserve the German traditions and language or adopt an American orientation in the language and the standardized content. (I could not find evidence from the available sources of any opinion questioning throughout the debate the very need for unification and standardization.) The pluralistic nature of American civilization passed unnoticed.

American Reform Judaism at the end of the nineteenth century redefined itself in the 1885 Pittsburgh Platform as a "religious community," rejected Zionism, and ignored the suffering of the Jewish people overseas as well as the needs of new immigrants. In broad terms the platform's intent was to promulgate the position that Reform Judaism was a distinct denomination, separate from ethical secularism and Orthodox Judaism. In the minds of Reform leaders of the time such as Kaufmann Kohler and Emil G. Hirsh, "not philosophy but science, not theoretical ethics but applied morality were the criteria that now measured the legitimacy and value of modern religion."[12] It is significant to notice that the platform does not make any reference to the US constitutional, cultural, or economic context. Kaufman Kohler was the zealous leader of the rabbinical group that designed the Pittsburgh Platform. Most of the content of this short document affirmed theological predications in an assertive language style that offered little theological depth and allowed for no dialogue. It was an optimistic document that advocated progress and a commitment to economic justice.

In many ways the platform legitimized the elitist status of the German-oriented Reform approach and attempted to immunize it from the influence of ideas brought over by new immigrants from Eastern Europe. A concise statement of the essence of what came to be known as "Classical" Reform was published in an article by K. Kohler, E. G. Hirsh, and D. Philipson: "Reform Judaism from the Point of View of the Reform Jew."[13] In this article the authors summarize the mission, scope, practices, and rituals of Reform Judaism that evolved in the nineteenth century in Europe and became the foundation for the American expansion. Reform Judaism was regarded by the authors as a modern addition to the Jewish heritage that emphasized, among other revisions to traditional rituals and practices, acting according to the moral customs of the surrounding environment, with little connection to the Hebrew language or to fostering a rebuilt Israel in the Holy Land.

The debates and polarization that followed the publication of the Pittsburgh Platform, in the last decades of the nineteenth century, diverted the attention of the movement from the plight of European Judaism and the need to assimilate immigrants to the United States.

The nineteenth-century evolution of the Reform movement in America can be seen as a Jewish reflection of the utopian and communitarian movements that emerged during America's development. I could not find any specific connection between the concepts promoted by the Unitarians or Owen's New Harmony movement, but we can assume that Reform preachers and rabbis were well aware of and influenced by them. The admiration that Unitarians and Owen's followers had for European Socialist thinking and Prussian public control of education and religion must have confirmed the ideas promoted by the German-educated rabbis and preachers and the top-down elitist philanthropic practices that supported the congregations.

By the end of the nineteenth century, conceptual controversies, personal animosities, and poor managerial abilities created divisions between lay and spiritual leaders and between different congregations. New Jewish organizations deprived of religious affiliation drew their support from the same population basis as the Reform movement and often advocated similar political agenda items. These divisions weakened the movement. By the beginning of the twentieth century, Reform Judaism remained frozen in ideological debates.

The arrival of large waves of poor, secular, Zionist, and orthodox Eastern European Jews by the end of the nineteenth century and the beginning of the twentieth century diminished the presence and impact that Reform congregations had on the Jewish public. These new immigrants also brought the interdenominational debates that dominated the Old Continent. In spite of some initial resistance to get involved, Reform congregations and individuals provided assistance to new immigrants, mostly through charitable organizations. I could not find evidence of any organized, movement-wide Reform initiative aimed to assimilate and integrate the newcomers into the Reform movement. One possible reason the Reform leadership maintained its distance from the newcomers was the self-serving intellectual and theological stand of the Reform rabbinate, as opposed to the aggressive—close to desperate—spirit of the newcomers. For many new immigrants, America offered more than freedom from oppression and discrimination. It also offered opportunities for personal success. In their minds, hard work and education were the ways to achieve personal success. Spiritual connection might have provided long-term community support, guidance, and a helpful sense of belonging. In the absence of spiritual connections, however, charity remained a limited relief which most people preferred to replace with rewarding work. The new immigrants were determined to succeed and to provide their children with a better future. In America, education was key for success, and the educated sons of immigrants became the next generation of Jewish American intellectuals and professionals. The ability of these immigrants to succeed by themselves distanced them from charity organizations to which they did not have any connection except for the limited material support.

Besides the reluctance to assimilate the new immigrants, the opposition of Reform to Zionism was another major divider between the two constituencies.[14]

It is during this period that the front organization of the Reform rabbinate, the Central Conference of American Rabbis (CCAR), promoted the transition from personal morality to social activism. Inspired by Emil Hirsh's advocacy and influenced by activist organizations such as the Christian Social Gospel progressive movement, the CCAR embarked on its Socialist trend.[15] The concentrated effort of the rabbinical leadership was increasingly focused on social justice and pacifism. This social activism was met with criticism and opposition from some Jewish business community leaders.[16] By adopting the class-warfare approach and rejecting the opinions and interests of the lay leadership, the CCAR added to the already growing tensions in the movement.

It is worth noting that the ideological advocacy on social and political issues was essentially propagandistic in nature. In its first social justice platform, in 1918, the CCAR published a fourteen-point resolution that read just like any Marxist manifesto published at the time.[17] Ambiguous statements such as "a more equitable distribution of profits of industry" are confusing and are open to many interpretations, none of which are religious. The rest of the points could be easily considered a labor union agenda. How could such a resolution—a political manifesto—be justified as an expression of divine faith? It was during that period that the CCAR and to a certain extent the Hebrew Union College (HUC) emerged as organizations in search of an ideology rather than a religious vision. This "applied" approach to reality was essentially political, not spiritual, and as such it brought into question the integrity of the mission of its advocates. In commenting on the rise of social issues in the Reform awareness, Meyer observes that "perhaps also the prophetic role was the rabbi's endeavor to forcefully reassert his own status against the wealthy businessmen who dominated his congregation and whose values reflected the capitalist ethos."[18]

In the tumultuous years of the first half of the twentieth century, the CCAR and the HUC did little to initiate and research original initiatives, either spiritual or applied. If social activism was important, why did the CCAR ignore the need to develop comprehensive plans for the absorption of Jewish immigrants? Such a project would have been an extraordinary opportunity to attach the concepts of Jewish Reform to the expectations of the immigrants for a new life in a new country.

In my opinion, the role and mission of a Reform rabbi is to provide moral inspiration and critique as a spiritual leader. Rabbis are neither trained nor equipped—and definitely lack the authority and responsibility—to provide political and socio-economic solutions. Reform Judaism could provide critical positions on national issues, but providing solutions infringes on the Reform principle of separation between church and state and undermines the moral status of the religious institution. Unfortunately, it appears that the CCAR was mystified by Socialist propaganda, and in its verbal enthusiasm to help the "needy" it lost its ability for critical religious thinking. In just one generation, the CCAR had to backtrack from or reconsider major elements of its agenda: pacifism, its labor advocacy, and its anti-Zionism. Nevertheless, searching for a social ideology rather than creating new theology remained a central attribute of the CCAR's agenda.

In retrospect, we find the Reform movement in the United States in the period between the two world wars adopting a dual existence: many congregations and their lay leaderships adopted an exclusive, comfortable "country club" mentality, while the rabbinic leadership advocated a "living room" Universalist, Marxist social activism, wrapped in Jewish narrative. At the same time, Reform intellectuals were influenced and challenged by other denominations that viewed Reform Jews as their natural partners; the enlightened Christianity of the eighteenth century was replaced with the belligerent activism of liberal Protestants, Jesuits, Jewish Socialists, and advocates of international communism. It was under the influence of such beliefs that parts of the Reform movement embraced Universalist and Socialist inclinations.[19]

The debated issues were clear and resonated immediately with the public. They did not appear to raise complex spiritual challenges and could easily motivate recruitment of financial donations and political support. These positions were in line with the activism of the American political left—Jewish and non-Jewish—and the pacifist position of the Franklin D. Roosevelt administration.

"Living room" socialism was attractive to well-groomed American intellectuals who were mystified by the Marxist utopian illusions and Soviet propaganda. Rabbinic social activism, advocated as a redeeming compensation for the "usury" wealth of the "wicked capitalist bourgeoisie," instilled in the Jewish laity an apologetic "Jewish guilt" for their economic success. This "guilt" was effectively used by activists to recruit resources for the promotion of their social ideas, which increasingly advanced anti-capitalist agendas focused on "social justice" and strong governmental intervention.

This Marxist narrative, wrapped in Jewish terminology of goodwill and charity and marketed to the Jewish middle class with flamboyant rhetoric, became a resounding motivational topic to preach from the pulpit. As mentioned above, this agenda was often opposed by congregations, yet in the absence of an organized lay leadership this opposition failed to have a significant influence on the movement.[20] The legacy of these trends is still with us and will be further discussed in the following chapters.

Simultaneous with the social activism momentum and the debate on Zionism, a more traditional concept was brewing in the rabbinic population. Rabbi Solomon Freehof proposed a concept by which as Reform congregants, "we do not begin with theology, we arrive at theology." Freehof's understanding was that customs and practices (*minhagim*)—such as Friday evening services, confirmation, men and women sitting together at worship—built the religion.[21]

At the same time, the rabbinical establishment continued to oppose the parallel Jewish reformist offspring: Zionism. Orthodox Judaism rejected Zionism based on its belief that only the Messiah can redeem the Jewish state. The Reform leadership, in comparison, while rejecting the Messianic approach, additionally viewed the establishment of a Jewish state as a competition to their current national identity. In the American context, this European nationalistic approach was quite strange. Most Americans considered their original heritage a contribution to the American melting pot and (with the noticeable exception of the impoundment of Japanese Americans into concentration camps in the Second World War) did not doubt the loyalty of citizens based on their origin.

Confronted with the need to improve its educational programs, the Union of American Hebrew Congregations (UAHC) showed some flexibility toward Zionist supporters and in the early 1920s entrusted its educational reform to a dedicated lay educator of strong

Zionist convictions and religious orientation, Emanuel Gamoran. Due to Gamoran's cumulative influence over the course of thirty years, the activism of leaders such as Stephen Wise and Abba Hillel Silver, and emerging evidence of the tragic events that were taking place in Europe, the Union and the CCAR started to soften their anti-Zionist positions.

On the theological front, Samuel Cohon, who inherited Kohler's position at the HUC, promoted "the religious consciousness of the individual, specifically with personal experience of the sacred."[22] By the mid-1930s, Cohon's positions were shared by the majority of Reform rabbis. The reorientation of Reform thinking resulted in the issuance of the Columbus Platform in 1937. The platform expressed the changes in Reform thinking as to rituals and practices, its social mission, and recognition of the Jewish claims for a homeland in Palestine.

The war effort of the Second World War and its political and ideological implications seem to have had limited impact on the pacifist thinking of the Reform leadership. Only after the Roosevelt administration issued its war declaration against the Axis did the CCAR concede to modify its pacifist orientation. Around the same time (1943), however, the Union appointed Rabbi Maurice Eisendrath as executive director and then in 1946 elevated him as the first salaried president and first rabbi to hold the position. Michael Meyer describes Eisendrath as follows:

> Never one to avoid a controversy, Eisendrath advocated absolute pacifism, a binational state in Palestine and a greater Jewish appreciation of Jesus. Beginning as a classical Reformer, he shifted his positions along with the movement: from anti-Zionism to Zionism, from anti-ritual to a limited fondness for custom and ceremony. But his religion remained

prophetic Judaism, his chief concern social justice and world peace.[23]

A striking feature of this period, between the 1930s and the 1960s, is the failure of the Reform movement to react to some of the most significant Jewish events of the time: the Soviet purges, the Holocaust, the establishment of the State of Israel and its war for independence. In spite of the historic magnitude of the events, the movement, and in particular its leadership, took no clear and determined positions on these issues. Especially disappointing was the dismissive and even hostile position taken by the Reform movement toward activists who called for the intervention of the Roosevelt administration to prevent the extermination of the Jewish communities in Europe.[24] A sad example is the refusal of asylum in the United States by the Roosevelt administration for the 937 Jewish and German refugees on board the MS *St. Louis*.[25] Roosevelt's cruel stance never became an issue for the social-justice-minded Reform rabbis. America had a free and aggressive press and yet little was brought up to criticize and combat the anti-Semitic evil that was taking over Europe and was present in parts of the Roosevelt administration. Instead of taking the forefront in investigating, exposing, and combating the Jewish tragedy, the Reform leadership was silent and remained consistent in their blind support of Roosevelt's policies. It is on this background that we can understand why it took the Reform leadership up to the late 1950s to finally accept the full drama of the Holocaust.[26] In comparison, the active and vocal involvement of Reform activists in the civil rights movement and in opposing the Vietnam War shows what could have been done to combat the Jewish extermination in Europe. Apparently, Reform social justice applied to everyone else except Jews.

The prosperity of the postwar period, along with Eisendrath's managerial diligence and efficiency, revitalized the Reform movement.

Much in conformity with the general trend of the postwar American society, Reform congregations patterned themselves along the typical lifestyle of the 1950s: extensive movement to suburbs and enrollment and attendance in religious centers.

In the period after World War II, Reform activism continued its tradition of affiliation with radical left-wing movements, in spite of the brutal Soviet occupation of Eastern Europe and the Cold War. As a movement, it continued to ignore the contradiction between its divine faith-based spiritual mission and the controversial political messages it supported. Occasionally, some messages reached ridiculous levels, such as Eisendrath's proposal to ask the American Jewish community to pay reparations to the African American community for slavery, while maintaining no Jewish guilt or obligation for slavery.[27]

Inspired by ideologies seeded in the nineteenth century, mid-twentieth-century secular left-leaning intellectuals in Europe and the United States continued to believe in an ideal state of affairs in which everyone could achieve everything one wished for, whether or not it could be achieved; others reached the conviction that they deserved to receive everything just for being present. European leaders, sustained by generous American aid and the tensions of the Cold War, adopted entitlements as the building blocks of a new kind of civilization based on the welfare culture, in which individualism and collective responsibility were replaced by legalized selfishness.[28] There were assorted versions of this concept (and in the last few decades we have witnessed the demise of all of these): the utopian communitarian/kibbutz version in Israel at one end, the Scandinavian welfare model at the other, and other intermediary versions in the United Kingdom, continental Europe, or Canada. The connection between these European sociopolitical concepts and the American Reform movement has been clearly stated in messages adopted by the Union for Reform Judaism (URJ) and the Religious

Action Center (RAC) social activists, a messaging that came at the expense of genuine religious action. These messages will be discussed in more detail in the following chapters.

In an article published in *Commentary*, Jack Wertheimer points out that

> until recently it was possible to find Reform rabbis and lay leaders active in both the Republican and Democratic parties, and the movement's pronouncements on matters of public policy retained at least a studied semblance of political neutrality. This is no longer the case. In recent years, Reform Judaism, at the prodding of its Washington arm, the Religious Action Center, has issued resolutions after resolutions in support of Left-liberal positions across an array of political and social issues.[29]

In the second half of the twentieth century, two developments offered signs of optimism regarding the reformative approach in America. The first development was the strong presence of new reformative interpretations, such as those of the Conservative and the Reconstructionist movements, as outgrowths of the original Reform movement. In my opinion, by providing new ideas and commitments within the Reform paradigm, rather than abandoning it, these movements strengthened the American reformation.

The second development was the significant change in perception toward the State of Israel. Reform Judaism did not take any major actions in support of Israel's Independence War or the Sinai operation of 1956. Neither was any significant solidarity action taken toward Israel in view of Eisenhower's negative position toward Israel at the time. The miraculous Israeli victory in the Six Day War of 1967 brought the Reform constituency to enthusiastically embrace the

Jewish state. The Reform leadership was compelled to recognize the vitality of Israel and created a Zionist link: the Association of Reform Zionists of America (ARZA). In the late 1970s it initiated a physical presence in association with one of the kibbutz movements in Israel. Still, the Zionist-applied activism of the Reform movement remained modest and hesitant. The official explanation was the hostility toward Reform Judaism by the Orthodox establishment in Israel. Again, this was a religious issue that could have been addressed effectively by energetic religious action in the field, both in Israel and in the United States. A careful reading of the situation leads me to believe that the position of the American Reform leadership was and is conditioned by deep reservations toward the Zionist mission, while the rank and file has become increasingly supportive of the State of Israel.[30]

The most important and encouraging aspect of the movement is that, in a true Reform spirit, congregations are sustaining vibrant local activities by focusing on providing religious and educational services requested by the public. Ultimately it is the energy and dedication of each congregation at the grassroots level that ensures the success and the future of Reform Judaism in America.

Notes

1. Eugene B. Borowitz, *Reform Judaism Today* (New York: Behrman House, 1983): 1: xix.

2. See "John Adams and the French Debate the American Constitution," a reading list at The Online Library of Liberty, http://oll.libertyfund.org.

3. See Meyer, *Response to Modernity*, 228; Dimont, *Jews, God and History*, 354.

4. See Meyer, *Response to Modernity*, 228–32.

5. See ibid., 232.

6. Ibid., 233–35.

7. See ibid., 226–27.

8. See ibid., 253.

9. The imported religious content from Germany was influenced by European ideological trends such as Romantic thinking, Universalism, nationalism, and socialism. These trends were seldom explicitly acknowledged by the various advocates but their presence is evident in the promotion of social action, the advocacy of social justice, and the support of trade unions. Also, we can detect an ethnic and nationalistic pride in the stubborn preservation of the German heritage.

10. See ibid., 237–44.

11. See ibid., 244–50.

12. See ibid., 272–73.

13. See a reprint of the 1885 Pittsburgh Platform online at http://www/jewishencyclopedia.com in the topic "Conferences, Rabbinical."

14. See Meyer, *Response to Modernity*, 293–95.

15. See ibid., 286–89, 310–13.

16. See ibid., 311.

17. See "The First Social Justice Platform of the CCAR" (from 1918) in Michael A. Meyer and W. Gunther Plaut, compilers, *The Reform Judaism Reader: North American Documents* (New York: UAHC Press, 2001).

18. See Meyer, *Response to Modernity*, 288.

19. See ibid., 310.

20. See ibid., 311.

21. See ibid., 324.

22. See ibid., 317.

23. See ibid., 355.

24. In the 1940s activists such as the Bergson Group called, through rallies and pageants, for a common cause in condemning the Jewish extermination policy deployed by the Nazis in Europe. In their effort to protect the Roosevelt administration, Reform leaders such as Rabbi Stephen Wise and lay organizations such as the American Jewish Committee demonized the Bergson Group. The most regrettable fact is that after the war, many in the Reform movement, as a justification for their silence, denied any knowledge of the Final Solution. (See Matthew M. Hausman, "Reform Angst Regarding Israel and Jewish Nationalism," article posted by Ted Belman on June 26, 2011, on www.israpundit.com. Available at http://www.israpundit.com/archives/37269.)

25. See http://en.wikipedia.org/wiki/MS_St._Louis.

26. See Meyer, *Response to Modernity*, 363–64.

27. See ibid., 368.

28. For the purpose of this book I adopted Erich Fromm's definition of a selfish person as provided in *Fear of Freedom* (London: Routledge, 1942), 100: "The selfish person is always anxiously concerned with himself, he is never satisfied, is always restless, always driven by the fear of not getting enough, of missing something, of being deprived of something. He is filled with burning envy of anyone who might have more. If we observe still closer, especially the unconscious dynamics, we find that this type of person is basically not fond of himself, but deeply dislikes himself."

29. See Jack Wertheimer, "What Does Reform Judaism Stand For?" *Commentary* (June 2008), http://www.commentarymagazine.com/article/what-does-reform-judaism-stand-for/.

30. The selection of Rabbi Richard Jacobs as president of the URJ raises serious concerns about the relationship between the URJ, Zionism, and the State of Israel. Rabbi Richard Jacobs is a committed political activist, an enthusiastic supporter of left-wing agendas in the United States, a leader in the New Israel Fund, and an outspoken supporter of radical left-wing groups and Palestinian causes in Israel.

Chapter 3: Faith in the Almighty or "Partners with God"?

> 12 [But as for] wisdom: Where can it be found? Which is the place for understanding? 13 Mankind does not know its worth; it cannot be found in the land of the living. 14 The depth says, "It is not in me!" and the sea says, "It is not with me."
>
> 23 [Only] God understands its way and He knows its place.
>
> 28 and He says to man: "Behold, the fear of the Lord is wisdom, and refraining from evil is understanding."
>
> Job 28:12–14, 23, 28

In the process of transition from a religiously neutral, educated, secular Jew to a Reform Jew, I found it necessary to ask myself how I explain faith in divine inspiration and the need for it in the twenty-first century.

How can I explain faith in the Almighty? I do not know. I cannot define it in my own terms. But I believe I can recognize it. As a child I was aware that we could do little to change our life. In an instinctive way I prayed, hoping that there was an Almighty of last resort able to help us escape the evils of communism. I had faith in my prayers, in the dedication and faith of my parents, and a miracle happened: we escaped safely. Nine years later I witnessed the anxiety of my mother who, like other mothers in Israel, prayed and had faith that we all would do our best to survive, that the strength of our spirit would prevail and a miracle would occur. And in 1967 the Six Day War miracle occurred. In the following years, we became confident, had fun, and forgot our prayers, and then in 1973, the tragedy of the Yom Kippur War befell us. Sacrifice, a spontaneous resurgence of faith, and the call of President Nixon's conscience to reject Secretary of State Kissinger's advice and allow urgent military supplies, saved Israel. This was another miracle and a harsh lesson for us all.

America is wealthy and mighty. Many believe that if you do your job and play by the rules you will be successful. Talent and dedication can make you wealthy. Apparently there is no need to pray or have faith in an inspiring spirit, and yet millions of Americans join congregations and rejoice in their prayers. What makes so many seek a spiritual experience that transcends the surrounding reality? It is uniquely American to find a wide range of religious pursuits. Yet, all address the mystery of one original, everlasting power that encompasses life and universe.

A number of sources made me recognize the limitations of our human intellect and accept the possibility of a transcendental, metaphysical existence. Philosophy of science indicates that our participation in and interpretation of data influences our understanding of findings and conclusions. Contemporary astrophysicists are searching for explanations of the creation of the universe and its behavior. Biochemists and life scientists are puzzled by genetics and the mysteries of life creation. Some scientists recognize that there might be forces and factors that the human intellect is not able to comprehend in a dedicated manner or study in objective ways.[1] In this complex context, the human mind has developed an ability to record and imagine but not always explain. Language and innovation are human achievements that are driven by an intrinsic need for which we can hardly provide a definitive reasonable cause.[2]

Human beings immerse themselves in the surrounding environment by experiencing the opportunities offered by nature to accommodate our life (J. J. Gibson's "ecological affordances"), are fascinated by human relations in time and space (see E. T. Hall's anthropological and ethological studies), and marvel at the existence of inexplicable dynamic phenomena.[3]

On the other hand, much of our knowledge has been revealed to human awareness by accidental encounters and incidents. Throughout history we have learned that in addition to science, art and religion can help us overcome the uncertainties of the accidental. Odo Marquard indicates a possible explanation of how we can address the accidental:

> One of the ways of dealing with arbitrarily accidental is certainly art: the use of form to reduce arbitrariness. And one of the ways of dealing with the fatefully accidental is certainly religion: the transformation of extreme situations into routines. Both of these, art and religion, attempt to master something: art (perhaps) masters arbitrary contingency, and religion (perhaps) masters faithful contingency.[4]

Mystical explanations based on pagan pre-Classical or Classical idolatry remain evocative and provide entertaining stories, albeit with limited relevance to my current spiritual search. On the other hand, the concept of the Jewish Divinity reveals itself as intriguing and amazingly responsive to our contemporary existence. Jewish Divinity is an infinite, abstract, primal notion, whose time-space identity encompasses the past, the present, and the future. It is omnipresent, revealing to us the magic of places and the intricacies of life, and it fulfills our spiritual expectations today as never before. The divine omnipresence makes each of us part of the divine spirit, an explorer of its infinite time-space existence, which we will never be able to exhaust. Understanding Divinity becomes a spiritual experience shaped by a continuous dialogue between the individual mind, the timely realization of surrounding facts and phenomena, and the individual and collective conscience. The evolution of the understanding of this abstract Divinity over millennia and the impact of this evolving understanding created a unique heritage that embodies Jewish culture. By becoming part of this spiritual experience and heritage, I am able to create a personal, spiritual construct that reduces my limitations and vulnerabilities.

My search brought me to discover Reform Judaism. Reform Judaism, by its own definition, indicated a process of adding to our heritage an understanding of our time through personal commitment within a framework of liberties. I believe that our Reform spiritual and cultural content stems from our Jewish faith. Faith is not an image; it is a construct of our mind. It is inspired by ideas and tested by self-examination, exploration, and self-experimentation. Faith inspires new ideas and encourages action. Faith requires freedom of mind, freedom of action, and ability for self-reliance. Having faith is our goal and part of our existence. Our faith is inspired by experiencing the Jewish Divinity.

In reading the 1999 "Statement of Principles for Reform Judaism" by the Central Conference of American Rabbis, I was impressed by one introductory sentence:

> The great contribution of Reform Judaism is that it has enabled Jewish people to introduce innovation while preserving tradition, to embrace diversity while asserting commonality, to affirm beliefs without rejecting those who doubt, and to bring faith to sacred texts without sacrificing critical scholarship.[5]

This introduction sets a clear reference for an informed spiritual experience in our modern context, a reference that is quite conservative. This approach reminded me of Roger Scruton's opinion:

> The conservative response to modernity is to embrace it, but to embrace it critically, in full consciousness that human achievements are rare and precarious, that we have no God-given right to destroy our inheritance, but must always patiently submit to the voice of order and set an example of orderly living.[6]

My anticipation was therefore for an inspiring dialogue generated by a diverse set of ideas and interpretations devoid of dogmas and prejudice.

The succeeding three sections of the 1999 Statement detail the attributes of the three components of the faith: God, Torah, and Israel. I was able to identify myself with many of the affirmative statements in those passages. The concluding paragraph in the "Torah" section, however, raised some significant questions and concerns. The following sentences surprised and disturbed me. The Statement introduces Reform Judaism as follows:

> Partners with God in [tikkun olam], repairing the world, we are called to help bring nearer the messianic age ... We are obligated to pursue [*tzedek*], justice and righteousness, and to narrow the gap between the affluent and the poor, to act against discrimination and oppression, to pursue peace, to welcome the stranger, to protect the earth's biodiversity and natural resources, and to redeem those in physical, economic and spiritual bondage. In so doing, we reaffirm

social action and social justice as a central prophetic focus of traditional Reform Jewish belief and practice.

Reading this paragraph carefully, I began to ask myself, what does the notion of "partnership" with the Almighty mean? Never in the history of Judaism have we humans, even prophets, "partnered" with Divinity. The whole book of Genesis is essentially dedicated to establishing the notion of our Divinity as singular, abstract, infinite, and omnipresent. Nowhere is our Divinity impersonated by idols or kings, as was common in antiquity and dominant in the religious perceptions of the rest of humanity for centuries thereafter. The dialogue between Divinity and Judaism takes place in our conscience and is transcendental in nature. The transcendental Tanachic Divinity was the power that enabled Judaism to survive in history and provided inspiration to the other monotheistic faiths. Moses and Judaism stood up against the pretended god-like embodiment of the pharaohs. Prophets, kings, and sages were humbled by the divine word. Placing humans on an equal status with Divinity, as the Statement does, defeats the belief in the supreme divine spiritual inspiration and deprives us of its ethical power. Our religious faith accepts a priori the supreme power of Divinity and addresses it in awe.

This Statement raises many unsettling questions. Does the leadership of the CCAR indeed believe it is entitled to position itself as equal to Divinity? Does it not understand the deliberate damage it is imposing on our faith? Does indeed the CCAR mean to attach these proposals as an integral part of the Torah, the canonized five books of Moses? On what grounds does this statement proclaim as messianic and prophetic such confusing and controversial current political notions as "social action" and "social justice"? Did the writers of this statement assume prophetic stature?

In addition to the content of that paragraph, I found the assertion that "we are obligated to pursue" a list of current controversial socioeconomic, environmental, and political issues totally contradicts the discursive position and open-minded approach implied in the first paragraph as to "affirming beliefs without rejecting those who doubt." Who are the "we" who are obligated to pursue the political message, and who obligates us to follow this political agenda—and why? In subsequent chapters I will address some of the items included in this political agenda in more detail. The question, however, remains: If Reform Judaism is open to dialogue, how can anyone "obligate" or be "obligated" to conform to an arbitrary manifesto?

Such assertive proclamations, inserted into a statement of faith, diminish the enlightenment and hope that Divinity can provide to our people. They replace humility with an arrogant, distasteful assertion of power. In its special position as "a partner with God," does the CCAR expect to obtain the absolute authority to decide what has to be "repaired in the world," how it shall be done, where and when? Does the CCAR assume the role of kings and tyrants when deciding the fate of their constituencies, in the name of "God and country"? Does the CCAR notice that such an absolutist position contradicts the First Amendment to the Constitution, which defends freedom of speech, and contradicts the affirmative, open-minded principles highlighted in the introduction of the very same 1999 "Statement of Principles"? In expressing my concern, I find support in Paul Feyerabend's opinion:

> My main objection against intellectual solutions of social problems is that they start from a narrow cultural background, ascribe universal validity to it and use power to impose it on others. Is it surprising that I want to have nothing to do with such raciofascist dreams?[7]

Political partisan opinions inserted into a statement of faith are subverting the integrity of the faith and can lead to extreme reactions as indicated by Feyerabend's language. If the leaders of the CCAR assumed that by interjecting political messages in their 1999 Statement of religion they would gain superior authority, they achieved just the opposite: they drastically diminished their moral authority.[8]

The challenging question remaining is to what extent individual rabbis identify themselves with the CCAR position and whether they are prepared to defend it. If there is dissent and rabbis recognize the major damage the 1999 Statement inflicts on our faith, action should be taken. If, on the other hand, the rabbinical rank and file remains inactive, it will invite further political divisiveness and polarization within the Reform movement. This is a serious situation, yet none of the questions or concerns expressed here were either noted or addressed in the 2004 "Commentary on the Principles for Reform Judaism"[9] that was written to explain the 1999 Statement.

In reflecting on this Commentary, I wonder if members of the current national rabbinical elite are attempting to transform Reform Judaism into a political instrument under their control. Is it their intent to use the clout and reputation of the Jewish Reform movement to gain a position in the national political arena? The goals listed in the referenced paragraph from the 1999 Statement are definitely not religious goals, and they are drastically contradicting Reform Judaism's tenet of separation of church and state. We must differentiate here between religious messages, "good deeds" (*tzedaka*), and partisan political action. Religious messages and good deeds are personal actions inspired by individual connections to our faith. Political actions, with their power games and manipulations, are organized efforts of special interest groups aimed at achieving civic goals within the public realm. In mixing the two, we corrupt the transcendental connection with our "inner" spiritual voice.

If we reject the tendency to politicize our faith, what should replace it?

It is unclear from the formulation of the 1999 Statement what meaning its proponents give to the word "Torah." The reference to the Torah alone is a narrow position, reactionary to the vision of Reform Judaism. Reform Judaism is based on the broad spiritual and cultural Jewish heritage centered on the Tanach and its commentary. The reaffirmation of the limiting prescripts of the Torah only is one that brings our faith back to an Orthodox tradition of outdated, confining, and dominant compulsion.

Reform Judaism recognizes that the Jewish Divinity is exceptional and awesome. It has neither shape nor form but rather creates humanity in its own image. Image does not necessarily mean a copy, a reproduction of the original, but rather is a representation of intent that, as such, does not mean a complete transfer of content. For instance, humans got life, but not immortality.

The notion of "image," more than merely the word for it, refers to a number of meanings: object-oriented meaning, descriptive meaning, or symbolic meaning. The object-oriented meaning of "image" is basically pictorial and attempts to provide a picture of the subject. Since Judaic Divinity is invisible and by definition has no shape, any attempt to imagine the Almighty as an object is self-defeating. Yet, human beings have a clear physical dimension; hence their image can be represented in objective terms and features.

Like the objective image, the descriptive image lacks the ability to include all the attributes of Divinity since, by definition, we are not the Almighty. We humans cannot be omnipresent and cannot describe an infinite identity; at best we can reach a partial description. Human imagination, unable to realize the full power of Divinity, has often adopted symbolic images that indicate a divine presence.

Symbols again are not a complete reproduction of the notion but indicate key aspects we can comprehend and accept.[10]

In this context, can images become idols? Absolutely, yet idols are artificial, static, man-made objects attempting to symbolize divine power. Their influence is conditioned by the power the public bestows upon them. This is why pagan idols have long lost their impact. On the other hand, natural features, such as cloud formations, light, and landscapes, being beyond the immediate human realm of comprehension, may inspire a sense of awe, a sense that can bring us closer to Divinity. The same considerations can apply to man-made imaginative experiences such as music or architecture. From its inception, Judaism has included in its rituals both architecture and music, initially in the Tent and later in the Temple in Jerusalem, with the clear intent to bring us closer to faith in the Almighty. The experience of the ritual artifacts, ceremonies, and places is real, interactive, and dynamic. These experiences translate into behavioral and spiritual phenomena that go beyond imagery; they are abstract and liberating; they facilitate our divine experience.

In addition, the empowerment of humanity with the ability to debate and even disobey their Creator is part of an amazing creation process intended to provide unique intellectual capabilities to human beings. Dialogue and debate are attributes exclusively assigned to humans. Through dialogue we become aware of the world and the power of the unknown, of astrophysics and quantum mechanics, biology and life and the mysteries of the Almighty. Classical gravity, evolution, and psychology can describe and even explain certain phenomena but are left wanting in addressing universal developments. Einstein's theories of relativity have survived so far attempts of refutation and yet do not fit other aspects of physics. We believe in the "Big Bang" theory and we experience life, but we still are unable to fully comprehend either one.

From its inception, Judaism has absorbed the complexities of divine presence as a reflection of the universe that surrounds us and makes us part of it. No other religion has embraced such an abstract concept, with such conviction, at such an early stage in human history. Our own thinking hence is not divorced from Divinity; on the contrary, it is an expression of the Almighty's presence in our inner spirit. Having the courage and perseverance to think, criticize, and evaluate our deeds brings us closer to the Jewish divine spirit. Realizing our mistakes and our successes is a reward that makes us happy, and happiness is a divine gift. God punished Adam and Eve and they gave birth to humanity. Was their sin an accident or part of an additional divine intent? Is the divine intention to assert its existence in the life of humans by encouraging confrontation? In the Jewish tradition, debate became an expression of freedom, a freedom that is God given.

Judaism started as a pragmatic process of building a people/culture/religion/nation through the implementation of a well-structured set of rules and regulations, the Torah. Educating the Jews to fulfill this regulatory code was a process that transformed a mass of escapees from slavery into a proud community. This revolutionary transformation was followed by a long, complex evolutionary process of adjustments, improvements, and reformation gloriously revealed in the scriptures of the Tanach.

In the United States, Reform Jews are an integral part of American civilization and as such operate on a dual basis: participation in congregational services and activity in the civic world.

There are two purposes for coming to the synagogue: to affirm Jewish identity and to search for spiritual enrichment. Both purposes are very much interconnected. Identity is achieved by spiritual and cultural interaction. The difficult question is this: What kind of faith-based spiritual enrichment can Reform Judaism provide us in the present complex life setting?

Current thinking has made us aware that purely scientific reasoning has difficulties explaining many natural and spiritual phenomena.[11] Personal soul searching and explorations in the way we perceive our surroundings may offer alternative approaches. Reform spiritual commentary can refer to the Tanachic heritage as an extensive report on multidimensional explorations that have enriched and guided our ancestors. Whether this experience is suitable and useful in our time is subject to different interpretations and opinions, yet as a cultural and national heritage it certainly provides us inspiration, pride, and confidence. The Enlightenment added to Jewish thinking and practices new understanding based on principles of reason and science. Reason and science framed our thinking into new determinist mind-sets that, while opening new perspectives, also showed their limitations. In the 2004 "Commentary on the Principles for Reform Judaism,"[11] it states that "Reform Jews are now liberated from the constraints of a religion based solely on rationalism, or a limited understanding of science." This comment is quite a radical departure from Reform doctrines since the Enlightenment. A broad understanding of life and science opens new opportunities for current theological reflections. For this purpose, a dialogue with the Almighty that inspires, gives confidence, and liberates is in the center of our existence and confirms the connection with the Almighty.

An alternative approach to rationalism is trial and error, which is also a divine way to guide us toward more inspiring perceptions. Can we discover divine inspiration in an accidental way (as much as we can grasp it) rather than as a premeditated will? Such a discovery can happen if we are open-minded, ready to communicate, and ready to investigate and reject dogmas and demagogy. The history of science brings us numerous examples of accidental breakthroughs and discoveries that required post-factum explanations. (Radioactivity and penicillin are only two well-known examples.) As already indicated, modern research is based as much on refutation of theories as on the imagination of the researcher and his or her ability to envision new ideas. Occasional demonstrations or political majorities are not acceptable operational modes of scientific validation.[13] In certain areas of inquiry, exploring traditions and common practices are sources of inspiration and survival.[14] All of these investigative venues, with all their uncertainty and mystery, may well be ways to bring us to gain new divine support. By recognizing the complexity of divine presence in our midst, Reform Judaism—Reform rabbis in particular—can bring to our congregations an improved and energized contemporary understanding of our religious faith.

The genius of the Jewish heritage is the richness of its experimentation since its inception. Accepting the approach that trial and error is not a sin but rather a way to search for improvement through self-initiatives, calculated risk, and imagination releases us from the bondage of determinism. In criticizing positivism, Feyerabend refers to Ernst Mach and explains that the scientific researcher, the key player in scientific development, should address research as follows:

> Entering the playground "like an attentive wanderer" ("wie ein aufmerksamer Spazierganger") the researcher develops his imagination, makes it nimble and versatile and capable of reacting to new challenges in new ways. Research, accordingly "cannot be taught," it is not "a bag of lawyers' tricks," it is an art whose explicit features reveal only a tiny part of its possibilities and whose rules are often suspended and changed by accidents and/or human ingenuity.[15]

If science can be liberated from positivistic rigidity, we can assume that religion, in particular Reform Judaism, can definitely be experienced "like an attentive wanderer." We need to emphasize, though, that nobody enjoys or is inspired by "wandering" in a desert, in a vacuum. The Jewish heritage provides us with the inspiring spiritual landscape from which we can start extracting new experiences and revelations.

By exercising our free will and creativity, "wandering" through the Jewish heritage, we may reach new spiritual revelations and be able to hear the "small inner voice" of the Almighty hidden in our deep self, and as a result, become closer to our Creator.[16] We must recognize that our "inner voice" can come to bear if we are able to appreciate our freedom of expression. But J. F. Lyotard[17] eloquently raises a question:

> Why would we have the right to freedom of expression if we had nothing to say but the already said? And how can we have any chance of finding how to say what we know not how to say if we do not listen at all to the silence of the other within?

The challenge we face is hence: Do we have anything to say?

The Tanachic message is complex. The element that brings its many attributes together is ultimately the transcendental awareness of a supportive Divinity. The Judaic Divinity is unpredictable, elusive, inspiring, and loves its Chosen People. One of the unique features of the original Jewish Divinity was and remains its monotheistic dimension. Polytheistic faiths provide comfortable identifications of the individual with specific issues, events, or natural features each represented by a specific god. This kind of identification enabled a direct and focused interaction, limited in scope. Greco-Roman pantheism developed a rich and intimate relation between gods and people, to the extent that it accepted the extreme beliefs that gods would engage in intercourse and procreate with humans. This sensual relation between gods and humans, this "partnership" between humans and gods, trivialized Divinity and caused the god or gods to lose their power to inspire trust, hope, and faith. In many ways, attempts to integrate political agendas in divine messages have a similar effect: these attempts use religious narrative as a package to market mundane agendas of special interest groups. It is hard for me to find spiritual faith in these gods.

Jewish Divinity is One. It is invisible and infinite. This overwhelming power is simultaneously intimidating and comforting. Divine power relies on our subjective belief in the presence of Divinity. For the believer, disappointing the Almighty might mean losing this supportive asset, losing spiritual freedom, with personal devastating consequences. In trusting the Almighty we may receive overpowering support anytime, anywhere. It is an asset each of us carries freely within ourselves everywhere, since Divinity is everywhere. This is the power of One and it is present in each of us and shared by all believers.

The acceptance of the One does not preclude the emergence of the contrarian concept of the other-one: evil. In a faith in which, from its very beginning, we witness dialogue and disobedience, these two aspects are embedded in the existence of the One. Our faith is shaped by the differences between the two. Tanachic heritage indicates that the One asserts its authority through debate, doubts, and choice; the other-one can suppress dialogue and impose conformity, provoke rebellion, and cause pain. Judaism exposes us constantly to this danger and tests us with our choices. It is through debate and choices, through trials and errors, through practices and beliefs that we become aware of the failure of the other-one and discover the might of the One. As Buber tells us,

66

Good and evil, then, cannot be a pair of opposites like right and left or above and beneath. "Good" is the movement in the direction of home, "evil" is the aimless whirl of human potentialities without which nothing can be achieved and by which, if they take no direction but remain trapped in themselves, everything goes awry.[18]

Home here represents a known reliable goal, while "the aimless whirl of human potentialities" tells us about intended or unintended confusing thoughts that bring us nowhere. The purpose of dialogue and trial and error is to clarify confusions and limit vagaries, ultimately enabling us to come "home."

If our Divinity encourages dialogue, this dialogue enables us to *speak out*, express opinions, and expect answers. The traditional approach for reaching answers was by interpreting the Word, written and oral, and conducting discussions in the community. Essentially these discussions were focused on deciphering the divine codes embedded in the scriptures and in the wisdom of our sages and rabbis. Through images and codes Judaism has searched and dissected divine messages. These searches have sustained and invigorated the Jewish people in the Diaspora for generations.

This process and the perceptions it generated inspired and found confirmation also in the thinking of Christian philosophers. Karl Jaspers reiterates in modern terms the wisdom of our sages. Jaspers recognizes that human existence is conditioned by the faith in Divinity, and while we cannot perceive Divinity as such, we can sense its effects, its anger, and its love.[19] In *Chiffren der Transzendenz*, Jaspers further explains that transcendental perception reaches us beyond being, beyond permanence, but as a by-pass through codes that enable us to discover a cosmology that might be unpractical but is liberating. The codes that trigger the search may be hidden in history and language, in our reality, or in our practices, and searching for them and deciphering them becomes a rewarding challenge. This liberation remains a remarkable riddle of human self-recognition and makes us reach new thinking spheres.[20] It is exciting to find out that the studies of the Talmud, Jewish traditions, and explorations in the numerical codes of the Tanach (*gematria*) are reemerging in modern non-Jewish thinking, and can enable constructive interfaith connections.

If our tradition encourages dialogue, implicitly it considers doubt as part of the debate. From Moses's doubts about his ability to fulfill the Almighty's requests to lead Israel, to the Book of Ecclesiastes and all the commentaries of our heritage, expressions of doubts are important aspects of our tradition. Doubt is mutual between Divinity and Israel. Job's righteousness and belief in the Almighty is tested, showing that divine doubt is another venue to confirm truth.

By its very nature, doubt leads to skepticism. Skepticism brings up the question of divine relevance in the Age of Reason. Skeptical doubt questions absolute authority—intellectual or institutional. Skeptical doubt is, in Odo Marquard's explanation,

> the balance, not only of conflicting dogma, but also of conflicting realities—which by that very fact (*divide et liberaliter vive!*) allows individuals freedoms and vouchsafes them the relief from the absolute that is also and above all provided, as Hans Blumenberg has shown, by the separation of powers in the myth.[21]

Does skepticism defeat the Judaic Divinity? No, on the contrary: doubt and skepticism are incentives for dialogue; dialogue enables us to express ourselves and as such exalts personal freedom. This dialogue is intimate and personal; it is abstract and transgresses daily reality. Yet, for our dialogue not to dissipate in the abyss, it must become aware of the inspiring power of Jewish Divinity as anchored in the Jewish heritage.

Reform Judaism is a voluntary, inclusive, and comprehensive spiritual venue connecting the Almighty and Reform congregants. This connection brings together a wide range of concepts, historic heritage, and practices. This connection is open to interpretations; it is an evolving connection that enables us to preserve the embrace of the Judaic Almighty while gaining new revelations on the place of Divinity in our life. This evolution from structured observant commitment to a voluntary Reform spiritual paradigm allows us to exercise a considerable degree of adjustment to related practices and rituals.

Our faith, by encouraging a continuous dialogue between congregants and by interpretations of our heritage, can answer doubts and provide a comfort by which the Almighty becomes a supporting factor to the spiritual quest of its people. The emerging dialogue creates scenarios that inspire individuals and communities to recognize and help themselves gain the faith in their spiritual path. The Tanach, a compilation of diverse and contradicting stories, a record of dialogues between Divinity and Israel, inspired Judaism to expand its thinking by adding additional experiences and scenarios, through the oral tradition and more. The historic evidence shows that the Tanach as a whole is not a plan. Even the Torah, with all its rules and regulations, is meant to be a guiding paradigm created in the desert and implemented in the Promised Land. Prophets and judges were expected to interpret these rules in the practical life of the people of Israel in the Promised Land. Skepticism is one inspiring source for interpretation that enables adjustments and reformation. The genius of this heritage is evident in the fact that two millennia after this heritage was canonized it has preserved its spiritual validity and power of inspiration.

Divinity made two promises to the Israelites: a land of "milk and honey" and the glory of the Chosen People. The challenge to Judaism—Reform Judaism in particular—is to find out what these promises mean throughout a history that has evaded straightforward answers to these promises.

For centuries, trust in divine support encouraged Judaism to overcome difficulties and acknowledge rewards. This is an abstract, spiritual relation, a relation of love. The history of Jewish love of the divine is rich in thinking and actions. Divinity designated the Israelites to be its Chosen People. Divinity inspired the Hebrew culture and the intellectual wealth of the Jewish spirit. It built the nation and established its state. It brought glory to Judaism and tested it relentlessly for centuries. People can debate the reasons for the need to be tested, its benefits and drawbacks. Yet here we are in the twenty-first century, facing a new era and wondering what is our path into the future.

Antique Judaism was a state religion in an agricultural culture. Orthodox Judaism evolved as a state-in-state culture, predominantly bourgeois, with a broad range of interpretations tied together by the Halacha. By keeping the Tanach and the Jewish scriptures removed from the public, traditional Orthodox rabbinical elite established a sacral realm whose mythical significance preserved the integrity of the faith, a faith constantly attacked by other faiths. The sacral realm also sustained the ghetto-based Jewish urban community structure, the absolute authority of the rabbinical leadership, and the cohesiveness of the Jewish public, struggling for survival in a hostile environment.

Evolving from the doubts of the Jewish Enlightenment, Reform Judaism in Europe attempted to discover modern ways to experience Judaism but failed when confronted with the entrenched European fusion between politics and religion. In the United States, Reform Judaism gained a new awareness for Judaism, thanks to the freedom of religion established in the United States' founding documents. The American open forum of discussions influenced Reform Judaism in its considering of a variety of ideas borrowed from other religions or inspired by the American context. The initial basic format for these discussions was the Reform congregational dialogue moderated by lay and rabbinical leaders. We can consider this mechanism a revival and improvement upon the antique synagogue culture. The Reform movement was and remains a pluralistic fabric of congregations connected by practices and rituals based on contemporary interpretations of the Jewish heritage. In addition to the congregational discussions, a federative format of discussion evolved as well. The result was and should continue to be an open-ended complex spiritual construct within which the parts and the whole of the space-time Jewish Divinity and Jewish heritage are in a constant process of dynamic interrelation.

Spiritual faith is individual, but it can be inspired by trained spiritual messengers, our rabbis. The role of Reform rabbis is to catalyze individuals and congregations into experiencing the Judaic divine faith. Rabbinic inspiration goes beyond knowledge: it is a talent, a gift that brings to us the spark that makes us experience, maybe only for a moment, the transcendental presence of the Almighty. An inspiring rabbi is like a lightning rod that attracts the lightning and transfers it to the grounded congregation. This is a gift given to the individual, a gift that serves our spiritual need but is not a divine attribute. The messenger is not the partner of the sender or part of the message. A Reform rabbi is a partner in the congregation and leads through inspiration. She or he is a humble and dedicated servant of the faith. The rabbi helps the community reach out and come closer to the Almighty. A gifted rabbi risks being consumed by the energy of the message. History shows that gifted rabbis most often are willing to take this risk.

It is beyond the scope of this work to attempt to explore the major subjects of inquiry mentioned in this chapter. My goal is mainly to identify conditions and factors that can guide us in envisioning and designing a sustainable spiritual Jewish Reform future. In this framework, religion is neither science nor philosophy, neither art nor technology. Religion may address each of the above, none of them, or all of them combined. Unique to religion is the belief that we humans can find help and inspiration through a combination of our own deep insight and a time-space transcendental revelation.

Notes

1. For a further understanding of these dilemmas see Robert J. MacCoun, "Biases in the Interpretation and Use of Research Results," *Annual Review of Psychology* 1998, vol. 49; and Eric Oberheim and Paul Hoyningen-Huene, "The Incommensurability of Scientific Theories," *Stanford Encyclopedia of Philosophy* (Spring 2009 Edition), archived at http://plato.stanford.edu/archives/fall2010/entries/incommensurability/.

2. A partial explanation for the difficulty in finding reasonable cause (if reasonable cause is necessary) for the emergence of major intellectual domains is discussed by P. Feyerabend, who notes that "knowledge is contained in the ability to perform special tasks ... The apparent objectivity of familiar 'facts' is a result of training combined with forgetfulness and supported by genetic dispositions; it is not the result of deepened insight." Paul Feyerabend, *Farewell to Reason* (London: Verso, 1988), 106–07.

3. The appreciation of natural features was always central in religious perception. Traditional science explained this interest mostly based on the assumption that ignorance of the scientific understanding of natural phenomena inspired

fear and awe. Human ecological studies show that people, in ancient times, already had an intuitive understanding of what the environment can offer, can afford, in terms of access, comfort, protection, and other resources. In ancient times these affordances were considered divine messages that priests were privy to identifying and enabled agriculture to develop and cities to be established. The perception and understanding of the meaning of the natural environment has emerged as an empirical and practical study area half a century ago. (See, for instance, J. J. Gibson, *The Ecological Approach to Visual Perception* [Boston: Houghton-Mifflin, 1979].) Today urban and regional planning replace religious rituals, yet the intrinsic meaning of places making people connect to sites remains a mysterious, even mythical, attribute.

4. Odo Marquard, *In Defense of the Accidental* (Oxford: Oxford Univ. Press, 1991), 121.

5. Central Conference of American Rabbis, "A Statement of Principles for Reform Judaism," adopted May 26, 1999, available at http://www.ccarnet.org.

6. Roger Scruton, "T. S. Eliot as Conservative Mentor," *Intercollegiate Review* (Fall 2003/Spring 2004): 53.

7. Feyerabend, *Farewell to Reason*, 305.

8. Recent press releases by the URJ and the RAC, full-page declarations in the general press, and the current websites connected to the Reform movement dedicated to certain political issues indicate a strong interest of our rabbinical elite in partisan political activism.

9. Central Conference of American Rabbis, "Commentary on the Principles for Reform Judaism," October 27, 2004, available at http://www.ccarnet.org.

10. For a further understanding of the notion of image in literature see P. N. Furbank, *Reflections on the Word "Image"* (London: Secker and Warburg, 1970), and for a reference work on image in art see E. H. Gombrich, *Symbolic Images*, vol. 2 (London/New York: Phaidon, 1978).

11. In the sciences the critique brought forward by Karl Popper, Thomas Kuhn, and others radically changed the traditional approach to scientific

investigation and validation. These lines of thought might also help to reconsider some theological thinking.

12. See Central Conference of American Rabbis, 2004 "Commentary on the Principles," 7.

13. The Inquisition rejected nonconforming theories and discoveries based on Catholic dogma not factual debate. It was a political decision intended to protect the established cultural power structure. In a similar way in our time, the assertion that human activity is responsible for climate change is advocated by a mixed international scientific and political establishment determined to manipulate science in order to enforce specific political and business interests. The president of the Czech Republic, an economist, has famously declared that global warming "has become a new religion or a new ideology and in that sense I think it's justified to compare it to other ideologies" (in "Freedom, Not Climate, Is under Threat," Reuters, December 11, 2007, as quoted in Christopher C. Horner, *Red Hot Lies* [Washington, DC: Regnery Publ., 2008], 213).

14. In this context we can consider anthropology and ethology as possible sources of inspiration.

15. See Feyerabend, *Farewell to Reason*, 188–89, which refers to Erich Mach's *Erkenntnis und Irrtum*, Leipzig, 1917.

16. Some might consider the source and inspiration for the "inner voice" in our traditions (David Hillel Gelernter, *Judaism: A Way of Being* [New Haven, CT: Yale Univ. Press, 2009], 124). Others may consider the Jungian and post-Jungian reference to self as well as symbols and their meaning (Andrew Samuels, *Jung and the Post-Jungians* [London/New York; Routledge & Kegan Paul, 1985], 98–100). In both cases the personal search for a spiritual inspiration requires dedication and conviction in beliefs that support faith.

17. Jean-Francois Lyotard. *Postmodern Fables* (Minneapolis, MN: Univ. of Minnesota Press, 1997), 121–22.

18. See Martin Buber, *Between Man & Man* (London: The Fontana Library, 1961), 103.

19. See K. Jaspers, *Introduction a la philosophie* (Paris: Librairie Plon, 1965), 46–52.

20. See K. Jaspers, K. *Chiffren der Transzendenz* (Munich: Piper, 1970), 42–44.

21. Odo Marquard, *Farewell to Matters of Principle: Philosophical Studies* (Oxford: Oxford Univ. Press, 1989), 17.

Chapter 4: Pride in the Jewish Heritage:
Particularism versus Universalism

6 For you are a holy people to Hashem, your God; Hashem, Your God, has chosen you to be for Him a treasured people above all the peoples that are on the face of the earth. 7 Not because you are more numerous than all the peoples. 8 Rather, because of Hashem's love for you and because He observes the oath that He swore to your forefathers did He take you out with a strong hand and redeem you from the house of slavery, from the hand of Pharaoh, king of Egypt.

Deuteronomy 7:6–8

Judaism originated as a mutual commitment between the Almighty and Israel, a commitment not based on the size of the people, or its quality (which is not even mentioned in the scripture), but because the Almighty made a promise to the forefathers. In other words, Jews and Judaism fulfill a mission designed and assigned to them by divine intent. The mission is essentially to be a designated people, "a treasured people," that implements the divine message. This is the religious essence of Jewish particularism.

The common faith basis of Jewish divine denominations is the belief in the Judaic Divinity. The uniqueness of the Judaic Divinity is in its abstract ability to inspire. The link that connects Judaic Divinity to its "Chosen People," the Tanach, is a complex, highly diverse, and pluralistic body of knowledge. For Reform Jews, the acceptance of the Tanach is by choice and accepting the Tanach makes the Jews become chosen. Accepting the Tanach and the related heritage is not a blind submission to its content but rather a wish to become part of its wisdom and contribute to it. It is a process of learning, dialogue, exchange of ideas, and ultimately, an act of conscientious love.

In the well-established Judaic tradition of interpretations and commentary, Reform Judaism is refining and improving our understanding of Judaism by addressing emerging knowledge. The Reform tradition is unique because of its open-minded, freethinking, and commonsense approach to our faith. Today, Reform Judaism acknowledges diversity in our faith by accepting and tolerating personal and congregational interpretations of practices and rituals. Affiliation and participation in congregations is voluntary. Interdenominational and interfaith dialogue is encouraged.

The 1999 "Statement of Principles" by the Central Conference of American Rabbis emphatically declares: "We are Israel."[1] Who is "we"? And who is "Israel"? In the "Commentary"[2] on the principles published in 2004, the CCAR clarifies that "Israel" stands for the people of Israel, the land of Israel, and the State of Israel. This declaration is wrong. We are not Israel; we are part of the people of Israel. We share the right of ownership in the land of Israel and we love the State of Israel.[3] We, me included, are Reform Jews, a distinct Jewish denomination, one of several Jewish denominations. In contrast to the Orthodox denomination, we recognize that our Jewish interpretation is neither exclusive nor obstructive; we do recognize the diversity of Judaism. Contrary to secular Jews, we embrace divine faith while attempting to include relevant aspects of the thinking of our time in our culture. American Reform Judaism has adopted the principle of the separation of church and state[4] and expects adherents of secular faiths to maintain and respect this separation as well.

Intrinsically, Reform Judaism recognizes the diversity of Jewish faith as an essential attribute of the Jewish heritage. In a 2011 newspaper opinion entitled "Reform Judaism Isn't an Island,"[5] Rabbi David Ellenson comments as follows:

> There is no magic bullet to resolve the challenges we face. Organizational reform is surely desirable, but institutional reorganization cannot accomplish the task of making Reform Judaism relevant to all Jews. Similarly, theology and vision are crucial. Nevertheless, we should not be naïve and assume that a commanding and compelling theology will inspire all Jews to participate meaningfully in Jewish life.

Life experiences are primarily personal and unique to the individual. The same applies to any religious experience and more so to Judaism. Reform Judaism branched out from Orthodox Judaism by emphasizing self-reliance and individualism. Self-reliance adds a new dimension to the diversity of opinions and interpretations characteristic of the Jewish heritage, widens the Jewish religious paradigm, and strengthens Judaic particularism. If we recognize that we cannot attract all Jews, it should also be clear that we cannot address the whole universe. Following this line of thought, I believe it is legitimate to question whether Reform Judaism can or should provide a universal, unifying faith.

Commentators of the Tanach and researchers of the Jewish heritage have debated whether the goal of Judaism is to be a separate, particular religion defining the Chosen People or to become an inclusive, universal faith for everyone. This debate can be reduced to two opposite attributes of the human intellect: dialogue or compliance. By definition, dialogue attempts to explore and experiment, innovate and inspire. Compliance induces conformity and comfort, obedience and stagnation. A separate, distinct position in the universe of ideas is prone to cause dialogue. An idea that is universally accepted results in conformity, compliance, and ultimately silence. For freethinking Reform Jews, Universalism is dead.

Congregational commitment can be sustained only as a voluntary aggregate of individuals who share, through dialogue, a consensus in divine faith. This consensus is not based on rational thinking but rather on a sense of belonging to a shared heritage and a shared belief in contemporary Judaic Divinity. Belonging to the congregation provides a feeling of confidence, pride, and comfort. The voluntary membership makes each congregation unique because of (a) specific attributes brought and shared by the congregants and (b) local conditions in terms of place and time.

By negotiating connections to other Reform congregations and by searching for and sharing similar feelings with other congregations— without losing the specificity of each congregation—we create the religious chain that brings together our religious denomination. These connections are most often not based on some predetermined rules but rather on a sense of shared destiny and spiritual views.

Each connection is unique and therefore it is difficult to identify any typical approach that can be rationally defined. Karl Popper indicates that "the universal, the typical, is not only the domain of reason, but it is also largely the product of reason, in so far as it is the product of scientific abstraction."[6] Reform Judaism is not a science, it is a unique spiritual relationship between Divinity and individuals, between individuals and between congregations, and hence it cannot and should not be universal.

Since its formal inception in the Sinai desert, Judaism recognized the duality between diversity and unity. Moses formalized the twelve tribes and at the same time established the Covenant, the Ark, and the rituals surrounding them as constitutional, behavioral, and ultimately symbolic unifying factors of Israel. Throughout its long history, Judaism evolved through interpretations and adjustments of its heritage into different traditions, particular though not separate: Israeli and Babylonian; Sephardic, Ashkenazic, and Yemenite; Orthodox and Reform. In Israel, the diversity is marked by such groups as *Haredi, Hassidic, Masorti,* Reform, and secular. In the United States, the Jewish public is divided into three main streams: Orthodox, Reform (including Conservative and Reconstructionist), and secular.

Many of these denominations, Reform Judaism included, have accepted but never had the courage to officially recognize the pluralism of the Jewish faith and the legitimacy of separate and particular denominations. The current exclusivity assertion adopted by each major denomination is not only unrealistic but also creates unnecessary interdenominational tensions. A formal recognition of the diversity in the Jewish faith will eliminate adversity and enable fraternal dialogue and cooperation.[7]

Dialogue is generated by diversity of ideas. Diverse ideas do not necessarily have to be exclusive. Art and architecture are two outstanding examples of how each of us can admire and appreciate highly different masterpieces, Classical or Gothic, Baroque or Modern, without dismissing one for the other. In music, we can love Mozart, Beethoven, and Gershwin with the same enthusiasm. Such diversities can raise questions, inspire new ideas, and generate a continuous dialogue.

History has witnessed alternating periods of active discourse and compliant conformity. In the civic domain, differences of opinion can be resolved by democratic action reflecting the discursive pluralistic scene or by an authoritative decision imposed by coercion. At times, dialogue and inquiry prevailed and provided humanity the path for survival, improvement, and development. It can be noticed that contemporary thinking has reached a stage in which many, though not all, are accepting the benefit of pluralism: the voluntary congregation of particular opinions, ideas, and beliefs brought together through dialogue and a shared sense of belonging.

One example of a positive dialogue among Judaism, Christianity, and civic society was the establishment of academic Judaic programs in the last quarter of the twentieth century. The success of these programs, in a short period of time, indicates the public's interest in the topic and its willingness to listen to and understand the Judaic message, without constraints or advocacy. It seems that the attraction of Judaic studies lies in their unique spiritual *authenticity* and *relevance*. For students in search of a better understanding of religious faith, Judaic studies provide an exposure to the sources and fundamentals of the monotheistic faiths in their original and quintessential form, undistorted by added scenarios and practices. In addition, the intellectual richness of the Judaic studies and their ability to address current situations in convincing ways offered new relevance to Judaism in our time. Still, we need to be careful what direction the content of the courses take. Are they providing an informative, balanced view of Judaism or are they propaganda vehicles for ideological messages wrapped in Judaic verbiage? Freedom of speech in academia is essential, yet it should not come at the expense of free, rigorous, authentic, comprehensive, and open-minded thinking on Judaism. Reform Judaism was, is, and should be a strong promoter of the open dialogue as a way to avoid abusing Judaism by preaching personal convictions in an attempt to brainwash the audience. Reform teachers and rabbis are uniquely positioned to be at the forefront of this constructive open dialogue.

Reform Judaism, as exemplified by the pluralistic character of congregations, has consistently reaffirmed its intrinsic freethinking and open-minded approach to faith. Modern Reform Judaism recognizes that each individual is unique and can make his or her specific contribution to the congregation. It also accepts the freedom of each congregant to exercise his or her own way of worship as long as one does not force others to follow it. Congregations unable to reach a pluralistic balance disintegrate. When a pluralistic agreement is reached, a congregation adopts a common denominator and shapes common practices and rituals.

Can we identify in the forthcoming post-"liberal," post-Marxist era, common grounds that can strengthen the particular character of our congregations, without being subjugated to each other or forced to follow the evil tyranny of one "party line"? Can we find comfort and hope in the dialogue between individuals as a spiritual venue to go beyond the known and the explicable? Additionally, can we explore the Jewish heritage and develop contemporary answers to current spiritual challenges? Can we redeem through dialogue family values that maintain sensitive and responsible relations toward children in our time and age? Throughout it all, can our Reform faith be inspired by our own experiences as revealed to us through our perceptions?

It seems that currently, many of these questions are marginally addressed by the Reform leadership, which persists in promoting political activism. The current political agenda promoted by the URJ and the CCAR eliminates dialogue and provides a power platform for select national elites who pretend to represent our religion. By attempting to create a uniform and universal movement, this elitism, reminiscent of nineteenth-century elitism, is wrong and foreign to the enlightened spirit of contemporary American Reform Judaism. The activist, partisan political direction adopted by the current Reform leadership takes on the dimensions of a reversed missionary action: it keeps a veneer of religious rituals while advocating a one-sided socioeconomic orientation and political content.[8]

Throughout our history we Jews resisted missionary pressure and suffered continual discrimination for declining offers of conversion and for maintaining our beliefs. Reform Judaism is not a missionary denomination. Universalist activism of the Reform movement in the last two centuries has been a controversial and divisive theme in the movement, especially since it contradicts the diverse, individualistic, and pluralistic character of the movement.[9] Other parallel streams of universal thinking, such as Catholic, Marxist, atheist, or environmentalist, preached the adherence to specific ethical codes that are essentially vehicles for a privileged group to assert power. Because of their power, greed, and restricted freedom, Universalist movements failed to achieve any of their goals, in particular that of global dominance. Our world today has more religious diversity and more national and ethnic identities than ever before. The American experience shows that only through pluralism, based on well-established freedoms and the defense of separate opinions, can discrimination and tyranny be avoided, bringing us closer to cooperation, prosperity, and personal security.

The Tanachic notion of the "Treasured People" or "Chosen People" indicates, between other attributes, that Judaism is a special religious idea between many other religious ideas. As such its mission is to be a participant and eventually a leader in the spectrum of ideas. The history of Judaism has confirmed the ability of our religion to do just that, often in difficult and painful situations. If Reform Judaism is aspiring to be on the forefront of modern religious dialogue it can achieve this position only if it preserves its spiritual integrity and does not pollute it with opportunistic political interests.

In this age of information deluge, exploding imagination, and inexplicable discoveries, many of the established truths can be put in doubt. A Reform approach, based on the recognition that our heritage is well tested by doubt, dialogue, interpretations, and commentaries, enables us to address new challenges with a reasonable degree of confidence, without undermining the integrity of our faith.

We must be aware that some of our interlocutors are still assertive and aspire to achieve global dominance and universal acceptance. Some Christian denominations, as well as Islam, Marxism, and environmentalism, are still continuing to advocate the universality of their faith with vigor and considerable intransigence. In spite of their variable degrees of inner diversity, many of these religious denominations are each united in their conviction that they represent the only valid, universal truth. Reform Judaism is and will be able to resist the totalitarian aspirations of these divine- or secular-oriented denominations by rejecting Universalism and sustaining Reform Judaism's diverse, pluralist, and particular approach to the Judaic faith. It can sustain its spiritual autonomy without undertones of victimization, in calm, dignified, and balanced ways, rather than with extreme vocal agitation and radical advocacy. Reform Judaism in America can present an authentic and inspiring Judaic faith, based on freethinking, respect for individual opinions, and Judaic particularism.

Being a distinct Jewish denomination, being particular, does not mean being isolated, parochial, or prejudicial. Separation does not mean exclusion. On the contrary, Reform Judaism can become a spiritual inspiration to aspire to spiritual excellence and to influence and lead through example. Reform Judaism can become an example for other denominations willing to preserve our pluralistic and democratic culture. Becoming a spiritual example is the ideal for any participant in a culture that fosters freedom of choice. The result is an evolving discourse rather than definitive proclamations, and rich and inspiring alternatives rather than an equalizing uniformity.

Notes

1. Central Conference of American Rabbis, 1999 "Statement of Principles."

2. Central Conference of American Rabbis, 2004 "Commentary on the Principles," 11.

3. The religious affiliation and cultural identification of Jews to the Judaic/Israelite heritage is a broad paradigm that enables us to connect worldwide. The State of Israel, with its unique patrimony of its Jewish holy and historic places and monuments and its Judaic culture, is our faith-based center of gravity. At the same time, those of us living in the Diaspora must remain aware of our civic commitment to our country of residence. Accordingly we can and should be a two-way bridge of friendship between the State of Israel and our state of residence.

4. For more on the separation of church and state, see chap. 5.

5. Ellenson, "Reform Judaism Isn't an Island."

6. See K. Popper, *The Open Society and Its Enemies* (Princeton, NJ: Princeton Univ. Press, 1971) 2:245.

7. Dana Kaplan discusses the challenges of Jewish denominations (see Dana E. Kaplan, *Contemporary American Judaism* [New York: Columbia Univ. Press, 2009], the chapter on "The Rise and Fall of American Jewish Denominationalism") and points out that Reform Judaism, by reintegrating the other reformist denominations, might remain the only divine alternative outside the Orthodox realm. I believe that this involves a matter of definition. If the Reform movement adopts a genuine open-minded national structure, without its current civic politicization, it might very well reach this status. Indeed, there are no fundamental contradictions between the pluralistic and inclusive concept of Reform Judaism and the other reformative denominations that historically were splinters from the main Reform movement. This process must be a friendly, collaborative process of partnership based on mutual respect and not a "corporate" takeover.

8. See the websites of the Union for Reform Judaism and the Religious Action Center of Reform Judaism. The pamphlets advocate notions that rely heavily on scientific theories, some of which are very controversial. As indicated before, this universal approach no longer suits the spirit of our time and the essence of our faith.

9. Inspired by Mendelssohn's attempts to convince the authorities that Jews can be loyal subjects and by pressures from local governments to "educate" Jews into the cultured life of Christian society, Reform rabbis, starting with Leopold Zunz, approached reformation by adopting elements of the Christian traditions (Meyer, *Response to Modernity*, 39; see note in chap. 1). Some of these elements were universal in nature (Ibid., 48) and evolved into a central opinion, following the Kantian influence. Enlightened Jewish thinkers attempted to prove that Judaism actually may become the ideal religion Kant invoked (Ibid., 66). This transition raised passionate debates and divisions in the Jewish public. In the United States, David Einhorn advocated the messianic mission of the Jewish people and its universal goal (Ibid., 246). His influence, together with others, shaped the long-lasting Universalist positions of the CCAR.

Chapter 5:   Separation of Church and State:
A Multidimensional Existence

> While as citizens, of course, we accept and respect the laws
> of the land, including those laws which include provisions
> as to which [we] were and are apprehensive, we reaffirm our
> long-established position that the principle of separation of
> church and state is best for both church and state and is
> indispensable for the preservation of that spirit of religious
> liberty which is a unique blessing of American democracy.
> This principle is shared by forward-looking elements of
> all faiths.
>
> Union for Reform Judaism, 48th General Assembly,
> November 1965, San Francisco, California

The European political scene struggled for centuries to merge the
authority and power of church and state and to determine the
priorities between the religious and the civic establishments. The
origins of this process were the traditional Tanachic and Classical
premises that church and state are compatible and able to integrate.
And yet there is overwhelming evidence that these two institutions
were incompatible on at least two levels: authority and values.

King and state derived their authority from physical power;
religion derived its authority from divine inspiration. In the Tanachic
tradition, church attempted to control the state by anointing the
king, while preserving a grassroots influence through the clergy and
its material and spiritual resources. Kings and state enhanced their

power by enrolling the support of the landed aristocracy and other interested parties. The two establishments remained interlocked in a long-lasting power struggle.

No less critical were the differences on value issues. Allegiance to king and state required a direct and tangible connection to the people. Even absolute kings had to convey their rulings to their allies and subjects in reasonable ways. Republics were even more committed to communicate and advocate their decisions and receive popular support. The interests of the state were local and mundane. The church, by representing a supreme will, expected a complete and absolute submission to supreme divine ruling as brought forward by the leaders of the church. The church's interests were universal and inclusive and were conveyed through mystical and spiritual means.

Two factors became game changers in the Western culture: the emerging power of cities and the Lutheran Reform. In this wider political field, the state power, the king, was able to have more choices and acquire more political leverage. Still, each state in Europe preserved its own state church. Often the presence of a Christian minority or other minorities complicated the situation. In some states, such as France or England, the king, the embodiment of the state, took over the local dominant religious authority while eliminating other religious alternatives. In Central Europe, the fragmentation of states allowed religious denominations to find patrons, and some Christian denominations became state-dominant forces. In many ways, the result remained inconclusive and rife with tensions.

The urban population increasingly nurtured skeptical views both on the monarchy and religion. This skepticism brought the bourgeoisie to encourage unconventional thinking and education and to attempt to gain autonomy or independent status.

Wherever it was tolerated, Judaism was in an exceptional position. The Jewish ghettos operated as autonomous urban theocracies with a strong mercantile foundation. The separation between the ghetto and the rest of the political scene made the Jewish community physically vulnerable but at the same time spared it the need to become a party in the continuous conflicts dividing the Christian bourgeoisie. The late Renaissance period was characterized by political consolidation that generated, in the eighteenth century, the European Enlightenment. From the Jewish perspective, this seemed to be an opportunity in Central and Western Europe to cross the separation boundaries between the ghetto seclusion and the Christian state. The intention was to consider Judaism as an additional religious minority with equal civic rights and responsibilities. This expectation added a tension to the already complex relations between the Catholic Church, the Protestant Church, and the increasing activism of the bourgeoisie.

The inability to reach a compromise between state, church, and the bourgeoisie exploded in the French Revolution. One of the main messages of the revolution was the separation between church and state and the promulgation of the principle of freedom from (state) religion. The revolution demonized the established religions and adopted secularism as its guiding belief, promoted with religious zeal. The persecution of traditional religious people and the revocation of Divinity as a spiritual fundamental had two unexpected consequences: it united and energized the divine religious opposition to the revolution, and it transformed secular ideas into a new set of beliefs, a new form of religion. In essence, the European republican movement, by adding a new set of (secular) religious beliefs, did not change the nature of the inter-religious confrontations; it just exacerbated them.

The new political developments offered Jews wider options for assimilation. Assimilated Jews who preserved a loose Jewish affiliation, or adopted secular or Christian beliefs, were able to succeed and rise to preeminence.

Still, the revolutionary spirit of the nineteenth century brought little or no fundamental change in the status of the European Jewish communities, traditional or Reform. I can assert that, in spite of extensive rhetoric to the opposite, Europeans over the last two centuries and into the present have struggled to find a formula to separate the civic state authority from enrooted religious beliefs and prejudices.[1] They still have not found a way to overcome the detrimental legacy of freedom *from* religion in their attempt to clarify the relationship between church and state. This controversy stands out when compared with the way the issue of separation of state and church has evolved in the United States.

The American Revolution adopted the principle of freedom *of* religion, which is quite different from the European principle of freedom *from* religion. A change in one preposition makes all the difference. The American approach recognized religion as a legitimate interest and provided the freedom to follow any religious denomination, while formally preventing the establishment of one official religion. It was the founders' intent to establish free religious practices and to prevent bringing to America the religious conflicts of Europe. For the first time in history, a new relationship between church and state was clearly defined: freedom through separation. This separation recognized the benefit of accepting the incompatibility between the two domains, while at the same time enhancing the validity and merit of each domain in its own right.

Different from civic subdivisions, traditional religions believe in an absolute, initial truth. Whether it is by putting faith in the supreme and ineffable existence of a divine Almighty or by believing in the sanctity of Nature or by pursuing the fundamental and comprehensive scientific truth, all these human endeavors seek a unifying, constant truth.

Contemporary thinking recognizes that it is very possible that human intelligence is unable to reach and comprehend the ultimate truth. As such, it accepts that our immediate truth might be somehow different than the total truth.[2] From this perspective, scientific research, through theory and refutation, attempts to come as close as possible to the ultimate goal. Believers in Nature pursue the same goal through perseverant discovery processes. The believers in a divine existence, in particular those following the omnipresent, time-space Judaic perception, enjoy the comfort of accepting transcendental Divinity as a starting point without explanation, and the rest is interpretation.

Historically, different religious interpretations pursue spiritual and political dominance by integrating all aspects of public and private life under one religious mantle: divine or secular/scientific/nature.

The equal constitutional status of all religions in the United States compelled religious denominations to recognize the prevalence of the constitutional civic authority as a protection of their respective liberty. It is most remarkable to notice the enthusiastic adherence of the American public to the principle of separation between church and state in the early years of the republic. Alexis de Tocqueville highlights this consensus and the support the American (Catholic) clergy expressed for this principle. He recognizes this principle as one key cause for "maintaining democracy" in America.[3] Over time, however, erosions in the consensus occurred. The proliferation of religious denominations invited competition for new followers. These competitions often induced religious denominations to adopt civic and political agendas, packaged in religious terminology, in order to attract and expand their membership. This activism often blurred the borderline between state and church activity and authority.

A democratic civic authority is expected to create the framework of political agreements for the performance of civic life and community governance. Religions are expected to provide visions of hope and spiritual support, enriched by critical thinking intended to inspire moral quality in the life of individuals and the community. Freedom of religion enables each individual to follow unobstructed any spiritual vision free from any public control. In a free society, political agreements and spiritual freedom can coexist separately. Civic concepts are mundane and material; religions are visionary and spiritual. The two notions dwell in different worlds. This positive incompatibility is a significant attribute of the educated, civilized person.

A helpful explanation of this human attribute can be found in Isaiah Berlin's doctrine of value pluralism and the incommensurability of incompatible goods. Berlin observes that human values may often not be combinable—for example, the demand for freedom of information and the need for privacy, or enjoying a Shakespearean sonnet and a sushi dish. We might enjoy both but we can hardly find common measures or dependencies. More sushi will not improve the sonnet or vice versa. Following the same line of thought, we may reach the conclusion that two values that are incommensurable cannot be compared, reasonably connected, or justified.[4] We may be able to appreciate each value on its own merit but we cannot rank them on a comparative scale. They are incompatible because they lack common measures. The remarkable aspect of the human intellect consists in its ability to recognize, produce, experience, and appreciate incommensurable values without much difficulty. The problem occurs when people are forced to choose between incommensurable values or attempt to merge them. As a matter of fact, by keeping such values separate we might enjoy them better, understand them better, and eventually expand them. From the point of view of the individual participant and possibly also from the perspective of congregations, if civic life and religious experiences are incommensurable, yet we can appreciate each of them in their own right, why attempt to merge them? Often the human mind is inspired and nurtured by the disparate and challenged by the different and the incommensurable. Separation enables perspective, prevents conflicts, and might trigger the human imagination.

The American Jewish population subscribes to two main divine religious approaches. Orthodox Judaism attempts to preserve, as much as possible, its state-in-state authority, including the preservation, as much as civil law allows, of the Halachic jurisprudence. Joining an Orthodox community is conditioned upon rabbinical scrutiny and approval and accepting and following Orthodox rules and leadership. Reformed Judaism officially recognizes the principle of separation of church and state and delegates conflict resolutions to civil jurisprudence. Joining and being part of a Reform congregation is a personal decision sustained by voluntary involvement in the congregation.

I would dare to comment that it is possible to see the relative decline in America of main Christian denominations (if we ignore immigration) as a result of their aggressive social activism and politicization that compromised their spiritual integrity. Research in the performance of religious denominations indicates that denominations with a weak spiritual basis are losing support and members.[5] Many such communities develop a "free-rider problem," which consists of a large number of members who do not participate in activities of the congregation but might take advantage of some of its services.

By allowing congregants a wide range of choices and options, Reform Judaism practices today a "consumer Judaism," to use Rabbi Michael Goldberg's term as quoted by Dana Kaplan. Kaplan, in focusing on the Reform denomination, agrees with Rabbi Eric Yoffie's belief that "Jewish doing" should precede theological statements. This approach is actually a traditional approach in Judaism. Orthodox Judaism mandates the following of the Halacha rules in day-to-day active application as an evidence of religious compliance.

In the designing of the Reform platforms, the Central Conference of American Rabbis has maintained the same Orthodox methodology, only changing the emphasis from *mizvot* (religious rules) to social action. The promoted social actions have strong civic characteristics and hence overlap with the out-of-church professional, business, or civic activities of the congregants. As such, these so-called "religious" activities lose their validity and momentum and may even alienate parts of the public. For instance, right now, the Religious Action Center of Reform Judaism advocates political content that positions it as a political action committee of an extreme wing of one of our major political parties. Such partisan activism polarizes the Reform constituency and throws the movement into the controversial and volatile political arena. The fact that other major denominations indulge in similar fallacies does not justify following in their footsteps.

Reform Judaism can and should distinguish itself by maintaining the separation between church and state and by enhancing its ability to project, from an unattached position, critical thinking enshrined in the richness of the Jewish heritage. A responsive Reform approach should focus on genuine religious action: a spiritual enrichment, visionary directions—essentially an interpretation and adaptation of the Jewish heritage to contemporary living. The Reform movement needs to recognize the issues that address religious interests and distinguish them from issues of nonreligious, civic interest. For instance, topics related to spiritual enrichment and ethics, the nature of family spirit, and comprehensive education are particular to our faith and involve the seeking of qualitative answers. On the other hand, issues such as security, justice, labor relations, and environment are civic in nature and scope and should not be included in a religious framing. The recent opposition of the Religious Action Center to including religious schools in the voucher policy in the name of the separation of church and state exposes a double standard. Does not the RAC's position contradict the strong interest Reform congregations take in religious education, individual choice, and parental responsibility? On the other hand, is not RAC's enthusiastic support for the Patient Protection and Affordable Care Act ("Obamacare") or for "cap and trade" legislation direct intervention in civic legislation and, as such, an infringement of the separation principle? Given the public sensitivity to these issues, involvement in civic and political issues, with all their embedded controversies, subverts religious ethical integrity, inclusiveness, and spiritual inspiration.

A precondition for operating effectively while maintaining important limits, such as the separation of church and state, is individual and public honesty. Honesty implies clarity of intent and no double standards. A conduct that performs on blurred boundaries and manipulates terminology is dangerous and counterproductive. Even worse, it might cause confusion and unwarranted conflicts with civic authorities and other denominations.

As citizens and member of civic society, Jewish individuals are and should be participating in the civic debates. They can contribute as part of citizens' groups or as volunteers for civic work and other similar activities and can fulfill sociopolitical missions. Yet, we should not confuse our identity as Reform Jews with our identity as citizens. The principle of separation of church and state established a personal dual identity: religious and civic. They are related but not identical. Civic life is determined by issues concerning the majority of the public and addressed by practical and feasible public management (politics). Religious life is guided by spiritual transcendental vision reflecting ethical and aesthetic perspectives. Maintaining the separation between the two is meant to be inspiring.

Respect for the separation between church and state applies with the same rigor to civic institutions and secular denominations. We are currently witnessing a renewed anti-religious activism initiated through civic institutions. Initiatives such as removing the words "under God" from the recitation of the Pledge of Allegiance, prohibiting the practice of male circumcision, the attempt to use labor laws to regulate the qualifications of clergy (*Hosanna-Tabor Evangelical Lutheran Church and School v. EEOC*, in which the US Supreme Court rightfully rejected the attempt), and the use of the Affordable Care Act to impose behavioral prescriptions in blatant contradiction to established religious tenets, are indications that secular movements, with the support of sympathetic political parties, are planning a reconsideration of the freedom *of* religion principle.[6] Apparently, this is a reaction to the current rise in the public's interest in divine denominations. Secular denominations, unable to compete and unwilling to recognize their failure, are starting to use legal subterfuges and scare tactics to impose their beliefs.

As history has demonstrated, the merger of church and state distorts reality, limits freedom, and engenders unwarranted, confusing, and abrasive positions that often culminate in conflicts. We have to recognize that humanity is complex and that imposing one-size-fits-all simple solutions is, in most cases, destructive.[7]

After a half a century of experimentation, the post–Second World War Western European welfare state, which is based on secular faith and Socialist ideological beliefs, is failing. The European welfare states survived economically as long as the American capitalist economy and its taxpayers were willing and able to subsidize them.

The Marxist Eastern European model failed because its communist ideology, aimed at equalizing society, proved to be a socioeconomic disaster and an oppressive, dehumanizing regime that became a human tragedy of historic proportions.

In both situations we can note a depressive spiritual vacuum nurtured by the official secular faith. The secular message failed because science cannot provide a holistic explanation for life and human existence and cannot fully resolve the mysteries of nature. Science might reveal unknown information and attempt to confirm specific ideas by refutation, but it cannot create new human realities. Human realities are created by the human spirit through inspiration and innovation.

In Tanachic times, following the Torah guidelines, Judaism in the Holy Land was actually operating along three separate and quite autonomous lines of conduct: first, the lay system led by elders, chieftains, and later the monarchy; second, the select religious establishment of *kohanim* and *levyim* which conducted the religious rituals and maintained the symbols of the faith; and third, the ethical and spiritual voices of judges and prophets. To my best knowledge this Tanachic institutional separation, with the authoritative and critical voices of the prophets fulfilling a "checks and balances" role, got its first adaptation in the founding documents of the United States republic.

Religious issues are essentially ethical and aesthetic visions of faith and reflections on Divinity, expressed by rituals and common practices. Let us recognize the genius of our Tanachic heritage. The Tanach provided us with a multidimensional culture as an awesome reflection of our abstract and infinite Divinity. This reflection, revolutionary at its time and controversial for many centuries, has become a highly suitable concept for our time. Inspired by the Tanachic precedent and reflecting modern thinking, Reform

Judaism raised doubts about the theocratic approach to Judaism maintained by Orthodox Judaism. The goal of Reform Judaism is to develop a modern understanding of our traditional Divinity as a suitable transcendental belief for our time. It is the study of this transcendental belief that can provide a comforting reference to inexplicable natural and human phenomena and become a spiritual anchor. This position is justifiable only if Reform Judaism provides its vision distinct from any mundane political debate; it nurtures the spirit and leaves practical solutions to the civic establishment, the politicians. Cleared of its political aberrations, Reform Judaism can promote the core message of its religious mission: spiritual and moral inspiration.

Reform Judaism, as an offspring of the Jewish Enlightenment, is ideally equipped to be in the forefront of defending the integrity of the US Constitution, the revered product of the Enlightenment. If such an approach is shared by other religions, separation between church and state can be achieved and ultimately foster the freedoms of speech and of religion.

Notes

1. The conflicts in the Balkans, in Belgium, in Ireland, to note only the most visible conflicts, have all had religious origins. Recently, the difficulties caused in Europe by unassimilated and uncooperative religious communities, mostly Islamic in orientation, indicate the inherent difficulty European states, from Norway to Albania, from England to Russia, have in dealing with religious diversity. The centuries-old religious discrimination has been replaced, in most states, by noncommittal, noninterventionist policies advocating tolerance for religious diversity. In reality, these policies discourage dialogue, encourage extremism, and sustain and exacerbate the alienation between religious groups. There is evidence that the secular European states are unable to overcome their deeply engrained local religious bias and to provide formulas

of national integration, let alone assimilation into the local culture. Again, the freedom *from* religion principle shows its failure to provide a suitable and sustainable answer to religious differences. In addition, historic religious/ethnic divisions have been aggravated by manipulating immigrant groups. Belgium is an outstanding example. In order to balance the influence of the Flemish population, Walloon politicians have encouraged immigration from ex-French colonies. The newcomers, however, are of Islamic denominations quite unfamiliar with the local culture and as a consequence they have added an additional layer to the local religious tensions. The political game has backfired and the situation in Belgium today is quite precarious.

2. Theories in evolution, ecology, ethology, and phenomenology offer explanations for life achievements and performance in our perceivable time-space frames of reference. Does this understanding apply in the same manner in the cosmic space or time frames measured in light-years? We can imagine unknown realities, but can we test and verify them with human tools?

3. Alexis de Tocqueville, *Democracy in America* (New York: Vintage Books, 1945) 1:319–26.

4. For a broader discussion on the subject, see J. Gray, *Isaiah Berlin* (Princeton, NJ: Princeton Univ. Press, 1997), the chapter on "Pluralism."

5. See Dana E. Kaplan "Reform Jewish Theology and the Sociology of Liberal Religion in America: The Platforms as Response to the Perception of Socioreligious Crisis," *Modern Judaism* 20, no. 1 (2000]: 60–77.

6. See Michael W. McConnell, "Washington Wants a Say Over Your Minister," *Wall Street Journal*, October 5, 2011, and D. Wuerl, C. Colson, and C. Y. Soloveichik, "United We Stand for Religious Freedom," *Wall Street Journal*, February 10, 2012. The essence of these constitutional violations is best captured in this quotation from the article by Wuerl, Colson, and Soloveichik: "Even worse than the financial impact is the breach of faith represented by Ms. Sibelius's decision. Her notion of an 'appropriate balance' between religious freedom and 'increasing access' to 'important preventive services' stands the First Amendment on its head." In other words, the Obama administration sees itself entitled to determine what is important in religious matters.

7. We witness current rhetorical attempts to replace the promotion of *freedom of religion* with the *freedom of worship*. Freedom of worship is a component of the practice of religion but does not include the cultural and psychological content that shapes religions. The elimination of the religious content deprives us of the dialogue necessary to bring spiritual comfort to individual congregants and voids any basis for interfaith understanding and dialogue.

Chapter 6: **Grassroots Governance**

People: Effective planning requires the active involvement and commitment of synagogue leaders and the participation of the clergy and key congregants.

Process: There needs to be a clearly delineated set of activities that facilitate the development of a plan involving key congregants in making decisions about the current and future state of the synagogue.

Cultivating the Future: Long-Range Planning for Congregations, Union for Reform Judaism[1]

One main cause for the split of Reform Judaism from Orthodox Judaism was the wish of Reform followers to have participatory governance. Participatory governance evolved into a shared, dual leadership structure: a lay board, with the rabbi's spiritual guidance. This arrangement was a radical evolution that elevated the lay leadership to an equal or preferred role to that of the clergy. This balanced leadership generated a novel checks-and-balances system that was different in many ways from the autocratic governance of the Orthodox community.

The transition, in the early nineteenth century, of Reform Judaism to America initially enhanced the lay-oriented governance by emphasizing the unique American principle of government "of, by, and for" the people—in this case, the Jewish congregants. The American sense of individual initiative and responsibility appeared to be prevalent in these congregations. This development was made possible by the civic framework of our constitutional republic that enabled freedom of speech and freedom of religion. Accordingly, each congregation operated autonomously and adopted local religious practices and rituals. The practices of each congregation seemed to enhance their own identity through interpretations inspired by practices of other religions or sometimes just through sheer innovation. Often these developments diluted the content and structure of the Jewish faith to an extent that it appeared to be indistinguishable from other surrounding denominations.

By mid–nineteenth century an opposite alternative emerged that focused on centralizing the governance of the movement. Inspired by the European tradition of central control of religion, Reform leaders, starting with Isaac Mayer Wise, initiated national organizations intended to unify the movement and adopt national standards of religious practices and rituals. Unified governance promised to provide quality services such as the education and training of rabbis and professional staff. In retrospect, we can see that, by its centralized intent, the unified leadership challenged the autonomy and American individualistic spirit adopted by the rank and file. In many ways, the unification attempted to limit the religious spontaneity and innovation of each congregation—unique characteristics of the Reform movement.

The national leadership that emerged was divided among three organizations: the Union of American Hebrew Congregations (UAHC), which later became the Union for Reform Judaism (URJ), the Central Conference of American Rabbis (CCAR), and the Hebrew Union College (HUC). The three organizations were meant to provide congregational support and operate on parallel tracks: the UAHC, based on lay governance, had a congregational orientation, the CCAR was conceived as a professional rabbinic association, and the HUC conducted the educational arm of Reform Judaism intended to prepare the religious cadre.

Following the example of Christian activism, the leadership of the Reform movement involved itself in the civic life of communities at large and became active in national politics.[2] The national organizations gradually evolved and became the message setters of the movement, producing a series of platforms, statements, and national initiatives. This assertion of power culminated with the selection of Rabbi Maurice Eisendrath as president of the UAHC. Eisendrath's ambitious and energetic personality enthroned in the movement a *kohanic* authoritative leadership that imposed its will over the dissent of congregations and other leading personalities of the movement.[3] He and his successors operated as CEOs of the movement and considered themselves the mind, the face, and the voice of Reform Judaism. The balanced leadership of the movement was negatively affected when the effective leadership—the presidency of the UAHC/URJ—became the domain of rabbis instead of lay leaders.

Historically, the kohanim were appointed servants of the Temple, not spiritual leaders. Prophets and judges, and later, rabbis were the recognized spiritual leaders. The kohanim distinguished themselves in the late period of the Second Temple by taking over the leadership and imposing a controversial authoritative regime. The current corporate governance of the Reform movement is characterized by its kohanic bureaucratic takeover of the leadership, a leadership that shows little tolerance for democratic debate on issues or leadership roles. This centralized process brought an unwarranted rigidity into the operation of the movement, a rigidity that is foreign to the intrinsic "open mind" premise of Reform Judaism. The URJ is increasingly performing like a public corporation with limited accountability to its grassroots membership and with diminished formal participation of the rank-and-file members and rabbis. In many ways, this type of governance, with its focus on "corporate" survival, rather than on spiritual leadership, is causing the movement to become a stagnant follower rather than an inspired leader. For much of the twentieth century the Reform movement was inclined to "play it safe" and follow the political trends of the day, even when these trends contradicted the interests of Jewish people. The corporate national governance style inspired some congregations to adopt similar corporate governance structures at the local level. Local kohanic governance is a first step in changing the participatory nature of a congregation to bring it closer to the authoritative, theocratic regime of Orthodox communities.

We should distinguish here between the Orthodox rabbinical authority and the emerging "kohanic" Reform rabbinical assertion of power. Since Jewish orthodoxy does not commit to the separation of church and state, the responsibilities of the rabbi are extensive and demanding. Different from the Orthodox rabbis, Reform rabbis glean their authority from their ability to participate in the congregational dialogue and by providing spiritual faith-based inspiration and moral support. The very being of a Reform congregation is conditioned by the balanced cooperation between the lay and rabbinical thinking. Its decisions are ratified by the congregation and represent the congregation. An unilateral top-down empowerment of the congregational rabbi, as a representative of the central authority, may transform his or her role from an accepted leader, who is an integral part of the congregation, to a kohanic agent, a sort of religious commissar, assigned to control the congregation. Reform Judaism questioned the absolute authority of rabbis or any central authority and replaced it with balanced governance. Any top-down unwarranted determinations in Reform Judaism would be dubious and lack validity.

Replacing the theological focus with political activism is endangering the dialogue that sustains our congregational structure. In addition to dividing the congregation along political lines, it might generate a divide between the lay leadership and the rabbinical leadership. Instead of working together in a continuous constructive dialogue, declarative leadership guided by top-down proclamations unsanctioned by the public at large enhances the kohanic empowerment of the national rabbinical elite and oppresses and frustrates grassroots participation. An example of this can be found in Rabbi Eric H. Yoffie's sermon to the 65th UAHC Biennial Assembly in 1999, in Orlando, Florida, when he proposed

> that this worship revolution be built upon the premise of partnership: rabbis will be its architects, cantors its artists, and lay people its builders. This has always been the way of our movement ... So it is critical that vested interests be put aside and that the laity be admitted into the dialogue, even as we acknowledge that Jewish wisdom is ultimately the rabbis' expertise.

These quotations indicate a fundamental contradiction to the essential tenets of Reform Judaism: the laity is not supposed to be "admitted" into the dialogue. The laity was, is, and should stay a full partner in the leadership dialogue, providing its own wisdom parallel and equal to the rabbinic wisdom. As I am an architect, I also must correct Rabbi Yoffie's understanding of architecture by indicating that an architectural project is a full collaboration initiated by owners and expert developers ("lay people") with whom architects and engineers collaborate to design the project. Other "lay participants," including public authorities and financial groups, criticize, review, and approve the project, whose execution is supervised by architects and authorities and built by expert specialists. The architectural analogy shows that even in the building industry there is no "tyranny" of one profession. The kind of "partnership" proposed in Yoffie's address, with its distinct separation of roles and implied hierarchy, is far from responding to the Reform perception of shared governance and the principle of checks and balances. Reform Judaism is "of the people, by the people, for the people," and the role of the rabbi is to inform, teach, and participate in the dialogue, not necessarily to lead the dialogue. In the Reform congregation, leadership—spiritual or managerial—should be acquired by inspiration not title, through congregational recognition and consent.

In my opinion, we can identify the kohanic trend as an ideological confusion. Christian Protestants were the dominant religion in the United States. As such they were in a dual situation. On one hand they took credit for establishing the tenets of the republic. As the dominant community, however, with the majority of the population, they had a controlling institutional presence in the political system. This duality could have been perceived as constitutionally unbalanced and raised the question whether this unbalance should be corrected by religious redistribution, or whether other means could be designed such as attention to ethnicity, race, gender, and more. We must note that, different from their European counterparts, American Protestants recognized the problem and took a leadership role in the multidenominational effort to sustain American pluralism.

Civic challenges are, by definition, political. They have a wide public outreach and, as discussed previously, including them in religious concepts contradicts basic tenets of Reform Judaism, specifically the separation between church and state. Reform Judaism was and remains a small part of the American mosaic. By adopting policies and actions that are focused on political issues rather than specific religious issues, the movement diminishes its uniqueness and wastes its resources. It is quite easy to identify, as negative consequences of political involvement, the accusations of illegality regarding the charity status of our congregations, of lobbying for special interests, of promoting one-sided propaganda, or of brainwashing students in religious schools and seminaries.

The URJ, as the front organization representing the lay constituency of the movement, is obligated to be an honest messenger of the Reform movement. It is not the URJ's role to create the message. The creation of the message is the prerogative of the grassroots. The operation of the URJ must be a rigorous reflection of the tenets and common practices of the movement as a religious organization. Its main mission is to help expand Reform Judaism, improve the communication between congregations, and promote the involvement of congregations in interfaith dialogue. The discipline required from the URJ leadership applies also to its affiliated organizations such as the RAC.

Sustained success and viability of our congregations in this age of interactive communications depends on governance that applies the very American principle of checks and balances between the lay and rabbinical views on religious concepts. This tenuous and complex balancing act requires sensitivity and a willingness for learning, mutual understanding, and compromise from all the participants. Achieving this balance enriches the congregation with a high level of civility and critical thinking. This process is a demanding and ongoing project intended to celebrate the Jewish dialogue, clarify spiritual and congregational issues with candor and mutual respect, reach an in-depth understanding of our faith, and foster strong connections within the congregation and between congregations.

It is in this context that I must express my disagreement with the assertion of Peter Weidhorn, the past chairman of the board of trustees of the URJ, in a 2011 column in *Reform Judaism*. In his opinion,

> If we are to have vibrant Jewish communities that will help our grandchildren live rich, productive Jewish lives, the institutions of our movement must lead the way. No individual and no single community can go it alone. We need to find the collective wisdom and creativity to reshape, redefine and re-envision our movement with the synagogue community at its very center.[4]

I do agree that we need to re-envision our movement, but the direction that will bring the desired revival is essentially opposite to what Mr. Weidhorn indicates. For more than half a century, the movement was under the influence of kohanic central leadership. This leadership stifled spontaneity and innovation in the congregations, reduced the diversity of ideas and practices, and replaced religious orientation and activities with partisan social and political activism. We have witnessed often enough a double standard adopted by the national leaders, between ideas that are preached and actions in the field. It is this kind of leadership that distanced individuals from the movement and wasted precious resources on lobbying for one-sided political agendas, in blatant contempt of the separation between church and state. Also, Mr. Weidhorn contradicts his own statement by emphasizing the importance of the national institutions while recognizing "the centrality of the synagogue community." If the congregation is central and its mission and duty are to promote the spirit of our faith, then national institutions should reflect and support this effort, not dominate it. It is indeed only the congregations in the field, their membership and their leadership that can energize the public, through direct contact, to join and become involved in the movement.

With all due respect, dignitaries and bureaucrats operating from Washington, DC, will never be able to reach out to the wide Reform public. Even a highly effective administrator, such as Maurice Eisendrath, would not have succeeded in his mission if it were not for the conformist public opinion of the time and the economic boom that swept the country after the Second World War. Present circumstances are totally different.

The political orientation of the Reform's national leadership seems to come as a replacement for religious vision. Vision is not achieved instantly. Vision can be achieved through a rich and exhausting process of education and study, well known to every educator. Reform vision has added to the dialogue between members of the clergy the dialogue with the lay membership. This process can be sustained only if both the lay and the rabbinical contributions are introduced in participatory, rather than assertive, modes. A participatory approach requires that both parties be educated in the virtues of dialogue. An ordained rabbi who intends to become a congregational rabbi must be able to inspire and sustain this dialogue. The participation of the lay members of the congregation in the dialogue is conditioned by their knowledge and their availability and ability to become involved. Reform congregants are usually educated and interested in participating in the dialogue. Creating the conditions to enable a wide participation should be one of the main objectives of the congregational leadership. The congregational inner dialogue often creates a specific congregational perspective. Civil, informed, and constructive dialogues between congregations will energize the movement. It is this multilayered dialogue that ultimately generates and sustains the uniqueness of the Reform movement.

Rabbis must be active moderators of constructive dialogues, be sensitive to the spiritual needs of the congregation, have a critical mind, be the first responders to spiritual crisis, and be able to notice and learn from previous mistakes. The rabbi is a leading partner (*primum inter pares*) with the members of the congregation. His or her mission is to reveal to the congregants the richness of our faith and inspire the congregation to appreciate the beauty of Reform Judaism.

A participatory process requires rabbis to be dedicated to fostering the process of dialogue. To achieve this goal, seminary teachers must see dialogue as part of their pedagogical mission. The main contributions rabbinic leadership can bring to the congregation are in providing divine faith in good times and in bad times, guiding individuals in their quest for religious participation, revealing the wisdom of the Tanachic heritage, and inspiring pride in the Judaic culture. A rabbi becomes the principal teacher and spiritual leader of the congregation by providing inspiration for all age groups. The rabbi is the spiritual counselor to the lay leadership of the congregation and participates with them in the design of the religious life of the congregation. The rabbi leads the rituals and should actively encourage lay involvement in leading ceremonies. Rabbis should not be ideologues or advocates of political agendas and should not be burdened by managerial tasks or community organizing. As salaried staff, the rabbi represents our faith, but he or she does not necessarily represent the congregation unless specifically empowered by the congregation for special occasions.

My personal experience in three different congregations—in Florida, Massachusetts, and now Colorado—has led me to believe that many in the Reform public expect an open-minded approach that encourages diversity of ideas, dialogue, and innovative interpretations of our Jewish spiritual heritage. In spite of the old-fashioned partisan "liberal" demagogy generated by special interest groups and uninspired political parties, the public, especially the younger generation, is aware that we are entering a new era. This new era presents its own contradictions: an extensive, even excessive, access to information marked by doubts about our spiritual existence, and a sense of uncertainty in our ability to secure our freedoms and prosperity.

It is in this context that the Reform movement should reconsider, in new ways suitable to our time, the management of our regional and national networks. Professional organizations such as the CCAR must remember that their main mission is to disseminate professional objectives and performance. Professional organizations do not represent the Reform constituency and should not make statements of opinion on behalf of the movement.

The management of congregational networks should be based on a balanced sharing of influence among congregations. In this context the URJ could fulfill an important coordinating role. This balanced management should be carefully monitored by the congregations to prevent any attempts of regional or national power grabbing. Such an approach also responds to the traditional American fear of "big government." The ability to institute credible, monitored, grassroots governance is central in the process of validation of our faith and movement.

Transparent, democratic, grassroots participatory governance was, and should remain, a strong attribute of the Reform congregations and the movement. The grassroots dimension is a spiritual, religious reflection of our American free-market, democratic, entrepreneurial, and innovative bourgeois culture. In order to preserve and enhance participation in governance, more effort must be invested in educating and promoting local lay leadership, particularly young leadership. In addition, the congregations, as well as the movement, must rigorously maintain a strict separation between church and state, between religion and civics. This separation will ensure an inclusive membership affiliation undivided by political agendas. To achieve this objective, some statutes and governance policies adopted by the national organizations in the past will have to be revised and adjusted to support congregations rather than undermine them. Through its grassroots outreach, centered on our congregations, Reform Judaism is well positioned to provide an uplifting and confident modern Jewish divine-faith message to the American Jewish public.

Notes

1. Union for Reform Judaism, "Enjoying the Fruits of Positive Change: The Five P's of Productive Planning," section in *Cultivating The Future: Long-Range Planning for Congregations* (1999, updated 2006), 15, available at http://urj.org//cong/finance//?syspage=document&item_id=14861.

2. See Meyer, *Response to Modernity*, 364.

3. See ibid., page 366.

4. Peter Weidhorn, "The Chairman's Perspective," *Reform Judaism* (Summer 2011).

Chapter 7:   *Tikkun Olam?* Try *Or Goim*

> I am HASHEM; I have called you with righteousness; I
> will strengthen your hand; I will protect you; I will set you
> for a covenant to the people, for a light to the nations.
>
> Isaiah, 42:6

Tikkun olam, repairing the world, is the current declared mission goal of American Reform Judaism:

> Reform Judaism affirms the central tenets of Judaism—God, *Torah* and Israel—even as it acknowledges the diversity of Reform Jewish beliefs and practices. We believe that all human beings are created in the image of God, and that we are God's partners in improving the world. *"Tikkun olam"*— repairing the world—is the hallmark of Reform Judaism as we strive to bring peace, freedom and justice to all people.[1]

Reform Judaism has a history of interpreting the Jewish wish for a better world as a call and a goal to assume public, interfaith leadership. Many leaders of the Reform movement have asserted that universal tikkun olam is our mission. This apparently simple wish raises significant questions:

- Who determines what is to be "repaired"?
- What are the criteria for determining the "repairs"?

113

- How does the public know what "repairs" are indeed necessary?
- How will the public know that the "repairs" were successful?
- What will be the reward for those who were able to make a successful "repair"?
- Do the leaders of the Central Conference of American Rabbis or the Union for Reform Judaism believe that they have the knowledge to determine where and how to implement tikkun olam?

We become aware that our house needs repair if there is damage or a malfunction of an item in the house. The repair is performed by a technician who follows the instructions of the manufacturer or established professional practices that allow for very little, if any, variations. If the repair does not follow the instructions, it is bound to fail. If the instructions are wrong, the repair will fail. The process of repairing is linear, deterministic, and does not allow for any individual contribution. Repairing, as such, is a regressive action, intended to reverse the trend to the previous situation. And finally, the provider of the service is handsomely rewarded for a job well done.

Presumably, tikkun olam likewise is intended to offer a practical, applicable solution to the realities of life and society. The leadership of Reform Judaism purports to have such a solution or set of solutions. The problem is that Reform Judaism is a religious denomination, which is meant to address spiritual concerns, not practical mundane matters. A political party would be better suited to attempt such solutions; this would fulfill the role of a political party with a practical platform and leaders that are politicians—managers of communities. If we accept this distinction on conceptual levels as well as with respect to the principle of the separation of church and state, the concept of tikkun olam is self-defeating.

On the other hand, because of its spiritual influence and moral stand, religion can and does have the ability to bring improvement in human life. There is ample historical, anthropological, and psychological evidence that human beings, as an animal species, are "bad": they are by nature cruel, aggressive, selfish, and greedy. Religion was one major step toward cultivating a more cooperative and compassionate human spirit. Initially religion did not "repair" anything, since there was nothing to return to; religion brought improvement in human behavior, by inspiring mutual respect, appreciation of spiritual values, and a sense of belonging. To believe, however, that religious enrichment inherently makes humanity "good" (the opposite of cruel, aggressive, selfish, and greedy) is naïve and dangerous. Recurrent historical evidence shows how often humanity can be easily misguided by an abusive leadership to engage in barbaric behavior in the name of religious beliefs. Even in our current civilized time, we are experiencing vicious acts of religious terrorism and brutal and destructive riots of angry and greedy religious groups.

Humanity has developed a dual capability for good and bad, a reflection of the divine/evil duality. It is up to the individual to decide what to be and to take responsibility for his or her acts. As Karl Popper emphasizes,

> In the case of a moral theory, we can only confront its consequences with our own conscience. And while the verdict of experiments does not depend upon ourselves, the verdict of our conscience does.[2]

If conscience plays a role in our understanding and our acting in life, dialogue with others and faith in our beliefs are central in our decision-making process. This discursive process does not aim to "repair" our spirit but to improve it.

Here we must differentiate between the notions of repair, improvement, and change. The Jewish Enlightenment had a goal to refine and *improve* Judaism by incrementally enriching it with the knowledge of the Enlightenment. Improvement does not necessarily mean change but rather means a conscientious, differential, and critical addition to existing knowledge, an addition believed to better fulfill goals and objectives. The promoters of the improvements believe that they are making "good"—that the new ways will raise the spiritual conditions of the community in a sustainable way. By nature, improvements take time: improvements require broad participation, education, and critical evaluation. Often, new generations find out that improvement is too slow, due to inherent resistance. To overcome resistance, Reform Judaism has often opted for a more radical approach: *change now.* Immediate change consumes resources, effort, and lives, but cannot secure better results. Change for the sake of change can have devastating consequences: it destroys the old and replaces it with something new that might be worse. Change can cause reactions aimed at eliminating the change. Often, results of radical change have to be repaired in order to become effective.

In my opinion, in a democratic culture and civilized society the only viable progressive notion is improvement. Improvement combines two components that appear to be contradictory: prudence and risk taking. It is important to note here that the act of repairing does not require either prudence or risk; it requires only compliance to preconditioned rules that determine that the repair was properly fulfilled. Change is centered on risk taking and little prudence.

In Reform Judaism, the final decision is shared through agreement between individuals and the congregation. In considering the role of the individual, we must recognize that humans are not only problem solvers, but also are problem identifiers and are problem tolerant.

As part of a congregation, members become aware of problems and issues and may tolerate them or attempt to recruit support to resolve them. This is in essence the civil approach to public cooperation. Civil improvement can be achieved only by prudent acts using persuasion to promote acceptable risk. The history of the last two centuries teaches us that rebellion and revolution inspired by the exuberance of inexperience, naïve idealism, or political maneuvers can have serious destructive consequences, both intended and unintended. These acts have to be taken seriously; unfortunately, more often than not, the results of such acts are difficult to "repair."

Currently, some in the Reform movement believe that by assigning themselves as "partners with God in tikkun olam" (different from partners *in* God), they have the authority to repair not only themselves, not only Jews, but also "the world." Is the political agenda included in the 1999 "Statement of Principles" and in the advocacy pamphlets of the Religious Action Center[3] the Reform spiritual message that is expected to inspire us in the practice of our faith? Who empowered the "battle ready" activists of the RAC to instigate, in the name of Reform Judaism, political obstruction and violence? How do we know that they advocate the correct solution?

Raymond Aron brilliantly describes the problem of this self-assigned righteousness:

A party which is always right must constantly define the correct line between sectarianism and opportunism. Where is this line situated? At an equal distance between the twin pitfalls of opportunism and sectarianism. But these pitfalls were themselves originally placed in relation to the correct line. The only way out of the vicious circle is a decree by the central authority which defines truth and error alike. And this decree is inevitably arbitrary, since it is made by a man who decides autocratically between individuals and groups; the disparity between the world as it would be if the original doctrine were true, and the world as it is, subordinates the truth to the equivocal and inscrutable decisions of an interpreter whose only qualification is his power.[4]

Authoritarian leaders, political or religious, justify their self-assigned righteousness by pretending that they can "repair the world." The message is that an outstanding leader has the expert knowledge to "repair" the system and make it work again "the way it ought to work." The repair process and its results are finite and their evaluation is absolute and predetermined by the leader. In contrast, improvement of a system has a given start, followed by a dynamic, open-ended work process. The expectation is that the improvements will perform in a measurably better way than before, a way that can be predictable or novel. Repairs address and follow predetermined formulas; improvements are results of learning from mistakes or innovative designs. The evaluation of an improvement is open for public critique and revisions.[5]

Traditional religious thinking followed the guidelines of leaders and attempted to repair the rest of the world according to their guidelines. The intent of Reform Judaism, following in the footsteps of the Jewish Enlightenment, is to improve Judaism by enriching it with contemporary thinking. Reform Judaism does not negate the historic Jewish heritage, nor does it promote a return to past traditions: it builds the Reform spirit on the Jewish heritage, it adjusts the heritage to our time and circumstance and, in the process, introduces improvements that mitigate between the inherited traditions and modern culture.

There is an important distinction to be made here between religious aspirations and political objectives. Humanity is blessed by a dual nature: on one hand we are able to dream and imagine, on the other hand we are able to solve problems and survive. Bad political leadership replaces problem solving with impossible dreams. The consequence of such policies is economic and physical disaster. Uninspired spiritual leadership that replaces vision with mundane action causes cultural decline. Religious leadership that replaces faith with controversial and confusing political agendas compromises the faith and undermines trust and credibility in the spiritual support that religion provides.

The journey of Reform Judaism, from its emergence as an offspring of the Jewish Enlightenment to its place in our present time, has been marked and marred by social and Socialist illusions[6] promoted under the generic and vague title of tikkun olam. In many cases Reform leaders were at the forefront of the explorations of these ideologies, often adopting a single-minded, extreme position, ignoring the broader context in which they were operating. In the nineteenth century, the American spiritual reality was ignored by many Reform activists, indoctrinated with European elitism, romantic idealism, and revolutionary activism. This activism distorted the religious essence of Reform Judaism and reduced its theological foundation to marketing of religion. Replacing faith with sporadic initiatives of mundane nature, along with defining any "good deed" as tikkun olam, trivialized the mission of the movement and its credibility.

American Reform Judaism and American pragmatism thinking were contemporary. and for the sake of this discussion, we may assume that "repairing the world," rather than improving it, may be considered a reflection of the American pragmatist point of view. William James affirms that "true ideas are those that we can assimilate, validate, corroborate and verify. False ideas are those we can not."[7] This statement would suit well the traditional Reform inclination to include science and practical rationale into our faith. However, can we expect to "validate, corroborate and verify" Divinity? Following John Dewey's opinion, Diggins explains that

> the pragmatist response to the modernist crisis of knowledge was to make truth not so much a matter of philosophical proof as one of rational acceptance. All that truth can possibly mean is the practical results of inquiry, and society informed by science is the best judge of what works.[8]

Critics of pragmatism pointed out "that ideas can be false and useful and true and futile; hence utility itself cannot be the only property of true ideas."[9] This criticism brings into question how the practical, utilitarian approach to "repair the world" can be verified and justified and by whose authority.

Pragmatism and neo-pragmatism reject theory and transcendental thinking as governing forces for the practices of real life. As such, the world is perceived only from one perspective: the existence in our reality, which is material and can be repaired. Somewhere, this perspective misses the American public's tradition and desire to have faith in supportive transcendental Divinity and to take an active part in the free market of religious ideas.

The exciting question is what activates the free market of ideas, religious and otherwise? Is it improved content, is it improved communication, or both? Religious content provides a set of beliefs, conjectures, and stories. Communications enable the transfer of the content to the public. Uncensored communication enables individuals to reach personal conclusions, adopt specific positions, and participate in the dialogue. Dialogue does not mean automatic agreement or consensus and it definitely does not mean compliance with convention. The challenge is to find a way to bring together the subjective opinions of each congregant and shape a common cause.

Since its inception at Mount Sinai, Judaism has put its faith in the power of the word. The Tanach and its companion written and oral heritage is a record of a wide range of divine and human conversations, a record that has inspired and supported us for centuries. This record is a venue to preserve and communicate, through the written word, our history and wisdom, and it also provides a spiritual contextual paradigm. It was this spiritual paradigm that, even in the dark ages of oppression, provided a freethinking framework that used discourse and dialogue to stimulate the imagination of its readers and practitioners. A constructive dialogue, based on a common heritage, can bring agreement and solidarity, and it may clarify disagreements and conflicts. In any situation, dialogue clarifies ideas, positions, and beliefs, a clarity that helps improve our spiritual life.

Reality shows that public dialogue can be silenced by the tyranny of the majority or held hostage by a subversive minority. Aimless debates can discourage participation and allow zealots to take over the discussion. In commenting on German philosopher Jürgen Habermas's belief in "communicative consensus," John Patrick Diggins notes that it

> is alien to the rebellious spirit of the American culture. It is also alien to the conservative prudence of the framers of the Constitution, perhaps the first political philosophers to realize that liberty depends upon diversity rather than unanimity, conflict rather than consensus.[10]

While some dispute the prevalence of the rebellious spirit of America, there is no doubt that America is diverse. Any degree of diversity and conflict is initially addressed by dialogue. The freedoms secured by the American Constitution made dialogue and public communication a key component of our democracy and culture. In the age of transparent means of communication, such as Twitter and other social media, we have increased evidence that communication is a major factor in our culture and a vivid expression of "the rebellious spirit" of American culture.

The uniqueness of the American civilization is its ability to accommodate pluralist diversity in free and productive ways. Pluralist diversity includes both compatible and incompatible values, matching and contradicting opinions, and common and individual positions. One accepted principle that ensures this diversity is the separation between church and state, as discussed in more detail in chapter 5. This separation enables people to collaborate and to perform civic activities unaffected by their religious beliefs and to follow their religious beliefs unrestricted by their civic occupations. Any attempt to "repair" the separation between church and state and merge them under one authority will limit freedom of speech and bring back the religious conflicts and prejudices that are still dominant in Europe.

In the continental European cultural context, civic conformity most often required affiliation to the state religion, divine or secular. Maintaining a Jewish identity remained suspect even in the most open-minded European communities. The attempts of Reform activists in Europe to ignore or change this context failed. We can find a recent example in the position taken officially by France in regard to French collaboration in the extermination of Jews during the Holocaust. For half a century, France denied any responsibility in the Holocaust. A few years ago, a supreme French judicial court changed this position and recognized the collaboration between French Vichy authorities and the German authorities in the extermination of the French Jews.[11] Due to the statute of limitations, however, the court exempted the French state from any obligation of restitution or compensation for property or suffering. Only after this decision was made public did some voices in the French intellectual circles start to discuss the moral implications of the French collaboration in the Holocaust, while being well aware that these discussions had no applicable implications. So much for French intellectual free dialogue, moral integrity, and repairing the world! Let us remember again that the whole European culture remains entrenched in a self-praising elitist model, with its strict, covert conventions that often merge secular beliefs with politics and justice.

It is also important to recognize religion as the human domain that addresses spiritual beliefs and speaks to the human soul and mind. Socioeconomic and political ideologies are intended to suggest solutions to practical problems. Let us briefly recall the origin of the notion of tikkun olam. Tikkun olam is a Talmudic judicial notion intended to help in dispute resolutions, mostly in issues related to divorce, issues that remained unresolved by the Tanachic law. As such, tikkun olam is not a religious commandment (*mitzvah*) but a judicial amendment. The social explorations of Reform thinkers and preachers in the last two centuries have expanded the notion of tikkun olam beyond its Talmudic definition to an all-encompassing Universalist pseudo-theology. Based on such premises, the URJ recently assigned to itself the role to *provide* "leadership and vision to Reform Jews on spiritual, ethical and political issues."[12] This objective, disseminated in a public statement, is blatant evidence of the infringement of the separation of church and state principle.

The urgency with which the URJ national leadership promotes tikkun olam makes me believe that the real goal of this agenda is to enable the leadership to assume an active role in the national and international political arena, conform to certain trends of the day, and be included into the "Universalist" culture as it is shaped by certain political elites in Washington, DC, or New York City. What appears to be lost on the Reform leadership is that, in our time, attempts to belong in the temporal political arena are self-destructive illusions. Similar to the failed attempts to implement quasi-socialism and environmentalism, a global effort to "repair the world" dilutes Judaism and brings it close to being absorbed and "converted" into the vagaries of political campaigns and economic speculations.[13]

In the twentieth century, the political elites achieved the nineteenth-century goal of empowering national identities. In the process they created a divisive international political landscape, a landscape rife with conflicts and corruption. Attempting to "repair" this divided world by advocating Reform Judaism is far beyond our ability. Much worse, an expressed intent to "repair the world" can bring us into a direct confrontation with local and national political, religious, and cultural interests. To the same extent that we prefer to preserve our religious identity, we should not intrude on the identities of other religions or cultures.

Promoting global tikkun olam also contradicts the autonomy of the Reform congregations in the United States. The American culture, and Reform Judaism in particular, praise individualism and freedom of association. Reform Judaism is an autonomous Jewish denomination that does not need nor is it expected to blend into any other religion. America enabled all religious faiths to operate independently and to stand their ground with pride, creating a diverse, colorful, and inspiring spiritual mosaic.

As a matter of fact, Reform Judaism in the United States has survived and even thrived, in spite of the confusing social and political messages promoted by the national leadership. One reason for the success of the Reform movement is the sensitive response of congregations for the faith preferences of the Jewish constituencies throughout the country. These preferences are shaped by practices exercised in the field, responsive local leadership, and an inherent wish to sustain Jewish living. Also, as an integral part of the American society, Reform congregations are making their constructive contribution, in their own right, to the urban communities and the capitalist system of which they are an integral part. Fortunately, so far the confusing and divisive political narrative of the national leadership has been limited to fringe journalism, left-leaning political circles, and polite conversations in the congregations, with minimal implications on the daily lives of the individual members.

The Reform agenda of tikkun olam focuses on issues that appear to be well grounded in our civic reality while ignoring issues related to personal levels, such as the conflict between individual freedom and conformity and between imagination and conventional thinking. These ideas were important to Reform activists who initiated the movement in America. Could the movement revive this spontaneity and innovation, enriched by current spiritual knowledge and erudition?

Tikkun olam can be envisioned as a wish to repair our spiritual Jewish world and as such tikkun olam may well become an individual challenge to improve ourselves as Jews, embracing and fostering our Jewish identity and virtues. Improving our spiritual view is more than repairing it; such improvement entails an enrichment of the spiritual wealth of each of us, in our own way, as part of and together with our congregation. Spiritual enrichment has been a long-lasting Jewish tradition, a tradition that we can and must preserve and modernize.

Traditional Judaism has accepted Divinity as a spiritual compilation of transcendental belief, history, storytelling, and legislation. On the other hand, Jews lived, survived, and thrived in real life by using practical, commonsense innovation and solidarity. Material life provided the framework within which to rejoice in the spiritual. Reform Judaism expanded this dual characteristic of Judaic existence, a pragmatic participation in public life and a private life enriched by a religious spirituality, out of the ghetto into public life. American Reform Judaism was able to implement the maskilim's dream of improving traditional Judaism and enabling us to become both full citizens in the civic society and proud Jews in the community. This project, which started as an attempt to improve European Jewish communities, has evolved in the United States as a grand spiritual design with exemplary results. A similar life pattern can be found these days in many American non-Jewish denominations and communities. Whether this American phenomenon is a result of the constitutional principle of freedom of religion, or was inspired by the Judaic existence, or both, is difficult to say. Yet its existence is a significant hallmark of the American culture.

The distinct, inquisitive, and contrarian existence developed by Jews in the Diaspora did not allow for the emergence of a wide supportive constituency. Yet, was not this the idea of the "chosen people"? As the chosen people Jews could inspire others through self-reliance and example—example that excels through its quality, virtue, wisdom, and beauty. Already in the Torah we are told about the admiration Balaam Ben-Beor expressed, on seeing the Israelites' camp, of the beauty of their settings in the desert: "How goodly are your tents, O, Jacob, your dwelling places, O Israel."[14] The Israelites stood out in the beauty of their camp, a beauty that impressed and inspired virtue, a beauty that could be an example to other people. This is the meaning of *Or Goim*—shining light for other people—an attribute of Israel, an attribute Judaism can share with others but not impose on others.

Throughout history, Judaism became a continuous inspiration to Christianity and Islam, nurturing their faith, practices, and rituals. Judaism influenced through discussions and debates, through cooperation and competition, through surviving persecution and oppression. Jews always hoped for a better world and dreamed that the world would live in peace and prosper. Jews prayed that people would see the light and join together to fix disputes and remediate wrongdoing. This prayer was part of the Judaic faith in divine inspiration. In Jewish terms, Jews were called to remediate their own conduct and fix their own house and as such be an example to their neighbors.

In the global context, the State of Israel, a brainchild of Jewish reformation, has achieved, in very difficult circumstances, results that are an example for many nations. Israel has achieved a remarkable free, democratic, and prosperous civilization, in spite of the constraints of being in a permanent state of war and surrounded by hostile tyrannies. Even so it has not been spared a large degree of envy and hate since it has exposed the inability of other states and regimes to match its achievements. Israel's situation shows that even being just Or Goim is not always well accepted in a prejudiced world.

The Reform Jewish congregations, with their active and successful participation in the free, prosperous, enlightened capitalistic culture of the United States, are constantly helping to improve the American culture. Rather than advocating the futile slogan of "repairing the world," the leaders of Reform Judaism, and the CCAR in particular, should recognize that Reform achievements are Or Goim: valuable examples and enlightenment to people. In providing Or Goim, Reform Judaism is a proud part of the great spiritual and material American "beacon to the world," a lighthouse of hope.

Notes

1. Union for Reform Judaism, "What Is Reform Judaism?" as posted at http://urj.org/about/reform/whatisreform/.

2. See Popper, *The Open Society*, 2:233.

3. "We know that crucial progress on immigration policy, climate change and gay and lesbian rights will be resisted, and that without a powerful chorus of progressive voices calling for change, we will remain mired in the status quo. One example: The battle—and it will be a battle—to roll back health care laws is about to begin, and there was no stronger religious or Jewish voice fighting to support these key reforms than the RAC, and we will need to strengthen those efforts in 2011." (From a letter sent by the RAC to congregants in December 2010.) As this letter indicates, the RAC has expanded its positions: no more "repairing the world" but instead radical political and environmental change. The RAC is already preparing for "battle" and expects us members to follow it.

4. See Aron, *Opium of the Intellectuals*, 109.

5. Modern history teaches us that ambitious political initiatives intended to "repair the world," such as the Napoleonic Wars and the First World War, "the war to end all wars," ultimately brought enormous damage instead of repairs. In contrast, the Marshall Plan was a collaborative visionary process between governments and between private and public enterprises. The plan was conceived and built to provide a broad and complex range of improvements. The historic success of the plan was in providing sustainable results on a scale and at a depth never achieved before. We must note that many of the major economic failures of the twentieth century were caused by wrong governmental decisions (see the history of the Great Depression or the mismanagement of the midcentury urban-renewal projects). Zealous ideological application of well-intended policies, deprived of an understanding of life realities and human nature, brought more damage than benefits. Top-down government and central planning seldom possess the knowledge and the intellectual breadth to address the complex issues of human development. Modern capitalism, with its broad distribution of actions, individual initiative, and entrepreneurship as well as its self-correcting mechanisms has brought more basic prosperity worldwide than any other economic system. Sustaining prosperity, however, requires the expansion of freedoms with all their political and spiritual implications.

6. See Meyer, *Response to Modernity*, 309–14.

7. As quoted in J. P. Diggins, *The Promise of Pragmatism* (Chicago: Univ. of Chicago Press, 1994), 133.

8. See ibid., 233.

9. See ibid., 234.

10. See ibid., 449.

11. On February 16, 2009, France's top judicial body, the Council of State, formally acknowledged the French government's responsibility for the deportation of thousands of Jews to Nazi death camps during World War II. See http://www.jewishvirtuallibrary.org/jsource/Holocaust/francedeps.html.

12. See Union For Reform Judaism, "What Is Reform Judaism?"

13. Michael Meyer in *Response to Modernity*, 366–68, describes the dilemmas encountered by the Reform movement, in particular the CCAR, in the 1960s and 1970s regarding topics such as the civil rights movement, resistance to the Vietnam War, the Six Day War, and the merit of the alliances with interfaith groups. These dilemmas and disappointments indicate the danger in mixing religion with political activism. A wise approach would have differentiated between issues of civic interest and issues of religious nature. Civil rights and the Vietnam War were civic issues. The survival of the Jewish community in Israel was a matter of Jewish solidarity, an essential spiritual and faith-based Judaic tenet central to all Jewish denominations, including Reform Judaism.

14. Numbers 24:5.

Chapter 8: Religious Action—Is It Social Action?

> The language of religion once aspired to penetrate the soul and open the heart. To what does the language of social science aspire?
>
> J. P. Diggins, *The Promise of Pragmatism*[1]

Social action has been a long-standing item on the Reform Judaism agenda. It is time to ask a simple question: Why do we advocate social action instead of religious action?

Reform Judaism is a religious denomination. Even its most politically active organization, the Religious Action Center, is introduced as a religious organization rather than a social action committee. The RAC definitely is committed to social action, so is the religious title just a cover-up?

For the sake of the argument, we need to clarify the meaning of the two qualifiers: "religious" and "social." The American principle of *freedom of religion* allows American citizens to adopt, without any restrictions, a double identity: as citizens and as independent believers. The United States is the first and only country that has adopted and fully and honestly committed itself to this enlightened principle. Reform Judaism has positioned itself as a religious entity within the applicable statutory legal framework. In particular, it is a Jewish religious denomination and a charity. These definitions have moral, legal, and tax implications.

Judaism has evolved as a complex and inclusive religious concept: it is a faith, a people, a culture, a nation, a civilization, and a state religion. Initially Judaism was conceived as a totalitarian and inclusive regime. The books of the Tanach indicate that Judaism in the Holy Land developed a more complex and flexible understanding of its tenets. The oppression and discrimination of the Diaspora forced Judaism to restrict itself to a highly cohesive spiritual discipline. The more liberal circumstances of the European Enlightenment offered Judaism the opportunity to modernize Judaism.

Reform Judaism in America, in respect to the principle of freedom of religion, has adopted as one of its key tenets the separation of church and state. As a consequence, American Reform Judaism is meant to focus its beliefs and interests on Judaism as a faith, people, culture, and civilization. This large array of beliefs and interests offers options for numerous religious initiatives and actions. Fundamentally, all religious activities, practices, and rituals are guided by a religious vision. We have clarified in previous chapters that Reform Judaism is a Jewish religious denomination with a Jewish divine foundation. Secular and universal perspectives, as much as they are part of the existing practices, are extreme interpretations of the faith. The two primary tenets—divine foundation and separation between church and state—provide a wide array of visionary development in the context of the Jewish heritage. In simple terms, the purpose of religious actions is to promote religion. In the case of Reform Judaism, religious actions address the enhancement of our faith as a modern reflection of the Jewish heritage.

Social action originated in nineteenth-century Europe at a time when Europe was in a period of major radical philosophical and political upheaval. New scientific and technological discoveries, romantic and nationalistic trends, the Industrial Revolution, and capitalistic expansions brought improved mass education, broadened the ranks of the bourgeoisie, and empowered it. The process was met with wars and revolutions, reaction and oppression, and an explosion of hope.

On the fringe of the debate between liberals and traditionalists were extremist anarchist, Marxist, and Socialist movements that advocated their beliefs. Their goal was the recruitment of various deprived groups and instigating them to rise and take action against the new bourgeois, capitalist establishments. Initially, this European activism defined itself as revolutionary action, symbolized by the 1848 revolutionary spirit. Revolutionary action became an established notion in Marxist practices when its zealous propagators adopted the role of professional revolutionaries and viewed themselves as the leaders of the future proletarian-dominated communist society.

The failure of classical Marxism to justify or fulfill its ambitious and absolute goals in industrial countries (Germany, Great Britain) forced the "late Marxist" advocates of the twentieth century to adopt a more subtle approach; instead of attempting to demolish Western democracy and capitalism through revolution, they aimed to subvert it by exacerbating any social or cultural conflict and escalating it into crisis mode. This approach received its initial theoretical basis in the empirical work of Max Weber, who gave the intellectual impetus to social action. According to this approach, *social action evolved into an activist approach whose purpose is to adapt reality to a social idea.* This transition is evolutionary and tactical: it attempts to reach its political goals by taking advantage of the freedoms promoted by democracy and by infiltrating major institutions such as educational and judicial institutions, media and cultural institutions; its tactics can be discursive (brainwashing in education, propagating "the big lie" in the media) or confrontational (obstruction, intimidation, riots).[2]

As part of the existing system the main sociopolitical ambition of social action was, and still is, to demonize and to discredit free-market capitalist and constitutional democracies; its goal is to replace democracy and capitalism with centralized, planned governance. Social action became the defining attribute of the secular, late- and post-Marxist ideology as expressed by thinkers of the Frankfurter School up to left leaning postmodernist critics of the late twentieth century. A careful review of Socialist-oriented social action reveals that its message is based on the belief that humanity behaves like a docile homogeneous flock guided, nurtured, and essentially controlled by the dominant power of an expert bureaucracy. This belief brings the Socialist utopia close to a messianic religion in which Divinity is replaced by tyranny. Leaders such as Lenin and Stalin, Mussolini and Hitler, and Mao and Castro did propagate just that. They were the great prophets of radical change and never ending hope. Social action, like revolutionary action, "did not adopt a Church. Why? Because it was a Church itself."[3]

Confronted by the zealous activism and recruitment of secular Socialist activism, some major Christian denominations sought to protect their proselytizing activities by adopting similar approaches. Some Christian groups (Jesuits, Protestants, Anglicans) adopted class-warfare rhetoric wrapped in charitable sermons and street activities. This adjustment responded well to their global reach and was and still is a modern continuation of the historical involvement of Christian denominations in state political activities.

Due to its incrementally phased development and manipulative tactics, social action became the realm of intellectuals who rejoiced in its speculative orientation and the opportunity to gain unrestricted political control. For intellectuals, social action did offer more than the theoretical study of social phenomena and causes; it also offered an opportunity to market their ideas and eventually become part of a power bureaucracy intended to implement their ideas.[4]

Deprived of the ability to provide constructive achievements, contemporary social action adopted inflammatory rhetoric and linguistic abuses. The failed Socialist ideologues force their supporters to adopt and distort, without any intellectual scruples, the meaning of notions such as "liberal" or "progressive." These qualifiers, taken out of their contextual content (liberal what?: economy, behavior?; progressive to what?: competition, standard of living?), are deprived of any defined meaning. Unfortunately some capitalist leaders fell into this demagogic trap and let Marxists appropriate such terms. A liberal economy is definitely not the planned economy Socialists advocated, and as the history of the late twentieth century shows, most progressive achievements for the improvement of standards of living in developed countries and especially in developing countries were due to enlightened capitalism. If linguistic vigilance is vital in political actions, it is definitely vital in religious actions, since religion is highly dependent on the power of the word.

Much of the enlightened Jewish public was caught up in the enthusiasm of the nineteenth century and developed high expectations for change or at least for improvement in its status and living conditions. Numerous Jews were prepared to sacrifice traditions and religious practices for the benefit of promises of Socialist dreams. Socialist affiliation became similar to a religious affiliation. An alternative venue was reformation. Reform Judaism attempted to provide a new way for Jews to preserve a Jewish identity in the emerging civic system. In the absence of a clear understanding of the Jewish identity and messaging, elements of social action became attractive elements in the rhetoric of Reform activists. It is no wonder that Reform rabbis and preachers, in their intellectual search to modernize Judaism, found social action and its content timely and effective. Social action became an ideal venue to subvert the authority of the traditional rabbinic establishment, replace it, and adopt self-determined rules of performance.

For centuries Judaism was prohibited from proselytizing or promoting its faith to the general public. This policy was imposed on Jewish communities as a condition for being tolerated in the ghettos and, over time, became an accepted way to preserve a distinct identity. The activist spirit of the nineteenth century created expectations for Reform congregations to be able to have an open presence in the general public. In order to sustain and expand their congregations, preachers and congregational leaders were eager to adopt and develop missions that could energize the membership. It is easy to understand that open Jewish proselytizing or public Jewish activism of any kind was still unacceptable where Christian denominations were state religions or at least dominant religions and where state governance had a long history of institutional anti-Semitism. On the other hand, addressing deprived Jewish groups in the new terms of the emerging social trends, justified in the language of Jewish traditional charity, seemed to be an acceptable public activity. European state church authorities were aware of what they considered potential subversive rhetoric and activities and applied various degrees of tolerance or restriction, up to banning or expelling certain speakers. The failure of European political parties in the nineteenth century to devise improved civil political solutions for the emerging society gave birth to and nurtured the need for street activism, class warfare, and revolutions.

In the nineteenth century, social activism promoting Universalism, scientific determinism, social justice, and tikkun olam was brought to the American Reform congregations by German-speaking radical preachers and rabbis. By the beginning of the twentieth century, it was the Reform rabbinate that promoted social activism.[5] Inflammatory rhetoric that focused on hope and change, wrapped in biblical narrative, could always find a receptive Jewish American audience eager to be inspired by European intellectual flavor. Social rhetoric and charity activism became increasingly dominant activities in the Reform movement because they brought monetary support to the promoters, recruited volunteers, and could be executed. In addition, these actions paralleled well the social action conducted by Christian denominations. Interfaith collaborations emerged. In contrast to Christian activism, however, Reform social action was not motivated by religious proselytizing.

Up to the middle of the twentieth century, Reform social action was not about Jewish faith, Jewish culture, or Zionism; it was predominantly secular and universal. Its mission was tikkun olam. Its operation was to broker and to redistribute resources by advocating philanthropy. The rabbinic and lay leadership adopted social action as a way to achieve civic and political impact in America.[6]

In this context I join those who doubt interpretations arguing the existence of "social" and Socialist rulings in the Tanach. Nowhere does the scripture advocate egalitarianism—just the contrary. In a succinct article published in *The Wall Street Journal*,[7] Rabbi Aryeh Spero points out that we can actually find clear support in the Tanach for enlightened capitalism. The Jews escaped slavery for a promise of prosperity ("milk and honey") and ultimately were destined to achieve it by themselves, free from Moses's authority. The Tanach definitely supports individual wealth creation, but mandates its development by accepting honest and fair rules of behavior and transactions.

Social action was often justified as a venue to offer help to the needy. A traditional Jewish religious activity is *tzedaka* (charity). We must emphasize from the outset that there is a significant difference between tzedaka and social action. Tzedaka is a personal act of help provided by an individual of certain means to another individual in need. Charity is meant to help those in need, a need caused by special unfortunate circumstances. Charity does not justify entitlements or abuse. Charity needs to be distributed with caution so that it does not discourage personal diligence, development, and competition. Charity should be dispensed with care and sensitivity in ways that prevent people from feeling patronized. The reward for giving charity is in the act itself and not in any payback, honorary or political. Ultimately, charity is an act of Jewish solidarity made by individuals and aimed at helping the survival of the Jewish people. Only an individual is entitled to take unrestricted risks with his or her personal resources and distribute personal wealth at his or her discretion. As such, individual charity can become an expression of religious action and the individual can become a righteous person.

Social action is a collective political effort to impose an idea on the public. Forcing institutional charity on the public—governmental charity in particular—as a social action is unethical since public resources are not made available to be used at the discretion of politicians or bureaucrats. A subjective and arbitrary governmental management process, based on subjective considerations embraced by a self-empowered elite, can be easily abused and corrupted. In our constitutional republic each governmental institution must fulfill its separate role in managing public life in accountable and transparent ways.

The RAC has used the concept of Judaic tzedaka to justify national and international regulation and aid. With few exceptions, institutional aid programs, especially long-term aid programs, have failed and have had adverse effects on donors and recipients.[8] Whether successful or not, these programs are fundamentally not created to instill spiritual faith but rather to achieve political and economic results. From a broader perspective, developments in the last half century show that purpose-oriented education and a culture of achieving success based on entrepreneurship, innovation, and free markets is by far a more efficient, sustainable, and rewarding venue of economic and cultural development than charity or aid.

Can our modern spirit enable a religious organization to provide divine faith-based action? Faith provides spiritual support. Pope John

Paul II's peaceful and uplifting spiritual message sent to the Polish population in their quest for freedom was an effective religious action that changed history. Another example is Prime Minister Menachem Begin's call, in the 1970s and 1980s, to Jewish communities to participate in the urban renewal of deteriorating neighborhoods in Israel. The enthusiastic response and involvement was inspired and motivated by religious affinity and Jewish solidarity, a genuine religious action. The action was based on direct connections between individual communities around the world and specific Israeli communities, with limited bureaucratic involvement of the Jewish Agency.

In comparison, a glaring lack of social or religious action was the Roosevelt administration's refusal to grant asylum to 937 Jewish German passengers of the MS *St. Louis* attempting to flee Nazi Germany in 1939. No significant action was taken to influence the administration's decision, in spite of the fact that the return of the refugees to Germany would have put their lives in serious danger.[9]

Many leaders of the Reform movement maintained, after the war, their ignorance on the Final Solution. Yet there is evidence that activists such as Rabbi Meyer Berlin agitated in the United States for the intervention of the US government on behalf of Jews in Europe.[10] Apparently, religious oppression of the European Jewish communities was not a sufficient social factor to cause action—illustrating the political nature, at the time, of the Reform leadership and its social action program, let alone religious action. The loyalty of the Reform leadership to the Democratic Party and to President Roosevelt prevailed, and no action was deemed necessary.

In contrast, the active participation of the Reform movement in the rescue of the Soviet Jews in the 1960s and 1970s was a religious action, an action of "sacred survival." It is worth noting, as Kaplan indicates, that Reform Jews were disappointed that the new immigrants from the Soviet Union "were more materialistic than the activists have expected."[11] Kaplan's observation reveals a deeper misunderstanding between the two constituencies. The "Russians" immigrated to America in hopes of improving their life after escaping a life of real oppression. They viewed America as the land of opportunity, of success, and of prospects of wealth. They came to America in the hope of becoming liberated citizens rather than victims. They had no sympathy for hollow social activist rhetoric or the identity politics of their hosts. They simply had had enough of this kind of rhetoric and had a hard time and little patience to test the sincerity of these social messages. The American activists were unprepared to face this kind of skepticism. Their social idealism did not prepare them to understand and address the concerns of the newcomers and their craving for a free life in an entrepreneurial capitalist civilization.

Today, Reform Judaism in America presents a new perception of Judaism to the greater public. Reform congregations are able to share the Jewish heritage with Jews and non-Jews in both formal and informal encounters. Americans of Jewish origin, disappointed by secular beliefs, are looking into joining divine faith-based communities. Reform Judaism, with its open-door approach to faith and to the bourgeois lifestyle of its congregants, can offer an inspiring and comfortable spiritual environment for those seeking modern *hazara be'tchuva* (return to the faith). The encouragement of the hazara be'tchuva quest and the person's assimilation into a Reform congregation is a genuine religious action.

The success of Judaic academic study programs in universities with students who have had little direct contact with Judaism indicates that, if given the opportunity, Judaism can offer an attractive faith-based spiritual vision. This process brings a major improvement to interfaith understanding and theological rapprochements between religions.

In addition to the religious activities mentioned above, conversion to Reform Judaism seems to be gaining momentum in our time. The Reform movement is a defined and separate denomination, but it is not exclusive. Non-Jews willing to adopt the Jewish faith and the Jewish identity, following a rigorous conversion procedure, are welcomed. Should this receptivity be transformed into an active proselytizing movement? History shows that proselytizing can rapidly create conflicts. On the other hand, if Reform Judaism performs and excels by example—Or Goim—and aspires to become an inspiration to others, many might voluntarily join Reform congregations. However, becoming an inspiring example requires a highly sophisticated and demanding spiritual enrichment.

We are currently in the midst of a culture war between the modern Judeo-Christian approach to religion and traditional Islam's approach to religion. I believe that if offered a free choice, millions of Muslims would prefer a modern, reformed Islam. The challenge for a reformative movement is the need to reveal the power of modern divine beliefs within the Islamic context. Reformed Islam is the best alternative to extremist Islamic fascism that has led Islamic activism in the last century. The development of Reform Judaism can be a living inspiration for reform-minded Muslims. A process that encourages an open-minded, free and candid religious dialogue between reform-minded Jews, Christians, and Muslims might become a constructive religious action of historic significance.

Reform Judaism has consistently reaffirmed freethinking and open-mindedness toward the evolving culture surrounding us. Modern living is multidimensional, and successful performance requires multitasking. Religion is one of these dimensions. As Reform congregants we have the commitment to preserve the principle of separation of church and state, separation between religion and politics. The misleading mixture of politics and religion currently promoted by the URJ and the RAC under the banner of social action is dangerous and damaging. If we want to maintain the integrity and vitality of Reform Judaism, social/political action has to be replaced by genuine religious visionary action. Jewish solidarity is far more authentic and effective if it operates on the grassroots level rather than through political lobbies. As citizens we have the right and obligation to participate in the political system. As religious congregants we have the freedom to practice our beliefs without the interference of the state or political parties. This is exactly what Reform Judaism stands for. Let us not undermine this historic achievement.

The role of Reform rabbis is pivotal in pursuing the spirit of our religion. They must be in the forefront of religious dialogues, be sensitive to the spiritual needs of the congregation, have a critical mind, and be the first to notice and learn from previous mistakes. Reform rabbis are bringing the Jewish heritage into our current life. The daily work performed by rabbis in congregations is religious action. For two centuries many rabbis were influenced by Socialist illusions. Free from these illusions, modern Reform rabbis can create Jewish reformative visions that address our time without sinking into the political abyss. If there is a role for the RAC it is to help our lay leadership and clergy "in the trenches" in their everyday activity, instead of searching for new wasteful "battlefields" in the arena of national politics.

In its initial phase, this process requires dedicated and enthusiastic seminary teachers committed to the Reform religious mission. The resulting graduates, the rabbis, should be able to perform as religious leaders, not as religious bureaucrats, community organizers, or political activists. The main contributions rabbinic leadership can bring to the congregation are to provide faith-based support in good times and bad times, guide individuals in their quest for religious participation, reveal the wisdom of the Tanachic heritage, and inspire pride in the Judaic culture in its modern context. A congregational rabbi becomes the principal teacher and spiritual leader of the congregation by providing inspiration for all ages. The rabbi is the spiritual counselor to the lay leadership of the congregation and participates with them in the design of the religious life of the congregation. The rabbi leads the rituals and should actively encourage lay involvement in leading ceremonies. Rabbis should not be ideologues or advocates of political agendas. As one of the paid staff, the congregational rabbi represents our faith but not the congregation unless specifically requested by the congregation.

Religious action is not meant to provide mundane solutions but rather to create an environment conducive to dialogue and understanding. By separating our religious action from other actions, Reform Judaism leaves the prosaic aspects of human activities to their respective domains: political action to the democratic system, economic action to the market, judicial action to the unbiased judicial system, and scientific actions to science.

Religious action can be the cause or the result of religious experiences. Learning and innovation, soul searching and celebration, sermons and rituals, dialogue and motivation, charity and solidarity are all components of Judaic Reform religious action. By revealing the beauty and wisdom of our heritage and future vision, Reform religious action embraces and energizes congregants, inspires its audience, and soothes our souls and minds. Reform religious action is about love and belonging which bring us closer to the transcendental inspiration of our heritage. By improving our ethical understanding and enriching our aesthetic experience, Judaic Reform religious actions allow us to enjoy the divine-given art of living and the poetry of life.

Notes

1. J. P. Diggins, *The Promise of Pragmatism*, 443.

2. Three events in 2011 illustrate the "social action" scenario: The riots in London, U. K., the riots in Cairo, Egypt, and the Occupy Wall Street riots in the United States. The riots in London erupted against the background of populist incitement against governmental austerity policies. Deprived of any realistic solutions that could replace austerity, the result was an outburst of violence. In Cairo, the social action was motivated by a genuine demand for democracy. It was remarkable that for the first time, demonstrators did not rally around the usual anti-American and anti-Israeli demagogy. However, parties unhappy with the democratic trend were able to distort the original message and divert the focus to subjects of hate. First, they incited anti-Israeli hate and as a consequence the mob burned the Israeli embassy. Next, the social action morphed into pogroms against the Copts. The Occupy Wall Street uprising, initially sparked by President Obama's class-war rhetoric and by the magazine *Adbuster* (David Brooks, "Let's Occupy Ourselves," in *New York Times* and *Denver Post*, October 12, 2011) of anti-Jewish inclinations, and inspired by extreme Marxist, environmental, and anti-globalization indoctrination, showed a lot of noisy actions with little content. The rioters, rich in anti-Semitic outbursts (see J. Neumann, "Occupy Wall Street and the Jews," *Commentary*, January 2012) conveniently ignored that most or all Republicans voted against the TARP and that the mortgage disaster was caused by distorted housing and lending policies initiated and pushed by the Democratic Party in its craving for power (see P. J. Wallison, "Wall Street's Gullible Occupiers," *Wall Street Journal*, October 12, 2011). This spontaneous outburst is now being exploited by left-wing special interest groups to promote their specific and unrelated causes. The examples mentioned here show that social action, for its own sake, often creates confusion, can be easily taken over by partisan demagogy, and causes violence while achieving little results.

3. Jules Michelet's dictum as quoted by Raymond Aron in *Opium of the Intellectuals*, 282.

4. It is helpful to pay attention to an observation made in this context by R. Aron: "How could progressive intellectuals refuse to offer their talents to a

State which proclaims the true doctrine, to the building up of a society which conforms with the hopes of revolutionary rationalism and which is generous to experts and men of letters—*providing they obey?*" Ibid., 291 (emphasis in the original).

5. See Meyer, *Response to Modernity*, 288.

6. See ibid., 309–14.

7. See Aryeh Spero, "What the Bible Teaches about Capitalism," *Wall Street Journal*, January 30, 2012.

8. The Marshall Plan and the aid to Japan are examples of successful programs. The success was due more to the discipline and the know-how of the recipients rather than the expertise of the donors. Aid to developing countries, provided directly by donor states or through international organizations such as the United Nations, was and remains inefficient, corrupt, and corrupting, and in many cases achieved opposite results to those intended. See the tragedy of the aid to African countries and Pakistan. The same criticism applies to many national welfare programs that reduced personal initiative and increased dependency on the government.

9. From recent studies on the topic (see C. Paul Vincent, "The Voyage of the *St. Louis* Revisited," *Holocaust Genocide Studies* (Fall 2011) 25(2): 252–89, doi: 10.1093/hgs/dcr038), we can learn that the US press, starting with the *New York Times*, reported extensively on the issue. In spite of its highly humanitarian nature, no "social action" and public pressure initiated by the Reform movement was on record to persuade President Roosevelt to decide in favor of the refugees. Rejected by the United States, Cuba (although twenty-nine passengers managed to disembark in Havana) and Canada, the passengers returned to Europe, first stopping in the United Kingdom, where 288 passengers were allowed to disembark. The remaining 620 passengers disembarked at Antwerp, Belgium, and found refuge in France, Belgium, and the Netherlands. Recent research indicates that only eighty-seven of the passengers that reached continental Europe escaped the Holocaust.

10. I could not find any evidence of cooperation between the Reform leadership and the efforts of Rabbi Meir Berlin (Bar Ilan), a leader of the Zionist Orthodox Mizrahi Movement, who in his yearlong visit to the United States (January 1943 to January 1944) attempted to persuade the US national leadership to react to the atrocities of the Holocaust in Eastern Europe. See Hava Eshkoli (Wagman), "The Zionist Aspect of Religious-Zionist Policy in Palestine in View of the Holocaust," *Yad Vashem Studies* 29 (2001).

11. See Kaplan, *Contemporary American Judaism*, 38.

Chapter 9: Social Justice—Is It Justice for All?

The road to hell is paved with good intentions.

Folk saying

This is the meaning of social justice. It means actions by the State in the name of Justice, which is to say under complete protection and immunity from review. Its end is dictatorship.

David Mamet, *The Secret Knowledge*[1]

The 1999 "Statement of Principles for Reform Judaism" by the Central Conference of American Rabbis emphatically proclaims that "we reaffirm social action and social justice as a central prophetic focus of traditional Reform Jewish belief and practice."[2] It is difficult to define accurately the meaning of "social justice." On the face of it, the notion indicates the intent to skew justice toward social considerations rather than being impartial under the law. If we accept such a bias, we open the door to a long list of biased justice: Halacha, *Shari'a*, environmental, economic, tribal, gang, animal, Marxist, National Socialist, and much more. In very simple terms, we reverse the achievement of democratic constitutional law and bring back a judicial system that reflects the preferences of a privileged group or a ruling class.

Supporters of "social" justice argue that their advocacy empowers deprived groups and supports denied causes. The question is: Why are those groups deprived and their causes denied? Helping the homeless or protecting rivers are noble and well-intentioned causes, but are they, by definition, products of criminal action that require judicial remedy? Holocaust deniers, polygamists, pirates, and jihad terrorists promote denied causes in our society. Should social justice protect these causes?

If social justice means preferential judicial treatment for a certain class of people, let's say the "working class," the questions are: Who is included in this class, why should they be preferred, and why should only this class be preferred? Should mechanics and firefighters, university professors and surgeons, nurses and bank managers, engineers and farmers, who all work very hard, be included and if so, who is excluded? Should politicians and rabbis be included, assuming that they also work hard? The distinction becomes very arbitrary and dangerously controversial.

In real terms, social justice is an academic and political declarative topic that has generated little or no critical feedback and is lacking proof of its effectiveness.[3] As it often happens with topics that assert scientific status but lack scientific evidence, the promoters of social justice deliberately impose their agenda on any possible domain while aggressively rejecting any attempt at critical dialogue. A parasitic imposition of "social justice" activism on an established domain, such as science, art, or religion, attempts to convey undeniable justification to "social justice" by placing it as a supreme notion above the very tenets of the domain. Instead of promoting a genuine, valid, and verifiable intellectual area open for criticism, "social justice" activists are becoming lobbyists for special interest groups willing to wrap their interests in the mantle of "social justice."[4] This vicious, self-serving circle and the vagarious nature of "social justice" can damage and corrupt legitimate intellectual domains.

Justice that is qualified raises the question of who has the authority to pass judgment and based on what criteria? The American constitutional democracy has established a clear process of judicial implementation. In the interest of impartiality, the US Constitution has determined the separation between institutions and the practice of checks and balances. Constitutional justice by definition is a formal process of dispute resolution based on the laws of the land: federal and state, county and city. If the water of a river is polluted, legislation can address it. If the causes of pollution are unknown, the problem may be resolved by technical solutions, not by a judicial process, since nobody can be kept accountable. Yet attempting to find a culprit based on assumptions and passing judgment in the court of public opinion is not justice; it is political posturing and manipulation.

The blood libel of the Jews and the assertion that humans cause global warming are examples of passing judgment based on partisan consensus instigated by interested parties. The scientific findings of Galileo and Copernicus were dismissed by political consensus, not scientific refutation. In the absence of any constitutional law, the Inquisition administrated its justice based on its political agenda. Our current judicial system may need improvement, but replacing "blind justice for all" with biased justice will achieve the exact opposite result.

If the notion of "social justice" is not seen in the judicial context but rather in an ethical context of welfare and charity, then the use of terminology is important. In chapter 4 we indicated, based on Buber's observation, that clarity is "good," representing the reliability of "home," while confusion is destructive, it is "evil." Purposely introducing inappropriate terminology such as judicial terms ("justice") and confusing language indicates the intent to subvert the system.

Some activists candidly assert that "the purpose of social justice is to empower disenfranchised clients and create sociopolitical change to dismantle the current status quo."[5] This language goes beyond the offer of individual charity and justice; it is a political message whose hidden agenda is perpetual revolution, reminiscent of the Marxist class warfare and its perpetual revolutionary tyranny. Such assertions bring us back to the vagaries of the European nineteenth-century revolutionary slogans with their devastating effects. The American constitutional system has been heavily criticized by its European detractors because it provides a strong defense of individual rights and liberties and limits government. American supporters of this critique, unable to change the Constitution by electoral suffrage, have justified attempts to change or subvert the Constitution by introducing linguistic or procedural manipulations.

Arbitrary judgments, linguistic deception, and procedural manipulations provide a distinct advantage to those who are able to use them for political purposes. Political regimes, organizations, and bureaucracies that do not intend to be accountable to their constituencies, who are interested in avoiding any evaluation of their performance, adopt "social justice" as an indisputable confirmation of their positions. Again and again, whenever this type of judgment was applied it weakened the public's liberties and deprived the needy.[6] These vague qualifications are creating discriminatory biases to be determined not by laws and an independent judicial system applicable equally to all but by partisan decisions and arbitrary regulations applied at the discretion of privileged bureaucracies. Ultimately these positions defeat the moral stand of their advocates.

In sociopolitical terms, social justice is a reflection of the welfare state. The welfare state is structured around entitlements. Entitlements, such as free housing, free health care, free education, and free food stamps may appear to be well intended and "just."

Yet these entitlements promote excessive consumption, perpetuate poverty, and reduce public participation. They stifle entrepreneurship and limit accountability while ignoring the limited available resources to fund them. The most detrimental aspect of social justice is its advocacy for arbitrary wealth redistribution. Wealth redistribution does not provide a remedy to the causes of poverty. It is unemployment and poor education that institutionalize and legitimize poverty.

The stagnant nature of "social justice," in economic and cultural terms, presents the opposite of the enlightened capitalistic approach. Briefly stated, capitalism is based on opportunity, innovation, and rewarding success. Modern capitalism is able to self-correct through trial and error, public criticism, and market verification. Informed capitalism is sensitive to public response and appreciates a regulatory environment that provides public safety and prevents damaging litigation.

Upon more careful scrutiny, we may recognize that politicians who promote the unattainable promises of "social justice" are more interested in their immediate electoral success than in the long-term sustained prosperity of their constituency. In their hands, the control of entitlements distributed under "social justice" becomes an unaccountable Machiavellian "poison pill" aimed at keeping their constituencies docile and dependent on the party line. The most disturbing consequence is that the failure of these unsustainable entitlements is most detrimental for those for whom these programs are supposedly intended.[7] The failure of the European welfare state and the vulnerability of the entitlements established in the United States bring us ample evidence on this matter. Rabbi Jonathan Sacks highlighted this crisis in an article published in *The Wall Street Journal*. Referring to the August 2011 rioters in London, Rabbi Sacks's opinion is that the truth is it is not their fault. They are the victims of the tsunami of wishful thinking that washed across the West saying that you can have sex without the responsibility of marriage, children without the responsibility of parenthood, social order without the responsibility of citizenship, liberty without the responsibility of morality and self-esteem without the responsibility of work or earned achievement ... It has been the culture of free lunch in a world where there are no free lunches.[8]

In various ways and formulations, for two centuries, leaders of Reform Judaism have advocated labor and economic issues or pacifist and environmental causes that were labeled as "social justice" rather than as political positions. Yet again it is difficult to separate such causes from their political nature or recognize them as legitimate judicial cases and more significantly for us, accept them as religious concerns. American Reform Judaism, by formally adopting the principle of separation of church and state, should delegate all these concerns to the civic domain and separate them from our religious practices.

The argument that social justice stems out of the Tanachic vision of justice is misleading. We have to recognize that *tzedek* means justice, not necessarily "social" or "environmental" or "animal" or "economic" justice. The principle that "justice follows justice" (*tzedek tirdof tzedek*) is emphasizing the importance of justice per se without any qualifiers. More important, modern American constitutional law has implemented many of the provisions of the Judeo-Christian judicial heritage. It is for this very important reason that Reform Judaism has waived its juridical authority in favor of civil justice; it has renounced the Halacha as a mandatory judicial system and has conformed to the civic constitutional judicial system. It is totally absurd, after renouncing the Jewish jurisprudence, to replace it with esoteric systems such as "social, economic, or environmental" justices. And again and again we must pay attention that these replacements contradict the Reform tenet of separation of church and state.

Reform Judaism has always prided itself on being exploratory and innovative. To follow suit so sheepishly after other "progressive" denominations and adopting outdated nineteenth-century ideologies in the twenty-first century is disappointing and wearisome. The insistence on the propagation of "social justice" advocacy raises doubts on the professionalism and motivation of our leadership. The question is what motivates the Reform leadership to subscribe with enthusiasm to these ethical aberrations?

In reviewing the language of the pamphlets of the RAC, it becomes obvious that "social justice" is used as justification for a partisan political agenda supported by the current selected leadership. This position contradicts the religious, divine faith-based nature of our denomination and as such is unwarranted and illegitimate. In my opinion, in the absence of a genuinely inspiring religious vision, the leadership attempts to assert its authority by imposing an arbitrary "political correctness" justified by the vagaries of "social justice." Cynical political activists capitalize on real or imagined public frustrations by perpetuating a sense of discrimination, injustice, and victimization. They do not hesitate to promise their constituency lofty future remedies conditioned by immediate compliance. In following this course our current leadership is making two crucial mistakes: they undermine their own status as religious leaders; and, more importantly, they endanger the religious integrity and the cohesiveness of the movement with outdated and compromised ideologies. It is time for the congregations to reconsider the mission and performance of the leadership of the URJ.

The current goal of Reform Judaism, as a modern religious denomination, should be to provide spiritual support, inspiration, and comfort. As a nonpartisan, informed and critical observer, Reform Judaism can be on the forefront of the dialogue between religion and civics, while respecting the principle of separation between church and state. In this dialogue, the role of religion—Reform Judaism in particular—is to assume an ethical monitoring position rather than direct and partisan involvement. Modern religion is not meant to provide solutions to civic and state issues but rather inspiration and moral strength to the public and its leaders. Religious ethical presence is achieved by dialogue and its merit is achieved through personal and congregational example, not political assertion packaged in vague and misleading terms such as "social justice."

Notes

1. David Mamet, *The Secret Knowledge* (New York: Sentinel-Penguin Group, 2011), 93.

2. Central Conference of American Rabbis, 1999 "Statement of Principles."

3. See Robert C. Hunsaker, "Counseling and Social Justice," *Academic Questions* 24, no. 3 (Fall 2011): 323, 335, doi: 10.1007/s12129-011-9242-y.

4. See R. Hunsaker, "Social Justice: An Inconvenient Irony," posted September 17, 2008 at http://sjirony.blogspot.com (and identified as reprint of "Counseling Today OpEd, April 2008").

5. Hunsaker, "Counseling and Social Justice," 329–31.

6. C. Y. Chang, D. G. Hays, and T. F. Milliken, quoted in Hunsaker, "Counseling and Social Justice," 328.

7. By definition, biased justice excludes those who do not conform to its definition. The excluded are left to survive the caprices of the rulers or the aggravations of the outlaws. Building a defense in these circumstances, if allowed, requires enormous resources intended to change basic premises included in the bias of the prevalent justice.

8. Jonathan Sacks, "Reversing the Decay of London Undone," Essay, *Wall Street Journal*, August 20, 2011.

Chapter 10: **Jewish Family:**
The Reform Spirit

> The love of belonging, as does the love of the wife with
> the narrow womb, impels one to service, attention, and
> consistency. It prompts one to greater understanding. How
> wonderful to have such an object of devotion.
>
> David Mamet, *The Wicked Son*[1]

As a lay person, I wondered how Moses was able to identify Jews
and communicate with them throughout the Egyptian empire. I've
found an informative hint in Exodus 12:1–10. The Torah recounts
that one of Moses's first acts, in his process of identifying the people
of Israel in Egypt, was the establishment of a ritual offering and the
request to mark the gate posts with sacrificial blood. If Jews were able
to mark the gates, this meant that they owned the property and were
not slaves of private Egyptians but Pharaoh's slaves. As such, they
were subjects of Pharaoh (their status can be analogized to how Great
Britain would later view its citizens as being subjects of the queen)
and had the same status as the majority of free Egyptians. If Jews were
homeowners we can assume that they were able to raise a family.

There is archeological evidence that ancient Egypt hosted
minorities, including Jews. If Jews lived in built homes, not rural
huts, it indicates that they may have lived in cities and performed
as skilled workers and merchants and engaged in other urban
activities. Ample available archeological evidence indicates that

antique Egyptian cities developed vibrant urban communities in which Jews might have had an active participation. If we assume that the Torah provides reliable information, we can speculate that Jews, in Pharaonic Egypt, were able not only to raise families but maybe also to maintain whole communities, even in oppressive times.

The significance for us of this understanding of history is in the recognition that Moses recruited and accepted Jewish following based on self-identification of each family as Jews: the voluntary mark of the gate posts. Those who were prepared to join the vision Moses offered were accepted and included. This voluntary commitment of affiliation, being a Torah statement, gives us an initial and significant indication on the nature of Jewish belonging.[2]

It was only much later, after the golden calf incident, that Moses recognized the need for extensive family- and community-oriented rituals. Many centuries later, however, when Jews were again wandering in exile, deprived of statehood and prevented from conducting open community rituals, they could find comfort in the original family offering: the festive meal of Passover. Also it is the festive meal of Shabbat that brings the whole family together in reverence to the Almighty, a meal that has preserved the Jewish identity and shared sense of belonging to the faith throughout the ages.

What is central in any Jewish family? The sense of belonging. And what brings together the Jewish family? The mother.

Traditional Judaism designated women as keepers of the family. Indications for this privileged status can be found in such traditions as lighting the Shabbat candles, the matrilineal descent to determine Jewish status, and the ceremony of the holy day of *Rosh Chodesh* (a reward for not encouraging the golden calf sin). These unique attributes are not only symbolic but also had important practical implications. In a prevalent cultural environment in which women's status was close to slavery, assigning a significant statutory role and functional definition (as carriers of the line of descent and as guardians of the Sabbath) was revolutionary.

As a matter of fact, antique, polygamist Judaism assigned the responsibility for the family life to women in their role as wives and mothers. In agricultural civilizations, managing a household, which often included several children and dependent relatives, was a serious and demanding endeavor, especially in difficult times. Managing the household required considerable knowledge of what has been described in modern times as home economics and family responsibility. For the protection of women, the family bonds were designed along rigid regulations intended to minimize family conflicts and limit the husband's options to abandon the family. These regulations were also intended to protect the well-being of children in a society that did not otherwise provide any family safety net. We also should remember that the Tanachic tradition included women in prophetic endeavors, the most revered status in antique Judaism.

We must be cautious when reflecting on the tribal culture of antiquity from the perspective of the twenty-first century Western civilization. As a matter of fact, even in our time, people living in Western-oriented civilizations have difficulty understanding current tribal life in countries and cultures where it is still practiced.

Until recently, preservation of the traditional family was one key factor that was common to all civilizations and respected over centuries: it was the best way to secure the survival and continuity of humanity. It is only in the last few decades that the importance of and need for the traditional family has been brought into question. The status of voluntary single-parent families, for instance, is a new development made possible by moral, legal, and economic changes in Western culture. Voluntary (in the Israeli kibbutz) or coerced (in Chinese communes) modern attempts to dissolve the family unit and replace it with communitarian child care have failed. Criticizing traditions out of their historic context is erroneous and misleading. Preserving historic family traditions isolated from twenty-first century conditions and situations is unsustainable.

Orthodox Judaism preserves an ambiguous two-tier system by which it does not deny the ruling of civic legislation so long as it does not contradict the verdicts of the Halachic court. Disregard of the Jewish court, in particular in matters related to family rules and rights, is tantamount to exclusion from the community. The key factor in the Orthodox tradition regarding Jewish identification is maternal descent. Since our focus is on the position of Reform Judaism, I will set aside further discussion or criticism of Orthodox practices.

Unlike Orthodox Judaism, Reform Judaism, in recognizing the demands of modern times, made three significant adjustments to the family concept. As a denomination it adopted a broad definition of family descent based on one parent (either mother or father being Jewish) and added the condition to have the child being raised Jewish. As a consequence, by adopting broader criteria for Jewish identification and affiliation, Reform Judaism accepted a more balanced approach enabling any parent to determine the Jewish affiliation. The educational requirement, raising the child with a Jewish awareness, mandates parent involvement and reinstitutes a family bond better suited to modern times. Did this recognition change the role of the mother in the family? Partially, yes, but at the same time, Reform Judaism has recognized women as equal partners in all endeavors, including religious practices.

As part of the application of the principle of separation of church and state, Reform Judaism relegated family relations to the civil legal system. This adjustment reduced the family status to a contractual agreement based on material benefits. The civil legal system gives priority to the well-being of the adult partners with certain safety considerations for the children

The third adjustment to modern living relates to a significant shift in ritual that is occurring in the Reform movement. Family rituals for boys and girls, such as name giving, bar mitzvahs, bat mitzvahs, and confirmations, performed as public celebrations, are becoming life milestones and individual bonds to the faith. The expansion of some of these celebrations to adults, such as late *bar-* and bat mitzvahs, are additional layers in the process of fostering an enduring faith. This process is marked by an increased involvement of women as leaders, participants, and promoters with a particular impact on children's education. These new developments can and will intensify the sense of congregational belonging.

Briefly stated, we can identify here a certain contradiction between the tenets of Reform Judaism and contemporary American reality. Reform Judaism recognizes the centrality of the family in the Jewish culture and faith. On the other hand, by acquiescing and conforming to the prevailing civic system it opens the family structure to the vagaries and temptations of the entitlement culture. It appears to me that current Reform practices might need some clarification and improvement.

As a matter of fact, Reform Judaism officially recognized the equal status of women in its rituals (shared sitting) long before feminism was a la mode and later recognized women in leadership, as rabbis. Still, the question remains whether these recognitions strengthen the family. Is the purpose of marriage the establishment of a family unit? Can the act of marriage be reconsidered beyond the civil record? Can and should religion and faith have a role in the formation of the family unit?

We also should consider these aspects: Can the religious ritual be enriched to create a process by which the partners are made aware of and educated to accept marriage not only as a material benefit and regular sex but also as a divine spiritual faith-based experience that becomes a shared bond for the family? Can we reestablish family values that enrich the commitment between the partners with divine spiritual and faith-based qualities?

Reform Judaism is proud of its adoption of the formal liberation of women (and men) from religious legal bondage. Now, after two centuries of experimentation, can the movement reinvigorate itself by injecting spirit and faith into this basic building block of Judaism, the family? Reform congregations have recognized for a long time that marital disciplinary regulations and sanctions are ineffective and detrimental to individuals, the family, and the congregation. A congregation based on voluntary participation cannot accept or afford chastising of its members in any way. Reform Judaism is better served by applying dialogue and persuasion rather than imposing stringent rules. In this context, let us consider how to improve the family-formation process.

The purpose of the family unit is the establishment of a relationship that in modern culture goes beyond reproduction and survival. The family provides a basic spiritual environment that brings people out of the loneliness created by the exhaustion of their field of work, the alienation of crowds, and the hyper exposure to information. A reformed modern family can recapture the missing support, intimacy, and spontaneity that were part of the tribal existence or the tightly knit antique or medieval urban enclave.

In our time we realize that even in a prosperous society, the need to administrate limited available family resources in economical ways revives an appreciation for personal commitments. In spite of the numerous experiments related to children's education, children cannot be left to be brought up without parental involvement. Neither communities nor the state have the resources or the appropriate tools to replace parents. On a cultural level, the history of the last two centuries shows us that reason, science, and planning can be part of the solution but not the entire solution. The factor that could provide the missing fostering support to the family is spiritual: a bond that brings people together by sharing common world views, perception, beliefs, and practices. In spite of all the reaction against divine religious practices promoted since the French Revolution, people crave a transcendental shared reference that brings the family back together as part of a community of shared beliefs. Religion is back.

In Reform Judaism, this spiritual bond is provided by the congregation, the temple, and its affiliated services. The current challenge faced by each congregation is how to create an effective connection with the individual family.

Reform Judaism recognizes and encourages marriage for the creation of a family cell, which remains the basic block in shaping personal and congregational life. This encouragement should not be understood as a rejection of singles. On the contrary, it invites singles to join the congregation and find their suitable partners while taking advantage of the shared faith.

Besides providing a convenient and informal match-making environment, what other contributions, constructive and preventive, can the congregation provide to the family? Establishing and sustaining a family is a long-term demanding enterprise that has to be considered with care, since it involves responsibilities for the partners, the children, and society. It should not be a career facilitator or status setter, features which can be achieved these days without the commitments of marriage. Suitable and effective answers to these questions may reduce the reticence to marry and to establish formal families.

In the last decades, mostly due to the benefits offered by the welfare state and individual legal protections, we witnessed the widening of so-called out-of-wedlock relations that may include a shared lifestyle and children. Can this form of relationship replace the "traditional" family? There are serious drawbacks, civic and religious, for out-of-wedlock relationships. But, learning from reality, instead of dismissing such relationships, the religious practice may formally incorporate rather than tolerate them, as part of the family-building process. Certain limitations would be advisable, such as the amount of time spent together by the partners, participation in the activities of the congregation, and delaying parenthood until after the solemnizing of marriage. By recognizing and formalizing this relationship in the congregational practice, the family-building process can be sustained and expanded and be open to spiritual enrichment.

In the spirit and traditions of Reform Judaism, the family-building process can and should be carried out on a dual track: by the rabbi and by the congregation. While the rabbi fulfills the spiritual and educational role, the congregation can provide the social support and advice. This process can provide the couple with experience, confidence, and mitigation of disagreements. If the relationship dissipates before marriage, there should be no sanctions, and the congregation should encourage the individuals to try again. This process, if successful, will reduce the number and the acrimony of divorces. By nature if a divorce occurs, it is public. Since the psychological impact of a divorce on children and implicitly on society at large cannot be quantified, this dimension is often ignored. If the separation process is started, rabbis are replaced by family counselors or psychoanalysts, and later in the process, by lawyers.

The congregation may or may not welcome the divorced individuals, on a case by case evaluation. For instance, irresponsible behavior of one of the partners should not disenfranchise the other partner; on the contrary, the congregation should provide compassion and support. This approach may appear more restrictive than current Reform practices adopted by certain congregations. Placing selective restrictions emphasizes the need to respect the effort invested in the process and preserves its rigor. A reasonable degree of agreed discipline usually strengthens the congregation and makes it more reliable in the eyes of its members.[4]

Many congregations already provide support for child care and early education. However, this effort should not be a separate process from the family life but an integral extension of it. Child-care programs can be expanded in scope through parental involvement. The goal of such joint programs is to instill and sustain a spiritual foundation in the family as a whole. Also, the congregational grounds, the temple or the school, may become a place for contact between separated parents with their children and possibly offer an environment for reconciliation. New approaches, methods, and techniques may be needed in order to reach effective results, but the effort is worth trying. We will discuss the implications of Reform Judaism's approach to general education in the following chapter.

I raised my boys as a divorced father. It was my belief that even in this asymmetrical situation we could preserve a family sense, a sense of belonging. This belief made me look for support by joining a congregation. I found support in the welcoming reception I received from the members of the Tifereth Israel congregation in Lincoln, Nebraska, who opened their homes and accepted us with warmth and friendship. The lack of maternal attention available to my sons compelled me to pay more attention to them than I might otherwise have done. My behavior was guided by a sense of responsibility to my children. What I learned from this experience is that single parenthood is a difficult burden on both the parent and the children.

In traditional Judaism the father was the provider for the family and the mother sustained the Jewish spirit of the family. Reform

Judaism has transformed traditional paternalistic Judaism into an affirming denomination that has adopted equal status for men and women. How does this equality affect the family and the members of the family? Today the mother has the opportunity to expand her status, responsibilities, and effort. What should be the responsibility of the father in the modern family? Should the reformed family formula promote interchangeable roles between parents or a new type of partnership?

A simple answer would be to recognize an equal partnership between the mother and the father. Modern reality, however, shows that a truly equal partnership is difficult and may be unwarranted. Mother and father each make different contributions and as such play different roles in shaping their mutual relations and in conditioning the life of children.

Can our rabbis, men and women, provide us helpful directions? Can our rabbis and theologians find untapped distinct aspects of modern man that can make constructive contributions to the family and congregations?

It might be helpful to encourage congregations to consider promoting private family rituals and practices that suit our time, including the opportunities opened by available means of communication. Daily or weekly time spent in the family, dedicated to the learning of a portion of the Jewish heritage, and family-oriented events focused on Jewish topics can become enticing and effective ways to foster the family by enjoying Jewish content. Even a daily prayer, blessing, or a similar practice that brings the family together in sharing a common spirit might provide the minimal family basic bond.

Finally, the role of the rabbi and the congregation in this process is to teach and to recommend rituals and practices, as well as to develop tracks of inspiring learning and to design events that will enable the family-enrichment process. I believe that the seeds of such religious actions are already in place. Concentrated and innovative religious initiatives that bring together families, including all their members, can provide a sustainable revival of the Jewish family.

Notes

1. David Mamet, *The Wicked Son: Anti-Semitism, Self-Hatred, and the Jews* (New York: Schocken, 2006), 137.

2. The question "Who is a Jew?" is the most divisive issue in contemporary Judaism. The assertion of Orthodox rabbinic leaders that Judaism is established only by maternal genealogical linkage has been rejected by Reform Judaism. Reform Judaism accepts paternal linkage and cultural enrichment. As indicated in the text above, the Torah canon supports this premise. The genealogical argument can be refuted also on the evidence that the origin of many Eastern European Jews is connected to converted local tribes such as the Chuzars (see Maimonides's recounting). It is possible to see that, in certain difficult circumstances, the maternal condition was useful in preserving Judaism. Today, however, in Israel and in Western modern civilization, the maternal exclusive restriction loses its significance and may become detrimental to the well-being and sustainability of Judaism.

3. The proclivity in welfare states for such phenomena as alienation, single motherhood, out-of wedlock relations and high rates of divorce, neglect and estrangement from children, drug abuse and suicides are well documented in professional sources. Welfare policies have not improved the situation and some researchers maintain that these policies may have worsened the situation.

4. Dana Kaplan indicates in his research that as "most Reform congregants have little idea what the movement's religious beliefs are, it will be difficult for them to pass on those beliefs to their children and grandchildren." Kaplan, "Reform Jewish Theology," 73 (see note in chap. 5). This outcome can be remediated by bringing forward clear and coherent theological Reform positions and practices applicable in the family.

Chapter 11: Freedom of Education and Reform Education

> 1 My child: If you accept My words and treasure my commandments with yourself, 2 to make your ears attentive to wisdom, incline your heart to understanding 3 [for] only if you call out understanding [and] give forth your voice to discernment, 4 if you seek it as [if it were] silver, if you search for it as [if it were] hidden treasures—5 then you will understand the fear of Hashem, and discover the knowledge of God.
>
> Proverbs 2:1–5

Tyrannical political regimes imposed on the public a "freedom" *from* educational choices by maintaining a uniform and biased education. A controlled educational system is part of the infrastructure that makes tyranny successful. Allan Bloom indicates that

> the most successful tyranny is not the one that uses force to assure uniformity but the one that removes the awareness of other possibilities, that makes it seem inconceivable that other ways are viable, that removes the sense that there is an outside.[1]

For centuries Judaism escaped the tyranny of the surrounding environment by practicing Jewish education; it found freedom *in* Judaic learning. Finally, the Enlightenment and democracy, in the name of freedom *of* education, offered the public various choices of education. This freedom was meant to open a wide range of educational options to the public and provide the freedom to choose the most suitable educational alternative from the free market of educational ideas and visions. We, in the United States, are fortunate to still have a variety of effective educational ideas promoted in a wide, comprehensive educational spectrum: public, religious, and private K–12; vocational and community colleges; state, public, private, and religious universities; and a range of continuing education options.

Education is a key part of the spiritual and cultural formation of our civilization. For those who are proud of our culture and civilization—the Western Civilization—the purpose of education is to enable young generations to understand and be able to participate in our civilization. The first step in reaching civility is, to quote Clive Bell, "the acquisition of self-consciousness and a habit of reflection."[2] Western Civilization was inspired by the Tanachic spirit, which introduced individual human beings as interlocutors with Divinity. In a recent article in *The Wall Street Journal*[3] David Mamet emphasizes, in his own metaphorical rendition, the symbolic importance of blocking of human sacrifice and questioning the divine message:

And God told Abraham to take his son up the mountain and kill him, as humans had done for tens of thousands of years. Now, however, for the first time in history, the narrative changed. The sacrifice, Isaac, spoke back. He asked his father, "Where is the goat we are to sacrifice?" This was the voice of conscience, and Abraham's hand, as it descended with the knife, was stayed. This was the Birth of the West, and the birth of the West's burden, which is conscience.

In our time, we are still witnessing, in particular in Islam, the praise of human sacrifice. This reverence of martyrdom only highlights how unique and vulnerable Western Civilization is. In this regard education can be one of the most effective means to protect and improve Western Civilization.

It is the function of K–12 education to inspire and to instill the knowledge and discipline necessary to reach the Western level of conscience and human dignity. In Judaism the Tanach, the oral tradition, and the rest of the Jewish heritage are powerful sources in achieving this goal. Reform Judaism adds modern interpretation to this sequence, while preserving the spiritual essence of the Tanachic vision.

Initial American education was community based in the spirit of, by, and for the people. Public education was introduced in America in the first half of the nineteenth century by the Protestant or Unitarian Harvard-based elite. Its members promoted public education initially as a rebellion against Calvinist orthodoxy and local common schools and later as a defense against what they considered the dangers of Roman Catholic influence.[4] The Unitarians were inspired in their drive by the Prussian model of public education, a model based on Hegel's authoritarian philosophy as well as extensive state regulations and intervention.[5] European state-controlled, centralized, public education systems achieved a high level of knowledge delivery. Their statist Hegelian conceptual approaches, however, also became an effective indoctrination tool that shaped Europe's civil and moral decline, culminating with the atrocities of the twentieth century.

One of the original arguments in favor of adopting public education in America was that state intervention and regulations would promote "natural and progressive" concepts of education to all students.[6] The definitions of "natural and progressive" concepts remained vague and received various interpretations according to the groups that controlled the system.

In the name of separation of church and state and inspired by the utopian ideas of the nineteenth century, public education has become a universal, noncommittal, politicized education system that increasingly advocates secular conformism and compliance. The management of K–12 education is dominated by teachers unions that often put their quest for financial benefits before their educational mission.[7] In many communities, federal- and state-imposed regulations have caused government authorities, school staff, organized educators, parents, and pupils to become disconnected and to operate on separate tracks. In the process, the following valuable elements are becoming secondary attributes of the system (if not totally dismissed): discrete local pedagogic experience and dedication; ethical discourse; students' individual responsibility, discipline, proficiency, and rigor; freethinking; and parental support.[8]

This heavily regulated but dysfunctional system is antithetical to the entrepreneurial spirit of enlightened America, a spirit that emphasizes federal, state, and local freedom of choice offset by public checks and balances. "Liberal" politicization and deconstruction of higher education into a wide range of esoteric topics, often replacing fundamental studies, is making the situation worse.[9]

The accumulated experience of public education in America, in particular in the last half century, shows that in spite of large investments in the system, public education failed and is failing in its learning mission (delivery and absorption of knowledge) as well as in its mission to advance civic responsibility.[10] We must point out that a failing enterprise is the most expensive enterprise. The success of innovative reforms recently implemented in critical locations such as Washington, DC, New York City, Indiana, and Louisiana indicate that innovative solutions can work if the public is prepared to make an effort to overcome entrenched economic interests and political favoritism.[11] At the same time, there is ample evidence that faith-based educational systems are more effective in engaging pupils and parents in the process and provide a more rigorous knowledge basis.[12] This brings us to the opportunity to consider the contribution and role Reform congregations can play shaping Reform education.

Jewish education is an essential component of building the faith-based identity of Reform Judaism and Jewish solidarity. Our congregations of independent thinkers and entrepreneurs—compassionate but not complaisant—expect our young generations to be fair, reliable, and competitive. Reform Judaism has recognized that a thorough knowledge of our heritage instills Jewish pride and confidence and fosters the character and the performance of our future generations. Reform Judaism inspires its members to reach a spiritual dialogue between the divine spirit and human conscience, a human conscience shaped by free thinking, integrity, innovation, and entrepreneurship. These core values of our movement can and should become guidelines for the design of a comprehensive Reform education system. It is not the objective of this chapter to discuss specific solutions for the educational system. The subject deserves separate, in depth examination. My intention is to clarify the existing problem and to point out the availability of alternative educational opportunities.

For the purpose of our discussion, I make a distinction between the existing academic Judaic studies and Reform faith-based studies of Judaism. Academic Judaic studies are intended to introduce Judaism to the wide public in general terms. By their very nature and academic restrictions, such programs cannot answer the demands of faith-based spiritual enrichment of practicing congregants.

The purpose of the leading academic institution of Reform Judaism, the Hebrew Union College, is to prepare a knowledgeable religious cadre. It is essentially a professional academic institution that is not intended to serve the wide Reform public. Recently there were reports indicating that the education provided by our rabbinical institution is causing rabbinical students to adopt hostile positions toward Israel.[13] It is possible that some students reach seminaries with biased opinions nurtured by prior secular, nondenominational educational institutions. It is the mission of the seminaries and their faculty to clarify and convey to the students the positions of the Reform movement. If in fact the objective of the pedagogical delivery was favorable and sensitive support for Israel's existential situation, the students' reaction is an evident proof of the seminaries' failure. If the students' position reflects the learning spirit in the seminaries as included in their curriculum or faculty opinions, the Reform public, supportive of Israel, should express its concerns. We can also assume that these negative perceptions receive encouragement from the so-called "constructive criticism" some leaders in the movement have toward Israel's policies. Again, we witness the same essential confusion between the mission of Reform Judaism as a Jewish religious movement and the preference of the national leadership for a Universalist faith and certain political affiliations. Subverting the Jewish character of our theological education with foreign, one-sided agendas will not serve well the performance of the movement or its credibility.

The establishment of a comprehensive Reform education would not be an infringement of the separation between church and state. As such, a K–12 Reform education can become an additional constructive component of the pluralistic cultural fabric of America—separate but not exclusive. Introducing a Reform K–12 education clarifies the differences, prevents confusion, enhances the opportunities for choice, and can provide an effective example of Or Goim in education. A comprehensive Reform educational framework may include the development of junior college options, either as autonomous entities or attached to existing academic institutions, as a type of Reform *beit-midrash*. An inspiring precedent can be found in the Berlin *Hochschule fur die Wissenschaft des Judentums* (College for the Science of Judaism, 1870–1942). We should be careful, however, in copying foreign precedents for the United States in the twenty-first century.

Currently, Reform congregations conduct preschool programs, weekend school activities, and alternative educational activities. There are very few K–12 comprehensive educational institutions with a Reform orientation, mostly due to the opposition of the Reform leadership to acknowledge the failure of public education.[14] We can detect a new awareness in Jewish non-Orthodox circles of the benefits a distinct Jewish comprehensive education may offer.[15] This is a constructive trend I hope will gain momentum.

The link connecting education to our faith is parental commitment. This involvement is formal, through supervising bodies, and personal, through the commitment of parents to their children and the system. If parents and congregations recognize that a faith-based education is preferable to a state-sponsored education, they should be willing to initiate and support Reform religious schools. An extensive K–12 Reform educational system— supported by a public system of vouchers or similar mechanisms[16] and philanthropic contributions—would provide a significant educational improvement. Its success would make the investment more cost effective than the current failing system. Failure is the worst investment.

The development and implementation of Reform educational programs should be the responsibility of coalitions of interested local congregations with the support of the Union for Reform Judaism and the Hebrew Union College. It is in and around these institutions that students, parents, and scholars can experience and explore the intellectual wealth offered by Judaism and reflect on the essence of our spirit and culture in the context of our time. We can expect Reform schools and *batay-midrashim* to become intellectual incubators for twenty-first-century Reform leadership and the Reform public. Tested and novel educational systems can provide the framework for delivering, understanding, and assimilating content and can benefit significantly, in academic and fiduciary terms, from incorporating emerging communication and information technologies in their studies.

A distinct educational system is only as good as the thoroughness of its content and the talent and dedication of its teachers. The study of spiritual and cultural heritage provides an inspiring foundation for developing content. Open- and critical-minded professional Reform teachers, with an established understanding of the history and tenets of Judaism and its current Reform interpretation, will ensure a sustained in-depth learning of the American Jewish Reform religious content and practices. The commitment to modern Jewish values can significantly help develop rigorous curricula and high educational performance. It is my conviction that promoting comprehensive faith-based Reform education is a rewarding religious action: a more effective, more accountable, more reliable, and more lasting spiritual and cultural enrichment than social activism or tikkun olam, with their political confusions, ideological vagaries, and mundane positions.

Notes

1. Allan Bloom, *The Closing of the American Mind* (New York: Simon & Schuster, 1987), 249.

2. Clive Bell, *Civilization* (England: Penguin Books, 1947), 41.

3. David Mamet, "Israel, Isaac and the Return of Human Sacrifice: Why Have Liberal Westerners Turned Their Backs on the Jewish State?" Opinion, *Wall Street Journal*, December 13, 2011.

4. See S. L. Blumenfeld, *Is Public Education Necessary?* (Powder Springs, GA: The American Vision Inc., 2011), 115.

5. See ibid., 152–55.

6. See ibid., 157–80.

7. See the 2011 violent protests by teachers' unions in Wisconsin and the persistent resistance of these unions to educational reform.

8. See C. Greer, *The Great School Legend: A Revisionist Interpretation of American Public Education* (New York: Basic Books, Inc., 1972); Blog: "Betrayed—Why Public Education Is Failing"; A. M. Carvalho and S. L. Paine, "Strategies for Rescuing Failing Public Schools: How Leaders Create a Culture of Success" (policy paper) (McGraw-Hill Research Foundation, 2011); P. R. McDonald, "Compton Parents Petition to Take Over Chronically Failing Public School through 'Parent Trigger' Law, Sends Shock Waves throughout the Nation," *LA Weekly*, December 8, 2011.

9. See Kevin Nestor, "A Great Trust Betrayed: The Politicization of America's Public Campuses," *Academic Questions* 24 no. 2 (Summer 2011): 194–208; Stanley Rothman, S. Robert Lichter, and Neil Nevitte, "Politics and Professional Advancement among College Faculty," *The Forum*, Vol. 3, Issue 1, Article 2 (Berkeley Electronic Press, 2005), available at http://www.bepress.com/forum.

10. See A. J. Coulson, "The Impact of Federal Involvement in America's Classrooms" (Cato Institute, February 2011).

11. Schools operating as part of the public education system are definitely not providing strength to our democracy; on the contrary, they are weakening our culture and civilization. A meaningful indicator of the disintegration of public education is the aggressive and violent greed of teachers' unions. A sign of the time is the teachers' unions' vandal occupation of the capitol building

in Madison, Wisconsin, in Spring 2011, to which they brought their children to witness and participate in this act of savage assault on democracy. In spite of all the vocal rhetoric, such behavior does not inspire respect for the teachers or provide confidence to the students.

12. See William Jeynes, *Religion, Education, and Academic* Success, Research on Religion and Education (Information Age Publishing, 2003).

13. See Gary Rosenblatt, "Alienation from Israel Hitting Liberal Seminaries," *Intermountain Jewish News*, May 13, 2011. See also Center Field blog: "Treat Antizionist Rabbinic Students Like the Four Sons," April 20, 2011, available at http://blogs.jpost.com.

14. See Rabbi Eric Yoffie's message to the 66th URJ Biennial, Boston, Massachusetts, December 8, 2001, available at http://rac.org/pubs/packets/schools/.

15. See P. Beinart, "The Jewish Case for School Vouchers," *Wall Street Journal*, March 30, 2012.

16. Wide access to comprehensive Reform education is currently focused around the voucher allocation policies. Given the wide recognition of the courts of the legality of vouchers, the opposition advocated by Reform activists appears to be motivated by political dogma and commitment to teachers' unions rather than educational and religious interests. For details see Rachel Aliza Ames, "The Private School Voucher Debate in the Jewish American Community: A Window into a Greater *American* Question," senior thesis, Barnard College, April 18, 2007, http://history.barnard.edu/sites/default/files/inline/rachelames-thesis.pdf.

Chapter 12: **Beyond Content:**
Reform Religious Rituals and Practices

1 Sing joyfully, O righteous, because of Hashem; for the upright, praise is fitting. 2 Give thanks to Hashem with a harp, with a ten-stringed lyre make music to Him. 3 Sing Him a new song, play well with sounds of deep emotion.

Psalm 33:1–3

Why do we pray? Praying is an expression of hope and faith in the power of the transcendental spirit that brings us confidence and brings us together. What is the source of our confidence? The Tanach and the Jewish heritage are our spiritual foundations that provide us confidence and vision, rituals and practices. Vision provides the paradigm of our hope and energizes our solidarity. Rituals and practices enable us to communicate and respond to our faith, and, so to speak, to "listen to our prayers."

Can prayers become reality? Sometimes, if we believe in our prayers and help ourselves to have the necessary dedication and care, we might be able to translate prayers into plans and execution. Jewish reformation was an effort to bring Judaism out from the stagnation of the Middle Ages into a new revival: making prayers for dignity, freedom and self-determination come true. Jewish reformation recognized that the first step is to believe in oneself and make it known: to have a message of hope. This message brought us Reform Judaism and Zionism.

From its inception, Judaism recognized the power of the written word: the most significant evidence of the Jewish belief was the covenant of the Ten Commandments—the *brit*—between Divinity and the Jews, written on stones. No symbols, no magical rituals, but a simple, straightforward, constitutional contract written in Hebrew, the Israelites' own unique language—a language preserved throughout decades of slavery or reconstructed in the Sinai desert. This very start required a revolutionary level of popular literacy and intellectual commitment. Legal tablets were already known in the Sumerian civilization and writing was widely used in ancient Egypt, though it was reserved for the use and benefit of the ruling elites.

Moses realized early on that in order to achieve his goal of establishing the Israelite culture, he had to fulfill two improvements on the brit: first, following the incident with the golden calf, the contract had to be enhanced with visual and behavioral signifiers, right there in the desert, long before reaching the Promised Land; second, enhanced education was essential and education required time. The Ark, the Tabernacles, and the Tent, the creation of rituals and the establishment of a permanent class of priests, kohanim and *levim*, provided the much needed connection between the faith and the Israelite public. The tablets became the mythical artifacts initially mobile and later confined in the secluded holiness of the Temple. The successful implementation of this concentrated design required a prolonged, evolving process of assimilation and adjustment. It took Moses decades to develop the full legal codex included in the Torah and to make it an integral part of the Israelites' patrimony.

Throughout the history of the Jewish people, the Word has attained a special appreciation in its own right: the canonized Tanachic Hebrew, with its exquisite narrative and poetry, became an object of art. The Tanach, the book that contained the story of Israel, became an object of deep reverence, enjoyed again and again by readers, an inspiration for thinkers and writers. The Jews became the people of the Book and the Book became an object of pride, a "must have" for generations. Its amazing quality was that it could be enjoyed "as such," in a naïve way, or become a source of recurring intellectual inspiration. Like a great painting or sculpture, the Book inspires our intellect and stimulates our senses. The Book brought and continues to bring satisfaction to a large array of individuals and groups often opposed and in disagreement in many ways, including in their understanding of the lessons they learned from the Book. Like a great symphony or a popular tune, the Book excited masses again and again to enjoy it, memorize it, and refer to it. The language of the Book is a quintessential artistic achievement, a true artistic masterpiece.

Starting in the nineteenth century, Jewish reformation entered a transformational path, questioning many of the established traditions, in particular religious practices and rituals. One ideological justification for the radical approach was the acknowledgment that from its inception and throughout its evolution Judaism invented and adopted cutting-edge concepts of its time. The source for this apparently revolutionary stand was of course the Tanach itself, the everlasting Judaic inspiration. Whether the historic circumstances of the nineteenth century in Europe were similar to the dramatic circumstances described in the Tanach is debatable, but the spirit of the time was inflammatory enough to make such assertions possible.

Technological achievements of the nineteenth and twentieth centuries enabled Reform Judaism to reconsider life practices— mizvot—that over time have lost relevance in areas such as health, communications, transportation, and more. Over the years some congregations have abandoned traditional practices, replaced them with new practices, or adopted a mix of traditional and new practices. Today, Reform Judaism recognizes the compliance to mizvot as an individual choice of each congregant. The current approach has been welcomed by the Reform public at large as part of the open-minded approach to religion.

Reform Judaism has experimented with a wide range of rituals, from traditional and new rituals to those adopted from other religions, from rituals supported by music, decorum, and discipline to minimal rituals. After two hundred years of experimentation, a balanced consolidation is emerging, with a slightly different emphasis in each congregation. Clearly, a sense of maturity emerging in the movement is noticeable and it is my sincere hope that it will be sustained in the future.

From the perspective of the lay congregant, rituals provide a sense of bonding among the members of a congregation. Introducing visual, tactile, and choreographic features into the rituals enriches their perception with a higher aesthetic dimension. Participation in the rituals as individuals or as groups (i.e., dancing with the Torah scrolls, singing in a choir) elates the congregants and moves them to rejoice in the spirit of our faith. If we can visualize ideas in our mind, we should be able to express them through suitable media, as well.

And let us remember, that in spite of Orthodox opinions, the Tanach confirms the existence of a range of ceremonies and rituals rich in artistic features intended to enhance the aesthetic experience of faith. In Tanachic terms, the Ark and the Tabernacle were visual statements that symbolized the Covenant. The Tanach describes—with enthusiasm—music and dance as modes of divine and popular expression. The Tanach made the architectural qualities of the Temple a key component of the Jewish ritual. The Temple was an architectural masterpiece enriched with extensive artistic decoration, song and dance; it was the apex of the religious rituals, a symbol of the kingdom, a visual and tactile representation of the faith. We must remember that the limitations on visual and sensory Judaic expression were imposed upon us by foreign oppressors interested in suppressing the Jewish identity and presence.

Visual representation using traditional or new media does not have to become religious idolatry; on the contrary, it can shape spiritual elements and compositions that enhance our religious practices and encourage participation in rituals. And, as much as the poetry of the text can provide an aesthetic experience, so can other artistic expressions convey our faith's messages in profound and inspiring ways. The literary, graphic, and printing craftsmanship of the Tanach makes it a work of art. Its ability to create extensive connections and personal identification—spiritual, philosophical, and sensual—make the text of the Tanach a work that is continually enjoyed. By recognizing the importance of the artistic and aesthetic qualities of the Tanachic heritage, Reform Judaism expands the reach of our faith into new spiritual territory. Artistic and aesthetic qualities become powerful means to validate Tanachic heritage and the Jewish Reform ritual.

This process of enrichment is not a trivial endeavor. The recipients of the experience, the congregants, are a broad-minded community with diverse ideas and opinions. Satisfying this public aesthetically requires a broad consensus on a highly subjective topic: art. Reaching agreement on public art is a difficult process. The opinion of a wealthy benefactor can carry much weight in the decision-making process. The majority vote in a select committee based on a compromise is another way to reach a decision. If resources are available, congregations have embraced a range of rituals and decorum to satisfy the preferences of different groups in the congregation. All these venues for rituals may provide rewarding aesthetic results on the condition that we know what is meant by aesthetic quality.

An aesthetic ritual might be appreciated through active participation or by its contemplation as a work of art. Artistic quality is conditioned on high quality of execution, fabrication, and performance, all of which require extensive training and dedication. We usually enjoy something that is well done. Quality control is a tough obligation but if achieved it brings confidence and pride to the congregation.

We must be aware that aesthetic quality is not limited only to the visual appearance of the act or object. Rituals may gain aesthetic merit through musical enjoyment, through inspired architectural and lighting experiences affecting the audience's sense of space and time, through accommodating and pleasant use, touch, and smell of furniture and interior decoration, and through the appreciation of the artistic qualities of ritual objects. We are expecting the Holy Ark (*Aron Ha'kodesh*) to be beautiful; it is an object that we enjoy looking at it in its presence, its place, its use, its content, and its symbolism. We can have a similar appreciation for a Torah scroll and many other objects of ritual.

Some believe that uniqueness and originality may add to the aesthetic experience by inciting curiosity and the enjoyment of a novel experience. Of course in this regard, each congregation needs to decide its priorities and how far it is willing to encourage novelty and stimulation at the expense of content and traditions. To be consistently effective, religious rituals need to reach the inner spirit of the individual while being shared by a whole group. This is definitely a high bar of performance that has to be carefully addressed. Therefore, new means need to be introduced in sensible ways, with care and sensitivity. An object or an event becomes beautiful if it fulfills its purpose and its presence is perspicuous and poignant. J. N. Findlay[1] tells us that

> by the perspicuity relevant to aesthetics I mean a presence
> to consciousness which has broken through to success and

mastery, whatever impediments and obstacles there may have been in the way of such a success, but which also involves a certain stationariness and arrest ... And by the poignancy which is relevant to aesthetics I mean not any and every shockingness or impressiveness, but the kind of shockingness and impressiveness that expends itself in vision, that in a sense luxuriates in the latter and that does not pass over into any far-flung reorganization of view nor into practical reorganizations. In the aesthetic situation, however feebly induced, one is necessarily rapt, caught up, fascinated, under the spell.

In following Findlay's guide, a genuine aesthetic experience of rituals helps us reach exhilarating feelings and may provide us with personal inspiring transcendental religious insight.

An important way to develop aesthetic enrichment is through the preservation and development of place-related monuments and ceremonies. The prolonged oppression of our faith has prevented us from developing or effectively preserving rituals and practices as physical expressions. Modern times have enabled us to revive some of this heritage.

As Reform Jews we experience our faith through human interaction, sharing our thoughts and feelings and helping people in need. We can reach out to aspire to divine inspiration through music and dance, architecture and the arts. We can reach out to experience Jewish Divinity by searching phenomenological and transcendental inspiration. Enjoying the features of Jewish special places and expressing an affinity for places of significance in our history is an inspiring experience. A place of religious significance is a destination that evokes memories and reverence and brings us closer to the Almighty. Memorable places acquire a unique identity that can generate specific rituals. For us as Jews, the most significant *makom* (place) is the Holy Land, which is a compendium of many marked and unmarked *makomot* in the process of being discovered. In the center of the Holy Land are Jerusalem and the Temple Mount.

Archeological excavations in Israel, and in places where Jewish culture flourished in the Diaspora, are starting to reconstruct the history of our physical presence and culture, bringing an expanding insight into our past presence. For two millennia we were forced to wander. Now we are empowered to settle and rebuild the Holy Land.

As part of the American religious mosaic, we are free to create places of worship, lighthouses of our faith. We must become aware that our own practices create artistic and architectural products that represent cultural values. Abandoning them for the sake of convenience or financial expediency becomes a historic loss and a devaluation of our spiritual commitment. For the sake of accommodating living trends, Reform Judaism in America has sold or abandoned numerous sites of worship rich in artistic achievements and history.[2] It is time to reconsider this "efficient" approach and include in our emerging practices the appreciation for our places of worship. It is in such places that we can find significant and irreplaceable expressions of our faith, in the accumulated historic value and aesthetic quality of their architecture and art. Regaining, preserving, and reviving significant places should be part of the preservation and development of our rituals and practices. We should not forget that one of the names of Almighty is Makom.

In a time and age in which culture is open to a wide and diverse range of choices with reluctance to accept limitations, how can a congregation be confident that its rituals and environment rise to a suitable aesthetic quality? The ultimate test of a successful aesthetic experience is whether the congregation participates spontaneously and willingly in the event and enjoys its features. Such a test, however, is after the fact and might involve costly risks in investment in people, materials, equipment, and technology. Are there alternative modes by which we can anticipate the aesthetic preferences of a congregation?

Reform Judaism has always been open to adopt new ways to reach its members and involve them in rituals and practices. In considering the effective application of existing and new rituals and practices, we may find help in current technological advances. Electronic media can simulate rituals in affordable, interactive virtual realities. We already have large amounts of information related to our faith available online. Individual congregants may become involved online, as observers or as interactive participants in rituals and congregational religious studies, enjoying services and celebrations in one's temple or visiting other temples. The High Holy Days may be shared between congregations and events in Israel. It is not difficult to imagine the emergence of virtual congregations operating in cyberspace.

Now, at the dawn of the twenty-first century, we may have reached the right moment to refine the form of our prayers, rituals, and practices. Liberated from oppression, we can experience our faith not only through actions and literary modes but also by enjoying its inherent beauty. Visual arts and music help us make our prayers, rituals, and practices communicative. Aesthetic fulfillment brings comfort in the reverence of our faith and catalyzes the belief in its power of redemption. We can enhance our religious experience by appreciating introspection and contemplation, rather than action; by finding inspiring insight in the resonance of music and color, poetry and artistic perfection; and by enjoying place making and the sense of belonging, taking pleasure in the beauty of our rituals and practices. Expanding beyond content into the beauty of our faith provides us an inspiring spirit that will enhance the spontaneity and candor of our prayers and bring us closer to our Jewish Divinity.

Notes

1. J. N. Findlay, "The Perspicuous and the Poignant: Two Aesthetic Fundamentals," in *Aesthetics*, ed. H. Osborne (Oxford: Oxford Univ. Press, 1979), 97.

2. Establishments of significant architectural and artistic qualities, such as a historic temple, are rare and deserve to be preserved. In return, these establishments can provide a place that brings people together because of its artistic and aesthetic qualities and as such sustains the community spirit. Contemporary urbanism recognizes the merit of significant places in shaping the identity of communities and conditioning land values and dwelling priorities.

Chapter 13:   **Belonging and the Pursuit of Happiness**

> Light is sown for the righteous; and for the upright of heart, gladness.
>
> Psalm 97:11

> Praiseworthy is person who has found wisdom, a person who can derive understanding [from it].
>
> Proverbs 3:18

The American Enlightenment, different from the European Enlightenment, was ratified by the founding documents of the republic. The Declaration of Independence declares the following:

> We hold these Truths as self-evident, that all Men are created equal, that they are endowed by their Creator with certain unalienable Rights, that among these are Life, Liberty, and the Pursuit of Happiness.

The Declaration provided a statement of faith that was close to the spirit of all settlers, Jews included. All three mentioned rights are spiritual and abstract, indivisible and omnipresent. These rights can be seen as reflections of the founders' biblical wisdom.

The pursuit of happiness is as inspiring as it is elusive and encompassing. It is the only right defined in dynamic terms, as a pursuit. This pursuit is simultaneously a spiritual goal and a call for action. And, amazingly, the authors of the Declaration recognized this dynamic about two hundred years before scientists discovered positive psychology! A genuine pursuit of happiness is motivated by personal attributes and talents. Teachers, leaders, or elites can reveal or inspire personal motivation but can never provide it. Numerous divine or secular attempts to impose top-down happiness have rapidly deteriorated into oppression—killing personal motivation and hopes for happiness.

In our open, mobile civilization, framed by an unbiased justice for all and liberties that secure equal opportunity and reward success, many people have achieved personal goals, such as wealth or professional achievement. Does the achievement of personal goals stop *the pursuit* of happiness? Some do, some do not. Those who enjoy the process of pursuit will look for new goals. Such later pursuits of happiness generated popular interest in charity and religion. For those exhausted by the effort of pursuing happiness, belonging can be the rewarding answer.

Modern Judaism is divided on the interpretation of the path to happiness. Traditional Judaism continues to believe in the happiness provided by the strict pursuit of the regulatory, introspective reflections on the Jewish heritage. Zionist reformation focused on national reconstruction with significant physical achievements and political challenges. Reform Judaism is at a crossroad.

Reform Jews join congregations as freethinkers and proud participants. We are neither victims nor oppressors. We cannot be controlled nor coerced. We engage in our religious beliefs with joy, confidence, and hope. Freedom to belong makes belonging a happy reward.

Reform congregations have had, from their inception, a strong interest in creating a congregational spirit that fostered cohesiveness and a sense of belonging. Belonging is a component of Jewish happiness. We often rejoice to meet a "landsman." Happy belonging is achieved by free choice, by interest and love—interest in sharing and participating. Love connects us to our faith, to our heritage, to the Almighty. People need faith as an explanation for the inexplicable and embrace religion as a spiritual support. We are grateful that we can find in our congregation, in our prayers, in our individual spiritual experience a sense of belonging and transcendental fulfillment through wisdom and through inspiring content and aesthetic enjoyment. We belong to Reform Judaism as an individual commitment reached by free choice in the context of our Jewish urban, entrepreneurial, open-minded bourgeois culture. We reach this sense of belonging through education and free personal discovery. We are different from our Orthodox brothers and sisters who love to revere their princely rabbis and are happy to conform to their Haredi confinements.

We have to distinguish here between two parts of Reform Judaism. One part includes the centralized bureaucracies of the national organizations, which assume an elitist position and believe they can predict and provide the "correct" idea of Reform Judaism. The other part is shaped by the Reform public that desires to find belonging and happiness in our religion, in our congregations, and at home. Lawrence A. Englander confirms this dilemma in an article entitled "In Search of Belonging."[1] In his opinion, "how Reform Jews confront the paradoxical nature of Universalism and particularism will determine the character of the Reform Jewish future." Englander maintains that

> we will have to go somewhat against the stream in a society in which the only constant is change, by creating a community that stands for something timeless. As in previous stages, our message is twofold. The universalist Mission of Israel ...

reminds us that we must settle for nothing less than *tikkun olam* ... The particularist side of the coin is that the Jewish people has a unique contribution to make in this effort.

The framing of Englander's concluding question as a dilemma between Universalism and particularism defeats its own argument. If we, as Reform Jews, believe in the freedom of the human spirit and take a historic perspective on human development, incremental change will bring constructive innovative improvements that reflect lessons learned from past mistakes. If we believe in the rewards a culture in change can bring, what is our right to pretend that we can *repair the world* by imposing on others a universal ideology of our choice? Improvement makes "repairs," with their confinement to outdated blueprints, unnecessary. As previously discussed in chapter 7, "repairing the world" is not a progressive act: you just fix what is there and at best bring it back to its previous performance. It is an activity with very little creativity, static in its goals, and possibly regressive, especially if the prior situation was not good (it deteriorated and needed repairs).

Persisting in "repairing" the same idea contradicts the evolving Reform spirit and promotes a misguided illusion of "timelessness." Compare repairing with building anew and consider which activity is more satisfying, which makes one happier. This is also the difference between "repairing" and "exemplifying," between "tikkun olam" and "Or Goim." Providing an example does not compel anybody to follow suit, contributes to the process of improvement, and might persuade others to follow suit or be envious. In a hostile situation generated by envy, the provider is at least gaining a degree of happiness by having achieved an improved result.

Is the current radical activist political agenda, as promoted by the Union for Reform Judaism and the Central Conference of American

Rabbis, providing venues for happiness? Political activity is dedicated to managing the possible and is usually based on compromise. Extreme political activity, with an uncompromising control of the institutions of government—as we witnessed on the national political scene in the United States in the years 2009–2011—causes partisanship and conflicts. Still, as long as the integrity of democratic elections is maintained, corrections may be made to such a critical situation. If, however, the party in power maintains its control by imposing an authoritative corporate managerial structure, grassroots democratic involvement and representation is ignored. Preventing or suppressing rank-and-file active participation in shaping the spirit and performance of the Reform movement is already affecting the very sense of belonging and commitment of many individual members.

Englander recognizes correctly that "loyalty to the Reform movement may be waning among younger generations of Jews who tend to dislike labels and prefer more fluid lifestyles." Yet, I must point out here Englander's intrinsic misunderstanding of the spirit of our time. Reform Judaism essentially was not based on "loyalty" but on affiliation and, ultimately, belonging. Loyalty is generated by disciplinary orthodoxy that follows a rigid ideology. Affiliation is voluntary, and love brings belonging. It appears that the tikkun olam indoctrination has blinded Englander and many of his colleagues and prevents them from enjoying the beauty of the Reform message: not "labels" or "blends" but a unique, dynamic, and inspiring spirit that pursues improvement, love, and happiness.

Happiness has many facets. A person may be happy by winning the lottery, being in love—even a good meal may make one happy for a short time. The Woodstock festival may have provided a moment of happiness to some participants, but could this happiness be sustained and to what result? Happiness is subjective. Often happiness emerges as a spontaneous act ("I am happy!") for which there might or might not be an immediate rational or causal explanation providing a reason to be happy ("It makes me happy."). It might be easier to understand happiness by just considering it as a specific human attribute. In this context, religious belief can become a happiness booster. Happiness can be shared as a group; see the numerous religious sects, cults, and movements whose members rejoice in their practices and rituals. Rituals and practices can reach an artistic quality that can generate an exquisite aesthetic experience: beauty that goes beyond pleasure and brings us happiness. Inspiring ecclesiastic architecture or music can provide a transcendental experience of awe and happiness.

There are numerous explanations of this subjective phenomenon, which has popular empirical confirmation over millennia. I have chosen to adopt here an explanation based on Jürgen Habermas's communicative theory and his reference to aesthetics. Art that reaches aesthetic qualities illuminates and communicates beyond its appearance; it transgresses the boundaries of our reality,

> in the direction of the decentering and unbounding of subjectivity. At the same time, this decentering indicates an increased sensitivity to what remains unassimilated in the interpretative achievements of pragmatic, epistemic, and moral mastery of demands and challenges of everyday situations; it effects an openness to the expurgated elements of the unconscious, the fantastic, and the mad, the material and the bodily—thus to everything in our speechless contact with reality which is so fleeting, so contingent, so immediate, so individualized, simultaneously so far and so near that it escapes our normal categorical grasp.[2]

Can we achieve through our belonging to our congregation and participation in religious rituals and practices "an openness to the expurgated elements of the unconscious" and reach a subjective happiness "that escapes our normal categorical grasp"? This is our individual challenge, the challenge of our rabbis, and the challenge of our congregations.

There is ample evidence from many religions that religious content and rituals can bring participants to shared experiences that infuse into them a state of excitement, elation, love, and transcendental visions, even revelations. These experiences, even if short lived, are considered happy moments. Is Reform Judaism aiming to achieve such experiences? The current political, practical, and mundane agenda advocated by the Reform leadership does not indicate such an intention. Universalist, political social activism is, by its very nature, partisan, controversial, and divisive, and it stands in opposition to the open-minded spirit of Reform Judaism. Reform Judaism has established as its mission to balance its civic commitments with its religious belonging. The balancing act recognizes the option for dual pursuits of happiness, separate but not exclusive. Civic happiness is a guarantor of religious happiness and religious happiness enriches civic happiness. Civic happiness is the city wall that protects religious happiness, while religious happiness is the spiritual market that energizes the city. This is our spiritual city, our spiritual Jerusalem.

Two human factors are instrumental in our spiritual Jerusalem: the lay leadership and the rabbi. The lay leadership provides the operational infrastructure of our congregation; the rabbi provides the spiritual leadership. In our search for happiness we need a solid operation, but little can be achieved without inspiration. The rabbi's goal is to bring vision to the congregation through understanding and feeling the spirit of the congregation. Vision is meant to stimulate the participation and the excitement of the congregation. By highlighting aspects of our faith in revealing ways, through words, music, and art, the rabbi can communicate a liberating spirit that "unbounds" the inner subjective self of the individuals in the audience and enables them to reach exhilarating transcendental experiences—experiences that can make them happy. Properly designed and executed religious actions can evolve into an active pursuit of religious revelation and happiness. Reform Judaism is sustained by its unique innovative spirit that fuses Jewish heritage and modern Jewish thinking and stands out by example—Or Goim—not by missionary assertiveness and political undertones.

It is not the purpose of this work to recommend specific solutions but to indicate opportunities. Reform Judaism is a young denomination that is open-minded and encourages innovation. Let us all contribute, with ideas and actions, in the pursuit of our religious belonging and happiness.

Notes

1. See Lawrence A. Englander, "In Search of Belonging," *Reform Judaism* (Summer 2011), 51.

2. Jürgen Habermas, "Questions and Counterquestions," in *Habermas and Modernity*, Richard J. Bernstein, ed. (Cambridge, MA: MIT Press, 1994), 201.

Chapter 14: **The Fraternal Dispute:**
Reform Judaism and Zionism

For from Zion will the Torah come forth, and the word of Hashem from Jerusalem.

Isaiah 2:3

2 Our feet stood firm within your gates, O Jerusalem. 3 The Built-up Jerusalem is like a city that is united together. 4 For there the tribes ascended, the tribes of God, a testimony for Israel, to give thanks to the Name of Hashem.

Psalm 122:2–4

The Jewish Enlightenment brought forward the Tanachic Word into modernity and became the spiritual source for the emergence of two reformative Jewish movements: Reform Judaism and Zionism. Reform Judaism defined itself as a worldwide Jewish religious movement inspired by the spirit of Zion. Zionism adopted a Jewish national, multidenominational orientation centered on Jerusalem and the Tanachic Holy Land. On the face of it, the two movements should have had a lot in common. In reality, Reform Judaism rejected Zionism and has fought against it for most of its history, sometime with vicious determination.

In Europe, Reform Judaism rejected Zionism out of fear that a Zionistic admission might prevent Reform Jews from being recognized as loyal citizens of the local state. In the United States, the German heritage of loyalty to the residing state, freedom of religion, the new civic confidence, economic security, and religious consolidation were considered by many rabbis and lay leaders as contradictory to the Zionist message. It is important to emphasize that in the true spirit of Jewish reformation, Reform Judaism was continuously debating the content of its faith. The approach toward Zionism was one of the key and prolonged debates, mostly between the adherents to the traditional, Classical Reform on the anti-Zionist side, and supporters of the Zionist project on the other side. Thanks to the perseverance of remarkable leaders such as Emanuel Gamoran, Abba Hillel Silver, Felix Levy, James Heller, Stephen Samuel Wise, Nelson Glueck, and many more, the Zionist message took root in many Reform congregations as well as in the HUC and to some extent in the CCAR. Still, the question remains why did not Reform Judaism in the twentieth century, in particular its leadership, become a strong ally of Zionism? The answer is complex and can be focused on two main aspects: ideology and authority.

It is possible to assume that one reason for the separation between the Reform leadership and Zionism stems from a subtle change that occurred in American Reform Judaism from its German original sources. While Reform Judaism in Germany aspired to be loyal to the state, the new American version was focused on universal ideals such as social or economic justice. These ideals had vague content and were elusive in their application, and hence were quite suitable for a noncommittal leadership. The Israeli realities required clear and committed decision making. The American Reform leadership was unprepared to make this effort. It is in this context that we can explain the limited connection developed, during the first decades of the twentieth century, between the "German" leaders of Classical Reform and the Jerusalem intellectual circles populated by refugees from Germany and Eastern Europe, which included internationally recognized thinkers, such as Martin Buber and Gershom Shalom. The two groups shared left-leaning ideological inclinations and a common cultural background. The difference: the Jerusalem group was committed to Zionism and was actively participating in the process.

Considering the fact that before the establishment of the State of Israel and immediately after its establishment, the dominant Zionist movement in Israel was the Labor movement, we can assume with reasonable confidence that the Reform movement of the time could have become a suitable, effective, and influential partner. This was a moment in history that offered an opportunity to express solidarity and implement religious action for Jewish people in desperate need of physical help and spiritual support. Yet again, as in the case of the Jewish immigration to the United States in the beginning of the twentieth century and the lack of Holocaust awareness, the mainstream of the Reform Judaism remained estranged from the Jewish reality and missed historic opportunities to lead. Developments related to Israel or Europe seemed remote from the home base. Religious solidarity and religious actions in the Holy Land were not perceived as essential to the Reform movement. As a consequence, Reform Judaism remained unknown to the nonobservant Jewish majority in Israel. For the Reform public, the State of Israel became more an abstract notion than a reality. We may speculate and ask whether the harsh realities of the emerging Zionist project in the Holy Land, its dangers and its sacrifices, might not have been a hidden reason for the reluctance of the Reform leadership to forcefully engage itself in promoting and committing to Zionism. Or, was it the assertive nature of the Israeli Socialist leadership that alienated the Reform leadership? Perhaps it was both.

In the decades following the Second World War, the Reform leadership was dominated by the assertive personality of Maurice

Eisendrath. Eisendrath was focused on exploiting the postwar economic and urban growth to expand the movement in the United States. Apparently this effort left little time or resources to get involved in expanding the Reform influence in Israel. In any case, the kohanic approach Eisendrath introduced in the Reform movement was not amenable to either a power-sharing approach or the compromises required by an active involvement in Israel. Unfortunately, by midcentury the focus of Reform activists was on the civil rights movement and the war in Vietnam rather than Zionism and the situation in the Middle East.

Orthodox Judaism considered the return to the Holy Land to be a commanding, final goal, but under messianic ruling. Yet, David Ben Gurion's diligence and political savvy translated the religious orientation of mainstream Orthodox Judaism toward the Holy Land into a significant recruiting argument in support of his Zionist project. The opportunity to play a significant role in determining the Jewish nature of the State of Israel, in parallel to Ben Gurion's Labor Party's Socialist orientation, encouraged Orthodox Judaism to become an active part of the Zionist movement. The Orthodox participation enabled Ben Gurion to establish his political power as a balance between the excessive demands of his radical Marxist allies and the aspirations of his political liberal-center-right urban opposition.[1] This historic development indicates again that socialism and Orthodox Judaism, in spite of their apparent contradictions, have a common goal: authoritarian political power. The Zionist orientation of the mainstream Orthodox movement left the ultra-Orthodox fringe as the only Orthodox opponent to Zionism.

The successful coalition between Ben Gurion's *Mapai* Party and the Zionist Orthodox parties defeats the Reform argument that Mapai's secular ideology was an obstacle in supporting Zionism. What Reform leaders failed to recognize was that socialism was a secular religion that could be influenced if addressed as such. The Orthodox parties recognized the religious nature of socialism and used it to their benefit. The result: for three decades Israel was led by a rigid authoritarian governmental coalition with a Socialist economy and an Orthodox Jewish orientation. By the same token, we must mention the significant contribution made by the Zionist Orthodox movement, in particular the Masorti segment, to Israel's economic and cultural development in building enterprises, towns, cities, and universities and in being deeply involved in the defense of the country. At the same time, the Reform leadership chose to ignore the existence in Israel of a large center-left urban, bourgeois, and liberal constituency. This constituency, with its alternative platform, could have been an alternative ally in launching a vigorous Reform participation in the Zionist project.

The remarkable success of Israel's performance in the Six Day War finally brought the Reform constituency to embrace the Jewish state enthusiastically. Also, disappointments in the performance of the alliances with Christian groups and with Black-Jewish partnerships brought a change in orientation. Meyer indicates that

> the entire concept of the mission of Israel—so long cherished by Reform Jews—now came under attack. Not all Reform Jews any longer agreed that the Jewish goal was to enlighten and aid non-Jews. The value of Judaism should instead be measured by what it gave to the individual Jew.[2]

It is my view that, at the time, the Reform leadership was only prepared to accept the State of Israel as the homeland of the Jewish people, rather than to endorse and become a full participant in the Zionist project.[3] It seems to me that the CCAR expected the Israeli variant of secular Judaism to provide solutions for the American religious crisis rather than the opposite. Even the enormous love the American Jewish community expressed for Israel was not enough to inspire the Reform rabbinical leadership to initiate a fundamental revision of its positions and open a substantive and constructive dialogue with the Israeli public, difficult as it might appear to be.

In the late seventies, with the ascent to power of the *Likud* Party and its centrist coalition, riding on a wave of national revival, new opportunities opened to connect the Israeli public with the Reform movement. The non-Orthodox Jewish public in Israel was evolving toward an open society and a free-market economy closer to the American world view: a civic, center-right orientation characterized by a rejection of socialism, an increased adoption of free enterprise and innovation, and a strong national conviction and eagerness to embrace a modern Jewish faith. Menachem Begin, the newly elected prime minister, was a man of faith, and proved to be far less doctrinaire than he was portrayed by his opponents. Begin's national housing renewal project, conceived as a joint venture between the Jewish Diaspora and the Israeli neighborhoods, was highly successful. Had the Reform leadership paid attention, discussed the various options evolving in Israel, and devised the adequate adjustments, they could have found a receptive partner in Begin's administration and gained a considerable and influential constituency. The responsibility for this fundamental mistake lies with the Reform leadership, in particular the CCAR, which was persisting in maintaining its proto-Socialist orientations. Also, the CCAR continues to blame the intransigency of the religious Orthodox establishment for its inability to grow the movement within Israel. In fact, without an extended, substantive, and active presence in the Israeli national project, this was and remains a weak excuse.

For the "silent majority" of the Israeli public, a constructive dialogue is relevant if it is based on tangible activities on the ground such as active participation in the expansion and integration of the Jewish immigration, establishment of new towns and industries, and active enrollment in the defense of the state. The alliance between the Reform movement and the declining kibbutz movement that took place in the 1970s was too late and out of sync with the Israeli reality.[4] The Israeli Movement for Progressive Judaism (IMPJ) was established in 1971. Only in the late 1990s, with some enhanced financial support, did the IMPJ start to become more assertive in the country and recruit adherents from nonobservant Israelis and new emigrants from the former Soviet Union. Predominantly, the Reform leadership preferred to address Israeli issues through speeches and patronizing political messages focused on Universalist issues, delivered from the comfortable distance of the American shores. We must remember that proclaiming "dovish" opinions regarding Israel's policy while living in the United States, with little firsthand experience of the real existential challenges faced by the Israeli public, did not bring much credibility to the Reform leaders then, nor does it now.

An indication of the gravity of the misunderstanding prevailing between the Israeli public and Reform Judaism can be found in the 1999 keynote address by Rabbi Richard Hirsh, retiring executive director of the World Union of Progressive Judaism, at the twenty-fifth anniversary of the transfer of its international headquarters to Israel. Four objectives guided Rabbi Hirsh's activity in Israel:

> Objective one: To move Progressive Judaism from the periphery to the center of Jewish life. Objective two: To demonstrate that as a movement we need Israel as the testing ground of Reform Jewish authenticity. Objective three: In the process of demonstrating that Progressive Judaism needs Israel, we shall begin to demonstrate that Israel needs

Progressive Judaism. Objective four: To participate in the ongoing process of responding to the critical question: What should be the Jewish character of the Jewish state?[5]

The four objectives delineated in his speech, constructive in their content and intent, indicate that after twenty-five years of official presence in Israel, Reform Judaism still remained estranged from local public opinion. Rabbi Hirsh correctly recognizes that "the ultimate test of Jewish authenticity for progressive Judaism lies in our efforts in Israel."[6] Religious influence is achieved by execution and implementation. Unfortunately, in the time since this speech was delivered, it does not appear that Reform Judaism has made much progress in fulfilling these goals in Israel.

A long series of proclamations and press releases published by the URJ, critical of Israeli public opinion, its democracy, the Knesset, and the Israeli government, did not help improve the perception and status of Reform Judaism in Israel. Material and ideological support provided to certain organizations that can be associated with the Reform movement, such as J Street and the New Israeli Fund, which support marginal extremist groups in Israel, are creating new obstacles in the dialogue between the Reform movement and the majority of the Israeli public.[7] The content and tone of many of these messages reflect a one-sided ideological bias, tainted by anti-Israeli left-leaning propaganda. Large portions of the Israeli native and immigrant population have had firsthand and long-lasting experiences with Marxist ideologies, Socialist regimes, and left-leaning demagogy in Israel and abroad. The Israeli middle-of-the-road majority is sick and tired of being preached into faked righteous positions, especially when the speakers are perceived as spoiled "trust fund kids" with little in-depth knowledge of either the topics they promulgate or the Israeli and Middle Eastern conditions.

It is interesting to note current attempts to rewrite history and hide the painful hostility Reform Judaism perpetrated against Zionism. The 2011 summer issue of *Reform Judaism* includes an article by Chaya Burstein entitled "The Ever-Evolving Faith."[8] The article noticeably omits the story of the "evolving faith" of the Jewish Enlightenment and the history of the relations between Reform Judaism and Zionism in the nineteenth century and the first half of the twentieth century. According to Burstein, Zionism appears with Israel's independence. The Arab political opposition to the declaration of the Jewish state and the war of aggression launched against Israel by the Arab states in 1948 is matched with the opposition of certain ultra-Orthodox communities toward Zionism. Amazingly, there is not a single allusion to the bitter opposition of the CCAR to Zionism and its prolonged reluctance to accept Zionism. Ignoring Reform Judaism's rejection of Zionism and placing the ultra-Haredi opposition to Zionism on equal status with the Arab aggression shows Burstein's deliberate bias and contempt of the historical truth. More than that, the fact that these biased omissions were not corrected by the editors of the journal raises questions on the intent and integrity of the publication.

Furthermore, in a following article in the same issue by Lawrence A. Englander entitled "In Search of Belonging,"[9] the author briefly mentions the Reform opposition to Zionism and attempts to frame it in positive terms by saying: "Reform support for Zionism—which the Central Conference of American Rabbis had endorsed in the Columbus Platform of 1937 by only one single vote—continued to gain momentum in the post-Holocaust years." To be accurate: the 1937 platform established a neutral position toward a Jewish homeland by endorsing the language of the Balfour Declaration rather than the Zionist national agenda. Englander continues by recognizing, without explaining, that "still, for the first two decades of Israel's existence, the Jewish state was a world away from the daily life of reform Jews in Manhattan or Montreal."[10] Interesting wording to minimize the long-lasting rift between Reform Judaism and Zionism and give it a positive spin.

The relation between Reform Judaism and Zionism and the Reform's attitude toward the State of Israel remains complicated. Reform Judaism's initial absolute negation of Zionism and refusal to conduct a constructive dialogue with its supporters was frank but wrong. Zionists, in particular Socialist Zionists, could be considered a brainchild of Reform Judaism. Rejecting such an offspring contradicted the premise that Jewish reformation responded to emerging events and needs of the Jewish people. A constructive dialogue can take place if differences, mistakes, and contextual conditions are recognized and acknowledged openly, honestly, and without distortion.

Currently there is a dichotomy in the American Reform public. A large section of the Reform public supports and identifies itself with the State of Israel, while the national leadership maintains a vague and controversial attitude toward it. In the "Commentary on the Principles for Reform Judaism," published by the CCAR, in the paragraph entitled "A Vision of the State of Israel," the authors assert the following:

> Our commitment to the State also implies a commitment to helping it to realize values which we as liberal Jews hold dear—peace with her neighbors and the full civil, human and religious rights for all citizens, Jews, Muslims, Christians and others.[11]

This comment is inaccurate, misleading, and insensitive. Minorities in Israel enjoy full civil rights, including the right of free assembly and speech, which are often used to express hate against Israel, Jews, and Judaism. Some minority groups do not exercise certain civic duties that are required of most Israelis, in areas such as military service and tax payments, and they are not sanctioned for that. Placing this inaccurate negative comment in conjunction with the peace process indicates the doubt the authors of the commentary have about Israel's dedication to achieving real, secure, and sustainable peace. In a tense region in which every word matters, making inaccurate comments can become a source of dispute and conflict. Such insensitivity indicates that the CCAR needs to take a more informed and careful approach in the formulations of its positions. These divisive situations can be mitigated if the Reform movement would bring forward clear and practical plans of action. Instead, we see expression of vague intent as those mentioned in the 2004 Commentary's paragraphs on "Strengthening Progressive Judaism in Israel" and "Israeli Jews Have Much to Learn from the Religious Life of Diaspora Jewish Communities."

The lack of relevant dialogue in times of need and the lack of clear planning and project implementation indicate that the Reform leadership is still unable to accept and respond in constructive ways to the Zionist project. Apparently, this numbness is attributable (again) to the dominant concern of certain Reform circles to gain political exposure in the United States. The current positions of the Reform leadership in reference to Israel lack credibility in Israel and raise significant doubts within the Reform rank and file in the United States. The selection of a new president of the URJ, who has shown, through his actions and speeches, a dubious attitude toward Zionism, does not help the process of realignment.[12] It is unfortunate that this rhetoric of Reform leaders encourages the recent fringe Jewish liberal anti-Israeli propaganda emerging in academic circles. Apparently, Israel is the new easy prey for the extreme left's venomous hate, a hate well received in left-leaning, pro-Arab European intellectual circles and the left-leaning press.[13]

The State of Israel is a Jewish state that includes four segments of Judaism: the nonobservant majority, the Orthodox minority, the fringe ultra-Orthodox, and a small Reform presence. Projecting Jewish aspirations shaped by American circumstances onto Israel, while ignoring its geopolitical, socioeconomic, and cultural conditions, is an unwarranted intervention in the internal affairs of a sovereign state, governed by a democratic political system. In Reform terms, such interventions suppress the dialogue between the parties, especially if the outside party adopts a patronizing tone. Therefore, it is unethical to advocate a dialogue with the Israeli public without understanding and participating, in a meaningful way, in Israeli life. Identifying the Jewish Israeli public with the fringe ultra-Orthodox is not only wrong but is vicious. Such distortions might serve well as a justification for Israel's bashers to build their careers and sell books.

Dismissing Israel's public opinion, its democracy, and its judicial system in such an irresponsible way is becoming a tool in the hands of long-lasting Islamic Fascist enemies of Israel, with tragic, even criminal consequences. The record of the Arab-Israeli conflict shows that the truth will come out and ultimately causes the demise of these hate mongers. If Reform Judaism is motivated to become part of the Israeli reality, it should give up its ambivalent positions and unequivocally recognize Zionism as a legitimate movement of the Jewish people and Israel as the Jewish state, not a bi-national state.

The recognition, by the Reform movement, of Israel as the Jewish state will be a departure from the separation of church and state principle. The historical, cultural, and political situation in the region mandates the integration between church and state and is intrinsically different from the situation in the United States. All the states in the region, with the exception of Lebanon, are dominated by state religions and religion is a central factor in their political orientations. The Lebanese national conflict is caused by the power struggle between its religious communities. European criticism of Israel on this matter turns a blind eye to the situation in the region and the excessive oppression of and discrimination against religious minorities in all Arab countries. The fact that all European states are still dominated, overtly or covertly, by secular or divine state religions makes the European argument quite hypocritical.[14]

It is my belief that, with proper leadership, the American Reform public could respond effectively, in practical ways, to the Zionist message and become a participant in the Israeli national project. Essentially, Israeli Reform Judaism could serve well the faith-based spiritual needs of the non-Orthodox Israeli public in their specific contextual conditions. If the Reform movement is able to recognize the situation in Israel as different from the American situation, a constructive dialogue may emerge with the Israeli public.

As part of such a dialogue, the Reform movement could advocate the adoption of equal opportunity and status to all Jewish denominations rather than attempting to gain similar privileges to those of the Orthodox denomination. Equal status and opportunity enable communities to have an equal judicial status and to promote their ideas freely. Such a request might require some legal changes in Israel.

The challenge here is to what extent the Reform movement is prepared to invest effort and resources to expand its presence in the Israeli public, adjust its positions to the Israeli reality, and achieve a significant electoral impact to reach its goals. Preaching trendy American concepts ex cathedra from air-conditioned think tanks in Jerusalem or Washington, DC, or expressing "constructive" criticism for the sake of criticism or for gaining political points in the American Democratic Party, will be useless and even detrimental.

The movement should roll up its sleeves and bring its message of faith to the non-Orthodox public by encouraging and initiating religious, cultural, and economic projects that can inspire and support the creation of active congregations. Such initiatives, in the framework of the Zionist spirit, might include organized immigration efforts to Israel, investments in industrial and agricultural projects, building temples and schools, and establishing congregations in Israeli towns and cities. These initiatives should not be considered charities or aid but rather viable religious and economic projects.

In addition to an extensive organizational effort, such a move will require an in-depth and insightful understanding of the Israeli public's opinions, its priorities and regulations. The implementation of such a national project should learn from the previous Reform initiative in conjunction with the kibbutz movement. The attachment to the kibbutz movement was utopian and doomed to fail along with the outdated rural communitarian lifestyle.

The urban nature of Reform Judaism will be well received in towns and cities of the Israeli countryside. My professional experience and personal acquaintance with residents in towns and cities such as Shderot and Maalot, Kiriat Gat and Arad, Hedera and Beit Shean, give me the confidence that these urban communities will welcome the contribution of a constructive Jewish modern American spirit. But caution: Israelis see this spirit as an open-minded dialogue, rich in innovation and entrepreneurship, with religious practices and rituals that suit the twenty-first century. No vagaries of social justice and Universalist multiculturalism will stick. Reform Zionist development should not be distracted by foreign-funded opportunistic activism and by slogans used by a vocal, nihilistic fringe minority and foreign agents in their attempts to make news.[15] The targeted audience should be the "silent majority" to which Reform Judaism indeed has a message to offer.

Reform Judaism must recognize that in a country that has emerged from the limitations of the welfare state with its Socialist confinements and reached a promising degree of capitalist prosperity, the objective is to sustain and improve the current direction. In Israel, a country the size of Delaware, poor in natural resources, in which most basic commodities, such as drinking water, have to be fabricated, incentives for innovation, hard work, and accountability are essential, and the best incentive for success is individual economic success.

Israel has achieved its emerging prosperity due to the genius of its population, in particular its young generation. It has consolidated its independence thanks to its Zionist dedication, has sustained its security through the determination and professionalism of its citizen-soldiers, and has fostered its democracy through an increased level of political transparency and critical thinking. This is the framework within which the Zionist Reform religious action must fit.

The non-Orthodox Israeli public is hoping to find a modern Jewish faith-based religious inspiration. Can the Reform movement still provide this inspiration?

American Reform activists and rabbis can become the catalysts for the creation of a local, broad-based Zionist Reform movement in Israel. In the Reform tradition, the initiative is individual and the application is one congregation at the time. Each congregation may be matched with a sister congregation in the United States. The connections should be congregants to congregants, not through New York or Washington bureaucrats. Country-wide distribution of congregations centered on the Reform temple, its adjacent institutions, and its activities can become a source of spiritual enlightenment and cultural progress in communities that currently are deprived of such inspirational services.

National issues such as a reconsideration of the Israeli educational system definitely deserve attention, but these problems will not be solved from Washington, DC.[16] Direct contacts and exchanges between American and Israeli congregants may create business opportunities and economic development. Success of individual projects in each community in Israel will enable the local public to improve its cultural life and reduce its dependency on major urban hubs. A secondary benefit will be a better population distribution throughout the country by strengthening of provincial towns. Ultimately, by creating a network of Israeli congregations throughout Israel, Reform Judaism will have the popular basis to influence the configuration of the Jewish character of the country.

To summarize, if the Reform movement is interested in having an impact on shaping Judaism in Israel, it has to wholeheartedly embrace the Zionist reformation and build in Israel an indigenous, well-rooted, productive, and loyal religious Reform movement.

Notes

1. "Messianic fervor—in tandem with a realistic Zionist policy, which sought to exploit the political circumstances of World War II in order to promote the Zionist cause—placed Religious Zionism at the forefront of the camp that struggled to create a Jewish state in Palestine. Whereas Mapai was torn between Ben-Gurion's synthesis of the political and the practical, and the extreme practical approach of Ha-Kibbutz ha-Me'uhad (which split into separate factions for this reason), Mizrachi and Ha-Po'el ha-Mizrachi maintained a broad and stable consensus on the statehood issue. In this matter—unlike on the induction issue—Mizrachi's position was in total contrast to that of Ha-Kibbutz ha-Me'uhad and the Left generally. In this respect, the leaders of Mizrachi/Ha-Po'el ha-Mizrachi fully sided with Ben-Gurion. They promoted and supported his policy and even attempted to advance it by means of the ideology and the special tools of Religious Zionism." Eshkoli (Wagman), "Religious-Zionist Policy in Palestine," 281–320.

2. See Meyer, *Response to Modernity*, 368.

3. Only in 1977 did the movement establish the Association of Reform Zionists of America (ARZA). Still, even today the presence of Reform Judaism in Israel remains benign with less than two dozen congregations.

4. The reader may gain a better understanding of the connection between Reform Judaism and the kibbutz movement in reading the paper of Michael Livni (Langer), *Reform Zionism*, originally published by Gefen publishing house, Jerusalem, available at http://www.michael-livni.org.

5. See Meyer and Plaut, *Reform Judaism Reader*, 33–35.

6. See ibid., 34.

7. Extremist organizations such as The New Israeli Fund, J Street, and their affiliated NGOs are not well received by the wide Israeli public. The association of Reform leaders and groups in the Reform movement with these organizations and their foreign activists and supporters does not help the dialogue between the Reform leadership and the Israeli public.

8. Chaya Burnstein, "The Ever-Evolving Faith," *Reform Judaism* (Summer 2011): 42–47.

9. See ibid., 48–53.

10. See Englander, "In Search of Belonging," 49 (see note in chap. 13).

11. See Central Conference of American Rabbis, 2004 "Commentary on the Principles," 14.

12. Before becoming the new president of the URJ, Rabbi Richard Jacobs participated in anti-Israeli demonstrations in Jerusalem organized by the Sheikh Jarrah Solidarity Movement. He also made controversial remarks regarding the Boycott, Divestment and Sanctions campaign against Israel. Behavior and declarations that might be tolerated in the United States as an expression of liberal indulgence and "constructive" criticism become significant political moves in the Middle East. Also, Reform leaders must recognize the difference between just sympathizing with Israel and being genuinely Zionist.

13. See Alan Wolfe's article entitled "Israel's Moral Peril" in *The Chronicle Review, The Chronicle of Higher Education*, Section B, March 30, 2012.

14. The European states' quest for freedom from religion has engendered a dual religious domination: an official secular religion and an unofficial affiliation of the public to the historic Christian denomination prevalent in each state. Many European countries acquiesce to the practices of religious minorities rather than allowing them to freely practice their religious beliefs. In some countries, religious minorities need special authorization to practice their faiths, which is provided on a selective basis (see Russia or Austria). For continuous religious conflicts in Europe, see the tense situation in the Balkans, Benelux, British Isles, France, Germany, Russia, even Scandinavia.

15. Some anti-Israeli organizations and some supporters of Hamas and of other terrorist groups are funded by covert European Union sources and extremist Islamic parties operating from Europe.

16. In an article published in *The Jewish Week* and reproduced at http://blogs.rj.org, August 27, 2009, Rabbi Eric Yoffie highlights the fragmented nature of the Israeli K–12 education. Education, like other cultural aspects of the country, definitely needs a revision in the twenty-first century. These initiatives need to be of, by, and for the Israelis. Reform contributions can be effective only when Reform presence in Israel will be substantive and perform as an integral part of the nation. In this framework, it would be helpful if the Reform movement would develop and adopt a comprehensive policy for a K–12 specific religious Reform education.

Chapter 15: **Being a Reform Jew:**
The Promises of Hope

> 21 For the upright will dwell in the land [forever], and the wholehearted will remain in it, 22 but the wicked will be cut off from the land, and the faithless uprooted from it.

Proverbs 3:21, 22

I am a Reform Jew. What do I expect from my religious faith?

Reform Judaism provides me with a Jewish faith-based spiritual environment that interprets the Jewish heritage according to a number of *promises* discussed in previous chapters. These promises may evolve and be adjusted but they must stay suitable to my Jewish environment. This suitability can be evaluated according to three criteria: *authenticity*, *relevance*, and *credibility*.

Eugene B. Borowitz, in discussing different opinions on our beliefs, provided me a coherent reference frame in support of the authenticity of Reform Judaism:

> I believe Torah arises from the relationship between God and the Jewish people, the Covenant, and I and other Jews are the living bearers of that relationship. As we accept the reality of God and identify our inner, personal reality with the Jewish people [by no means, thereby, sacrificing our individuality] we share in the relationship which creates contemporary Torah.[1]

In order to proceed from this frame of reference, it seems important to clarify four terms: *Torah, God, relationship,* and *living bearers.*

Let us start with the word "Torah." The common reference to the word "Torah" is Moses's five books. The key objective of these books was nation building: transforming a large group of ex-slaves into a coherent and cohesive people united by a shared culture, a common goal, and a clear set of disciplinary rules. A textual acceptance of this heritage in our time ignores the historic developments that have occurred in Judaism since the Torah was given to the Israelites and the settlement of the Promised Land.

A nation, a people, a culture evolves and adds additional layers to its heritage. For our ancestors, in the first century of the current counting, it was undisputable that Jews and Judaism are defined not only by the Torah but by a much broader statement of faith and cultural heritage represented by the carefully selected books included in the Tanach. This specific canonized collection includes highly controversial scriptures of exquisite literary quality, scriptures that tell their story with high eloquence and power of conviction. The Tanach's inspiring ethics and aesthetics indicate that there is much more in the Tanach than nation building. As such, we can see in the Tanach our foundation as a people, as a culture, and ultimately as our faith.

By recognizing the Tanach as the foundation of Judaism, we not only expand our perception of what we are and what we stand for, but also we expand our commitment to who we are and what is our covenant. In modern terms, we expand our spiritual contract to include realities that go beyond the original definitions of the Torah: the Tanach introduces us to existential challenges that confront our identity and offers diverse and complex life and faith options that are still relevant to our time. Considering this point of view, the whole Tanachic heritage becomes the cultural foundation that shapes our being as a people and can provide individual metaphysical inspiration due to its mythical messages, its aesthetic experiences, and its commentaries.

In addressing the Torah, we address Divinity's role. The Torah indicates the Almighty as one force, infinite and yet connected with humans. In the context of the creation of the nation and the shaping of the Torah, it is quite easy to understand why Moses needed the help of an authoritarian spirit. Moses's Divinity was not a recognizable idol, since idols can be patronized by the people. Mythology tells us that idols can multiply and can adopt individuals and that humans can become gods. This was the Egyptian precedent. Moses understood that such a personalization of the supreme authority could be divisive and defeat his purpose: a new nation with a new spirit, a new people with a new faith.

In the Torah the Almighty is invisible but quite evident and participatory; its presence is tested through acts of God. The Almighty is part of the environment, it appears as a cloud or as thunder, a bush or a miracle, and it physically empowers Moses.

The notion of God, the Almighty and its divine presence starts to evolve with the settling of the Promised Land. Later, the kingdom, and the evolving historic process of the migration of the Israelites out of their country, as well as their return and reconstruction, required new dimensions in understanding of the Almighty. After the original settling by the Israelis in *Eretz Israel*, the Almighty already seems to start to recede from its straightforward status and direct connection with its people. The tribes consolidated their condition and became less vulnerable. In life circumstances that were more secure, with less threatening challenges, divine intervention was not always necessary: people could solve their problems by themselves.

The revelation of the supreme power became more complicated and complex. Divinity transformed from an elementary force standing firm above its people into a complex, multifaceted spiritual concept. Jewish Divinity preserved its unified and unifying identity and its supporting power, but it added a multidimensional spirit that could address the intricate, conflicting, and contradictory issues challenging the people of Israel. In the Tanach, the supreme power is more elusive; it becomes more and more a perception and a vision fulfilling an inspirational role and a promise of hope. This spirit is conveyed to the people through messengers and leaders rather than direct acts of God. Yet, to complicate the matter, the Almighty might still be in direct contact with righteous commoners such as Job.

The history, the prophecies and the literature included in the Tanach attempt to illustrate the complexity of our Divinity. The complications and contradictions of the Tanachic notion of Divinity should actually not come as a surprise. The Jewish Divinity was defined from its inception as a complex entity. The term God in English does not capture the powerful essence of the Hebrew holy name that conveys the attribute of spatial infinity, dynamic evolution in time, and the open adaptation for changing conditions. The Tanachic Divinity does address all these perceptions and as such it enables Judaic Divinity to preserve its constant presence. It is hence this complex notion of Divinity that sustained its inspiration for generations that followed.

In regard to the notion of *relationship*, Borowitz adopts Buber's understanding of the relationship between Divinity and Jews. He presents it as a relation of love. Borowitz expands on his characterization of the love relationship by explaining that

because we share our people's historical relationship with God, Torah may start with us individually, but cannot end until it includes our people and a concern for its tradition.[2]

I feel that we can expand Borowitz's references to the "Torah" and "its tradition" to include the whole Jewish heritage, the Tanach, the Talmud, the connected vast body of commentaries attached to the oral tradition, and cultural contributions developed up to the present time. I believe this expansion is consistent with Borowitz's position and as such brings us to Reform Judaism.

Borowitz highlights that Reform Judaism recognizes its believers to be "living bearers" of the faith rather than observant followers. The notion of *living bearers* marks the radical change that occurred in Judaism due to the Enlightenment and the Jewish emancipation in the nineteenth century. Observant, orthodox followers of Judaism feel that they have to conform to a construct that is not only a divine concept but also a structured, committed real-life organization following strict traditional rules. The meaning of this distinction is quite obvious: as *living bearers* we are not compelled to conform to rigid authoritarian traditions and undisputed rabbinic ruling. We embrace our faith through conviction, out of our own free will, unconstrained, with an open mind and with love. We are replacing rigid regulations with a personal commitment to carry the burden of Jewish convictions. Such a position involves the constant participation in open and evolving dialogues based on the search for adequate answers that merge our beliefs in Jewish Divinity with contemporary spiritual challenges.

Orthodox Jews have the benefit of being immune to this debate due to the protective shield of their construct that separates them, in many ways, from the surrounding debates. The open paradigm of Reform Judaism is exposing Jews to challenging debates that constantly test, improve, and foster our faith. This position enables Reform Judaism to be an equal and distinguished partner in the global religious landscape, a partnership that provides a dignified and efficient promotion by example of Judaism.

Borowitz helps us understand the *authentic* nature of our faith. But, is our faith still *relevant* to the concerns of our time and the aspirations of our era?

A couple of factors come to mind in support of the relevance of our faith. One is the overwhelming pride and conviction that Reform Judaism has in Jewish history and traditions. Reform Judaism continuously adds to the existing heritage novel interpretations and commentary based on a modern freethinking approach to the scriptures and the Jewish heritage, open to the spirit of our time and place. This evolving body of Judaic commentary is instrumental in achieving current relevance.

Another relevant factor is the possibility Reform Judaism offers to conduct our spiritual life in an open-minded congregational format governed by a balanced dialogue between lay and rabbinic opinions. American Jewish Reform stemmed from a dual sense of individual and congregational empowerment. In essence this perception is highly relevant and still prevalent in our movement, though it is being challenged by groups interested in centralized power and bureaucratic control of our freedom of faith and our resources.

In the twenty-first century, an age of immediate individual participation through mass communication of information, the pluralistic, diverse essence of the movement becomes highly significant, inspiring, and effective. The new means of communication enable wide participation and dialogue, education, and organization on local and regional levels without centralized controls.

The twentieth century drastically changed the living circumstances of Judaism. On one hand we witnessed the physical destruction of our people in the Holocaust, the spiritual and physical oppression and corruption of our faith by the communist tyranny, and the extermination of the Jewish heritage in Islamic countries.

These crimes occurred while the world, including Reform Judaism, remained mostly silent. On the other hand, the Zionist dream came to be realized in the establishment and consolidation of the State of Israel. The relations to these historic events are two testing grounds for the *credibility* of the movement.

An additional factor affecting the credibility of the Reform movement is the way in which it applies its own standards of performance.

In previous chapters we discussed the contradictory relationship between the political agendas of the movement and its religious essence. Such contradictions and ethical double standards, deployed by the leadership on a variety of issues, harm the credibility of the movement. By distancing itself from politically loaded civic issues, Reform Judaism can take a more objective and impartial view of the issues. In this role congregations can review, discuss, and reflect on all aspects of the issues without taking sides. A rigorous implementation of this separation can provide Reform Judaism with a unique, ethical recognition within the contemporary religious mosaic and add moral authenticity and credibility to our faith.

Reform Judaism distinguishes itself from Orthodox Judaism by emphasizing the individual commitment to faith. It is through personal reflection and conviction to our faith that we realize our identity. It is this personal realization that enables us to engage in dialogues with other individuals who share or dispute our faith and identity.

Our congregations are as strong as the dialogue among the congregants is binding and inspiring. But we should not confuse a responsive dialogue with social action. Social action eliminates dialogue and replaces it with consent and compliance to a specific idea; it transforms the congregational assembly into a regimented crowd controlled by a single force or leader. Such a brainwashed crowd blurs its individual identity and responsibility; it replaces divine inspiration with the blind energy of the mob. Our Divinity does not expect regimentation. The strength of Reform Jewish Divinity stems from the continuous informed and inspiring dialogue between the spirit of the Almighty and the individual.

I believe that the majority of the Reform membership shares my belief in the discursive merit of our faith. The one-sided ideological position adopted by some national leaders is divisive and distorts the very *authenticity*, *relevance*, and *credibility* of Reform Judaism.

Can we mend ("repair") our credibility gap? And how?

I submit that mending our credibility would be a significant act of "repairing *our* world" for us and the Judaism we believe in. Credibility can be restored if we apply the unique tenets of our movement with honesty, clarity and rigor.

The first step in reforming our way of thinking is by recognizing previous mistakes. It is remarkable to point out a public recognition made by two outspoken advocates of social action on the dilemmas embedded in social justice. Albert Vorspan and Rabbi David Saperstein recognize that

> the certainties of yesterday have become the ambiguities and conflicts of today, especially when one right collides with another right. This is true for all Americans; for Jews only more so.[3]

Furthermore, they say,

> in these circumstances, we may have to walk a moral tightrope, yes, but we cannot escape our Jewish mission. With greater modesty and less certainty than in the past, with more tentativeness and greater tolerance for dissenting

views, we still bear our historic Jewish burden to face the world and its pain head-on; to engage in endless study and moral debate; to cherish human life and pursue justice; to enhance the life of the mind and to struggle to be God's partner in repairing this broken and incomplete world.[4]

This two passages indicate with considerable clarity the intrinsic confusion that pursuing social activism, social justice in particular, has brought to our faith. On one hand, the authors recognize that the issues are ambiguous and controversial and require more modesty and more tolerance for dissenting views. On the other hand, the authors continue to maintain that they seek to be "partners" with God and repair "this broken and incomplete world." Are these ambitious goals responsive to the recommended modesty and tentativeness? Why are they so confident that as Jews we have "to face the world and its pain head-on"? As Jews, a religion, a culture, a people, and a nation, we can be progressive and achieve improvement but we do not have to take responsibility for the whole world.

The two authors adopt a very confident position asserting that we, Reform Jews, know what is broken in this world and that our mission is to repair it. I wonder where this confidence comes from. We, and especially our leadership, were wrong on many issues discussed in previous chapters. The two authors themselves list issues in which the Reform leadership took controversial positions. We can be proud of our achievements and offer them as positive examples to others. It is absolutely wrong to impose "head-on" our views or achievements on others. As opposed to tikkun olam, Or Goim means illuminating the world, not burning the world.

A disappointing act that followed the publication of the article by Vorspan and Saperstein was the very assertive and arrogant 1999 CCAR Statement of Principles. The continuing statements and activities, up to the present, of the URJ and the RAC only confirm that the leadership has chosen the path of assertiveness rather than prudence, modesty, and tolerance. Right here we can find the path for improvement: let us learn with honesty and diligence from our failures and mistakes. Let us speak out without fear, with an open mind, without constraints. Let us listen to our critics with tolerance and humility. Let us focus on our constructive contributions, spiritual and real-life achievements, rather than destructive criticism for the sake of criticism. Modesty and tolerance require self-restraint and leadership by example, not assertive, controversial, divisive activism and demonizing rhetoric intended to "steer the flock."[5]

Ultimately, Reform Judaism is a dynamic spiritual path that should not be restrained by ideology or interested parties: Reform Judaism is the modern academy of Jewish Divinity intended to illuminate and inspire the thinking, the feeling and the actions of each participant in his or her own right. In this we can be inspired by Moses's leadership as recounted in the Torah.

Moses was and remains the ultimate prophet that "saw the Almighty face to face." And yet Moses was never anointed and his descendants did not get any privileges. In spite of his divine inspiration, Moses remains human and is never adorned by superpower mystic. Considering that leaders at the time, like Pharaoh, were revered as gods, with supernatural status, Moses's human status is remarkable. It is possible to detect in this rendering a clear intent not to create a personality cult. The Torah describes Moses as a man who had his hesitations and made mistakes.

We learn to see Moses as a determined leader, but ultimately as a *mensch*, a concerned human being, the role model for Jewish leadership. It is unfortunate that little of this aspect of the Torah has been promoted in Jewish and non-Jewish leadership inspired by the Holy Scriptures. Even in our time leaders are more inclined to pretend to have "immaculate" and supreme status not only in dictatorial regimes but also in democracies, in Jewish organizations and in Israel.

From this perspective it is difficult to sympathize with those in the Jewish Orthodox denominations who revere rabbis with blind submission. It is also disappointing and unacceptable to see some Reform leaders, from Rabbi Eisendrath to Rabbi Yoffie, adopting assertive positions bordering on arrogance in the name of our denomination. The Torah ends by praising Moses's humility and puts trust and power into its Chosen People to rise to the occasion, cross the Jordan and start a new future by themselves. Let us all remember, "Never again has there arisen in Israel a prophet like Moses, whom Hashem has known face to face."[6]

Our movement performs predominantly through local autonomous congregations. Preserving this grassroots concept is essential. However the vast geography of the country and the increasing alienation between the congregations and the national leadership has created a lack of dialogue and proper representation of the congregations' opinions on the national arena. Correcting this separation will require recognition that any national spokesperson or any support for a national policy must have a valid and verifiable confirmation from a significant majority of congregants in good standing. The system of representation and elections is still to be determined, but it has to be congregationally based, democratic, comprehensive, clear, accurate, transparent, and protective of the privacy of individuals. In our information age, such a process is feasible and can be devised economically with high efficiency and effectiveness.

The United States demonstrated that free people can build a free and creative civilization better than ever before. Its benefit is that it can be constantly improved and defended from forces of evil. Adopting a position that provides a worthwhile example (Or Goim), Reform Judaism can bring verifiable improvement, moral strength, and ethical integrity and, as such, convey a constructive, inviting, and unifying message of hope. In this context, leading by example means replacing the assertive message of social activism with a message of love: love of the Almighty, love of our Jewish heritage, and love of humanity. Love means the ability to share without losing one's identity, sharing between congregations, and sharing with other faiths.

Religious love is more than emotion: it is a spiritual exchange of values that provides criteria for solutions. It remains the mission of the American civic world to devise the applicable solutions. As Reform Jews we can be proud of our vision for sustaining and reinvigorating our faith in modern times. As Jews we stay humbled by our heritage and in awe of our divine inspiration.

Notes

1. See Borowitz, *Reform Judaism Today* 2:131.

2. See ibid., 2:130.

3. See Meyer and Plaut, *Reform Judaism Reader*, 159.

4. See ibid., 160.

5. The defensive and assertive attitude of the national Reform leadership is well illustrated by an exchange of opinions between Joel Alperson and Rabbi Eric Yoffie published in the *Intermountain Jewish News*, August 5, 2011, page 4. Mr. Alperson brought forward the argument that in his opinion Reform Judaism is in danger of becoming irrelevant because of the emphasis on tikkun olam and social justice. Mr. Alperson's position is this: "If Jews continue to prioritize these social-political efforts over proven religious

practices, we must have the courage to acknowledge that we have substituted all these secular causes for Judaism." Rabbi Yoffie's reply starts with "I have no patience for survival Judaism" and proceeds to highlight his opinion that "Social Justice is G-d mandated in precisely the same way that Shabbat observance and Torah study are G-d mandated." As a lay congregant I have a few concerns about this dialogue. Mr. Alperson's argument may be painful but it is legitimate and was expressed in a civil way. Rabbi Yoffie's reply was arrogant and dismissive, totally unfit to a civil dialogue. As for the holiness of social justice, I take offense and totally disagree. Shabbat observance is the topic of the fourth commandment. Justice (let alone "social") is not part of the Ten Commandments. Rabbi Yoffie quotes Jeremiah 9:24 and with all due respect, it does not stand up to the Torah test. For the sake of the argument, Rabbi Yoffie seems to confuse Tanachic justice with "social" justice, a modern qualifier of justice. In addition, Rabbi Yoffie ignores the conflict between social justice as a practice of Reform Judaism and Reform advocacy for the separation between church and state. As far as tikkun olam is concerned, let me remind the reader again that it is not a Tanachic notion but a Talmudic one of limited significance. I would like to direct the reader back to chapters 7, 8, and 9 for a more detailed discussion of these topics. Finally, it is disappointing to see the past president of URJ, a leading representative of our movement, adopting such a defensive and intolerant attitude toward a colleague and providing the readers with misleading opinions that bring into question his positions as a leader and a rabbi. It is hard to find in Rabbi Yoffie's reply the expected sense of open-minded dialogue we as Reform Jews constantly praise. Such an attitude can be most detrimental to the reputation and credibility of Reform Judaism.

6. Deuteronomy 34:10.

Chapter 16: **Jewish Reform Thriving:**
The Reform Galaxy

> The wise will shine like the radiance of the firmament, and those who teach righteousness to the multitudes [will shine] like the stars, for ever and ever.
>
> Daniel 12:3

European Reform Judaism emerged, evolved, and survived as a diverse and fragmented movement shaped and constrained by hostile political and religious environments. State religions, elitism, inherited privileges, and the misleading principle of "freedom *from* religion" were all operating against the essence of Reform Judaism. I believe the failure of the European Reform movement can be encapsulated in two key mistakes: (a) the futile attempts made by various components of the movement to transform its exceptional Jewish essence into a Universalist social action suitable to the whole world, and (b) the movement's acceptance of controversial secular ideas that blinded it to real-life developments of cardinal significance for Judaism.

The great achievement of the European Reform was its very survival throughout the nineteenth century and the beginning of the twentieth century, a survival that provided inspiration for the American Reform Judaism.

Did the Universalist mission of tikkun olam, with its social activism and political rhetoric, provide a constructive spiritual content in helping Jews in need in the last century? As mentioned before, the twentieth century offered several critical opportunities to test this mission. I have already briefly discussed the failure to provide substantive help in the tragic events that devastated our people in the last century. The active participation in the protests against the Vietnam War and the involvement in the civil rights movement show what we could have expected from the Reform movement if it had remained faithful to its religious mission. We did not see such actions regarding the Holocaust or the Jewish purges in the Soviet Union. We must point out that the support for the Jewish emigration from Russia was a Jewish, Israeli, and international effort, not specifically an item on the Reform movement agenda. In every critical situation of the twentieth century, the Reform movement failed to fulfill its stated objectives or make a significant difference. The message of tikkun olam, interpreted as Universalist social activism directed toward the world at large, remains a burden on the American Reform movement: it has dismissed Jewish particularism and blurred the ability of Reform Judaism to take a leading role in key Jewish challenges.

Yet, without much fanfare, Reform Judaism, reflecting the American spirit, has added to its Jewish heritage three significant framing tenets discussed in previous chapters of this work: (a) it is a grassroots movement of the Jewish people, by the Jewish people, for the Jewish people; (b) it embraced the freedoms of speech, of religion, and of unbiased justice for all under the constitutional law by voluntarily relinquishing judicial practices to the civic authority and formally adopting the principle of separation between church and state; and (c) Reform Judaism has relinquished the elitist European approach to religious thinking, with its authoritarian and exclusionary rulings toward religious practices, and institutionalized instead in its congregations, as its basic governance practice, the principle of "checks and balances" between lay and rabbinic leadership. In addition it established welcoming procedures for those interested in joining the Jewish heritage and the Jewish destiny.

By absorbing these tenets, the American Reform movement is evolving into a diverse "galaxy" of congregations spread all over North America. These autonomous congregations are becoming interconnected by multiple webs of shared interests, dialogues, and rituals on a local, regional, and national scale. By nurturing dialogues between faith and individuals, between individuals and the congregation, and among congregations, Reform Judaism can find reliable spiritual answers for our time. Reform Judaism recognizes its status as a distinct religious denomination in the Jewish religious spectrum. It does not compete for dominance in any religious sphere and it can inspire Jews and non-Jews by example—an example of ethical discourse, not political doing, of aesthetic enlightenment rather than physical intervention.

As Reform Jews we might want to recognize, in Buber's words, that

> true membership of a community includes the experience, which changes in many ways, and which can never be definitely formulated, of the boundary of this membership. ... With my choice and decision and action—committing or omitting, acting or persevering—I answer the word, however inadequately, yet properly; I answer for my hour. My group cannot relieve me of this responsibility, I must not let it relieve me of it: if I do, I pervert my relation of faith, I cut out of God's realm of power the sphere of my group ... In my decision I do not look away from the world, I look at it and into it, and before all I may see in the world, to which I have to do justice with my decision, my group to whose

welfare I cling; I may before all have to do justice to it, yet not as a thing in itself, but before the Face of God; and no programme, no tactical resolution, no command can tell me how I, as I decide, have to do justice to my group before the Face of God.[1]

In our faith, the dominant connection remains the connection between the individual and the Almighty, between us and our heritage. This connection rolls on and aggregates with other individuals, creating the human fabric that shapes our congregations and faith. In this context we need to recognize that a congregation is not a corporation but a voluntary association of people who share an idea, a religious commitment. Reform congregations are characterized by their freethinking and open-minded approach to faith and life. This open dialogue is sustained by the shared agreement that Reform Judaism operates of, by, and for the congregants and that its conduct is monitored by checks and balances between the lay and rabbinic leadership.

To reflect and foster this open-minded spirit, it might be helpful to democratize the congregations and make their operation more transparent. The current corporate management is quite patriarchal and opaque and stifles wider participation, in particular of young and new members. For the same reasons, the current application of the same corporate approach on the national level is definitely wrong and counterproductive.

In an era of instant communication, there is no need to be structured along stiff hierarchies and definitely not "unifying" stifling and wasteful national bureaucracies. Communications enable individuals and congregations to share resources and to seek and provide inspiration and support. The picture that we can envision here is of a conglomerate of separate entities that support each other through their "gravitational" fields. The shared interpretation of our heritage is the "gravity" force that keeps the network of Jewish Reform congregations together. No central force can or should dominate our spiritual and structural configuration and blur its aura. Service institutions, such as educational institutions, rabbinical seminaries, and research institutions, are necessary. Any such institutions should become additional "stars" in the "galaxy" but not dominant centers of gravity.

In a free, democratic, constitutional republic like ours based on limited government, well-informed congregations, versed in Jewish traditions with good discursive abilities, can best sustain and expand our faith, spirit, culture, and existence. Our responsive and sustainable identity can be enhanced by reforming the Union for Reform Judaism into a national council with a limited number of lay members, each elected for limited terms, as regional representatives of local groups of congregations. The office of chairperson may rotate among the council members, and the deliberations of the council should be public. The mission of the council should be the well-being and development of the movement. Any reference to political activity should be impartial and devoid of interfering activism or political lobbying.

On a similar note, the CCAR may adopt a representative model and focus its attention on issues of religious spiritual commitment and the preservation of the integrity of the religious tenets of Reform Judaism. The CCAR should promote Jewish faith-based ethical dialogues but refrain from overt or covert political content. The art in the religious dialogue is to delineate the boundary between ethics and politics.

Modern Reform Judaism is building on top of traditional Judaism, from which it inherits its complexity and to which it adds new dimensions. The open-ended spiritual opportunity and tolerance provided by Reform Judaism enables each congregation to become home to a specific modern Judaic vision while at same time enjoying the "galactic" vicinity and the affinity with other congregations of similar or different interpretations. The power of this paradigm is: (a) its moral integrity, spiritual richness, and open-minded Jewish religious understanding; and (b) a representative commitment to the rank and file, structural flexibility, and the ability to expand our membership.

We must emphasize again that the Tanach and the Jewish heritage remain at the center of our Judaic vision. The Tanach can be read simply as history while enjoying its quality as a literary masterpiece. We can read the Tanach for its descriptive imagery, envision the scenes, imagine and experience in our mind the dramas of its poetry and prose, absorb inspired scenarios, conceive thinking venues, and be exposed to symbolic forms. The appreciation of the beauty of the Tanachic message and language—in its storytelling and prophecy, in the proverbs and the lamentations, in its rhyme and prose—is key in establishing the foundation of this heritage. To appreciate best this heritage, it is imperative to achieve a command of the Hebrew language. Beyond the Tanach, our whole heritage is an extraordinary story of cultural evolution, an exceptional historic record, rich in achievements and masterpieces. In navigating the uncharted waters of modern faith, Reform Judaism, guided by the Jewish heritage, is powered by the energy of our constitutional freedoms and sparked by the inherited tradition of interpretations and reflection, commentary, and dialogue. I firmly believe that American Reform Judaism has the historic opportunity now to reconsider its own objectives and reform its vision by enhancing its unique spirit of faith.

American Reform Judaism with a free, balanced, authentic, relevant, and credible Jewish divine faith-based religious spirit and practices, liberated from political commitments, can generate a timely faith paradigm for our era based on its pluralistic and participatory nature that is evolving through learning and innovative customs, faith, and peace of mind (or *Gemut*).

This paradigm needs to be shaped by the active contributions and creative participation of both congregants and rabbis. The mission of our rabbis is to inspire and catalyze this participation by developing creative and constructive dialogues that preserve the Jewish divine religious faith separate from, but not ignorant of, the civic life. The contribution of congregants to the dialogue can include, but not be limited to, real-life critical thinking enriched by an educated knowledge of the Jewish heritage. The Jewish heritage, from the Tanach and Hillel the Sage, Maimonides and Rashi, Mendelssohn and Geiger, Ahad Haam and Buber, to our contemporary thinking, offers a vast source of inspiration to improve, adjust, and reform our faith. In my mind, this process makes us a unique constituency: a constituency that chooses and accepts to be part of the Reform challenge. Success in the pursuit of this challenge will lead us toward realizing our aspirations to become *"Am Sgula"* (an excellent people) and as such to be an example, a light to all people—Or Goim.

Notes

1. "The Question of the Single One," in Buber, *Between Man & Man*, 92.

Glossary

Note: *The definitions detailed below were selected and compiled by the author from various sources and express the author's opinion on the notions.*

Capitalism: A type of political regime based on a supply-and-demand competitive market performance. A capitalistic society requires an educated constituency, a democratic electoral system, separation between institutions of government, and checks and balances between governmental operations. Capitalism offers individual opportunity in a mobile society with a competitive culture aimed at rewarding success based on innovative ideas and personal abilities.

Communism: Socialist regime based on the governing belief that all individuals are entitled to receive rewards according to their needs and to perform according to their abilities. Communism failed to achieve its goal as a result of is faulty economic rational.

Divinity: The belief in a metaphysical, omnipresent existence; "God Almighty."

Ecology: The study of the relationships between organisms and the environment.

Ethology: The study of the relationships between animals, including humans.

Faith: Honest, strong belief.

Halacha: Jewish traditional law codex.

Haredi: Orthodox Jews (Israel).

Haskala: General education (Hebrew). The Haskala movement promoted the adoption of the ideas of the Enlightenment and the popularization of the Hebrew language.

Liberalism:	In the United States (currently): synonymous with socialism; Classical: laissez-faire, unrestrained capitalism; general: freethinking, entrepreneurial orientation.
Maskil[im]:	In Hebrew: educated person (persons). The notion referred to Jews who acquired a general academic education as part of the Jewish Enlightenment.
Masorti:	Conservative, close to Orthodox Jews (Israel).
Phenomenology:	The study of the conscious experience perceived from the subjective or first-person point of view.
Progressive:	In the United States (currently), an ambiguous term indicating Socialist tendencies.
Religion:	A system of faith and worship based on a set of beliefs with cultural implications. Divine religion subscribes to the belief in a transcendental, omnipresent, metaphysical existence. Non-divine religions subscribe to the belief in specific cosmic forces such as nature. Religious idolatry is subscribing to the belief in discrete mythical, superhuman powers, heroes, or personalities. Secular religions, such as Marxism and environmentalism, are based on non-metaphysical ideas adopted as beliefs.
Science:	Knowledge acquired through observation, experimentation, and verification of physical facts. *Science of religion*: a scientific study of religions. *Science as religion*: a pseudo-scientific study that replaces facts with beliefs.
Socialism:	A type of political regime based on governmentally planned and controlled use and allocation of resources according to predetermined standards of need, performance, and rewards. Socialism requires individuals to conform to regulations and standards established by a career bureaucracy unaccountable to the public. Governing standards are conceived according to scientific knowledge whose scientific validity is determined by the career bureaucracy. Socialism offers uniformity of ideas, little or no competition, and an equalized, economic safety net based on pre-established standards of living. Democracy is not a prerequisite for socialism.

Tanach:	The Hebrew Bible (*Torah Neviim Ktuvim*), a selection of Hebrew scriptures canonized after the destruction of the Second Temple and divided into three main parts: the Torah, the five books dedicated to religion and nation building; the *Neviim* (Book of Prophecies); and the *Ktuvim*, a collection of literary and philosophical books.
Torah:	The first five books of the Tanach, the books attributed to Moses.
Welfare state:	State governance pursuing a diluted Socialist model focused on extensive entitlements.

Bibliography

Books

Aron, R. *The Opium of the Intellectuals*. New Brunswick, NJ: Transaction Publ., 2003.

Bell, Clive. *Civilization*. England: Penguin Books, 1947.

Bernstein, Richard J., ed. *Habermas and Modernity*. Cambridge, MA: MIT Press, 1994.

Bloom, Allan. *The Closing of the American Mind*. New York: Simon & Schuster, 1987.

Blumenfeld, S. L. *Is Public Education Necessary?* Powder Springs, GA: The American Vision Inc., 2010.

Borowitz, Eugene B. *Reform Judaism Today*. New York: Behrman House, 1983.

Braunfels, Wolfgang. *Urban Design in Western Europe: Regime and Architecture, 900–1900*. Translated by Kenneth J. Northcott. Chicago: Univ. of Chicago Press, 1988.

Buber, Martin. *Between Man & Man*. London: The Fontana Library, 1961.

Deleuze, Gilles. *The Fold: Leibniz and the Baroque*. Minneapolis, MN: Univ. of Minnesota Press, 1993.

Diggins, J. P. *The Promise of Pragmatism*. Chicago: Univ. of Chicago Press, 1994.

Dimont, Max I. *Jews, God and History*. New York: Simon & Schuster/Signet, 1962.

Feiner, Shmuel. *The Jewish Enlightenment*. Translated by Chaya Naor. Jewish Culture and Contexts series. Philadelphia: Univ. of Pennsylvania Press, 2003.

_____. *Moses Mendelssohn*. New Haven, CT: Yale Univ. Press, 2010.

Feyerabend, P. *Farewell to Reason*. London: Verso, 1988.

Fromm, E. *Fear of Freedom*. London: Routledge, 1942.

Furbank, P. N. *Reflections on the Word "Image."* London: Secker & Warburg, 1970.

Gelernter, David H. *Judaism: A Way of Being*. New Haven, CT: Yale Univ. Press, 2009.

Gibson, J. J. *The Ecological Approach to Visual Perception*. Boston: Houghton-Mifflin, 1979.

Gombrich, E. H. *Symbolic Images*. London/New York: Phaidon, 1978.

Gray, J. *Isaiah Berlin*. Princeton, NJ: Princeton Univ. Press, 1997.

Greer, C. *The Great School Legend: A Revisionist Interpretation of American Public Education*. New York: Basic Books, Inc., 1972.

Hall, E. T. *The Hidden Dimension*. New York: Doubleday, 1969.

Horner, Christopher C. *Red Hot Lies*. Washington, DC: Regnery Publ., 2008.

Jaspers, K. *Chiffren der Transzendenz*. Munich: Piper, 1970.

_____. *Introduction a la philosophie*. Paris: Librairie Plon, 1965.

Jeynes, William. *Religion, Education, and Academic Success*. Research on Religion and Education series. Information Age Publishing, 2003.

Kaplan, Dana E. *Contemporary American Judaism*. New York: Columbia Univ. Press, 2009.

Lyotard, Jean-Francois. *Postmodern Fables*. Minneapolis, MN: Univ. of Minnesota Press, 1997.

Mamet, David. *The Secret Knowledge*. New York: Sentinel-Penguin Group, 2011.

————. *The Wicked Son: Anti-Semitism, Self-Hatred, and the Jews*. New York: Schocken, 2006.

Marquard, Odo. *Farewell to Matters of Principle: Philosophical Studies*. Oxford: Oxford Univ. Press, 1989.

————. *In Defense of the Accidental*, Oxford: Oxford Univ. Press, 1991.

McCloskey, Deirdre N. *The Bourgeois Virtues*. Chicago: Univ. of Chicago Press, 2006.

Meyer, Michael A. *Response to Modernity*. Detroit, MI: Wayne State Univ. Press, 1995.

Meyer, Michael A., and W. Gunther Plaut, compilers. *The Reform Judaism Reader: North American Documents*. New York: UAHC Press, 2001.

Mumford, L. *The City in History*. London: Penguin, 1966.

Osborne, H., ed. *Aesthetics*. Oxford: Oxford Univ. Press, 1979.

Popper, K. *The Open Society and Its Enemies*. Princeton, NJ: Princeton Univ. Press, 1971.

Samuels, Andrew. *Jung and the Post-Jungians*. London/New York: Routledge & Kegan Paul, 1985.

Schorske, C. E. "The Idea of the City in European Thought: Voltaire to Spengler." In *The Historian and the City*, edited by O. Handlin and J. Burchard, 95–114. Cambridge, MA: MIT Press, 1970.

Spotts, Frederic. *The Shameful Peace: How French Artists and Intellectuals Survived the Nazi Occupation*. New Haven, CT: Yale Univ. Press, 2008.

The *Tanach* translation used is *The Stone Edition*, General Editors: Rabbi Nosson Scherman and Rabbi Meir Zlotowitz, published by Mesorah Publications Ltd., 1998.

Tocqueville, Alexis de. *Democracy in America*. New York: Vintage Books, 1945.

Tuchman, Barbara W. *A Distant Mirror: The Calamitous 14th Century*. New York: Knopf, 1978.

Articles, Statements, and Reports

Beinart, P. "The Jewish Case for School Vouchers." *Wall Street Journal*, March 30, 2012.

Brooks, D. "Let's Occupy Ourselves." In *New York Times* and *Denver Post*, October 12, 2011.

Burnstein, C. "The Ever-Evolving Faith." *Reform Judaism* (Summer 2011): 42–47.

Carvalho, A. M., and S. L. Paine. "Strategies for Rescuing Failing Public Schools: How Leaders Create a Culture of Success." Policy Paper. McGraw-Hill Research Foundation, 2011.

Central Conference of American Rabbis. "Commentary on the Principles for Reform Judaism," October 27, 2004. Available at http://www.ccarnet. org.

———. "A Statement of Principles for Reform Judaism," adopted May 26, 1999. Available at http://www.ccarnet.org.

Coulson, A. J. "The Impact of Federal Involvement in America's Classrooms." Cato Institute, February 2011.

Ellenson, David. "Reform Judaism Isn't an Island," Opinion. *Jewish Daily Forward*, March 25, 2011. Posted March 16, 2011, at http://forward.com/ articles/136236/reform-judaism-isn-t-an-island/.

Englander, Lawrence A. "In Search of Belonging." *Reform Judaism* (Summer 2011).

Eshkoli (Wagman), Hava. "The Zionist Aspect of Religious-Zionist Policy in Palestine in View of the Holocaust." *Yad Vashem Studies* 29 (2001).

Hausman, Matthew M. "Reform Angst Regarding Israel and Jewish Nationalism." Article posted by Ted Belman on June 26, 2011, on www.israpundit.com. Available at http://www.israpundit.com/archives/37269.

Hunsaker, R. "Social Justice: An Inconvenient Irony." Posted September 17, 2008, at http://sjirony.blogspot.com (and identified as reprint of "Counseling Today OpEd, April 2008").

Hunsaker, Robert C. "Counseling and Social Justice." *Academic Questions* 24, no. 3 (Fall 2011): 319–40, doi: 10.1007/s12129-011-9242-y.

Kaplan, Dana E. "Reform Jewish Theology and the Sociology of Liberal Religion in America: The Platforms as Response to the Perception of Socioreligious Crisis." *Modern Judaism* 20 no. 1 (2000): 60–77.

Leon, Abram. *The Jewish Question*, chap. 4, "The Jews in Europe after the Renaissance," http://wwwmarxists.org/subject/jewish/leon/ch4.htm.

Livni (Langer), Michael. *Reform Zionism*. Jerusalem: Gefen publishing house. Available at http://www.michael-livni.org.

MacCoun, Robert J. "Biases in the Interpretation and Use of Research Results." *Annual Review of Psychology* 1998, vol. 49.

Mamet, David. "Israel, Isaac and the Return of Human Sacrifice: Why Have Liberal Westerners Turned Their Backs on the Jewish State?" Opinion. *Wall Street Journal*, December 13, 2011.

McConnell, Michael W. "Washington Wants a Say Over Your Minister," *Wall Street Journal*, October 5, 2011.

McDonald, P. R. "Compton Parents Petition to Take Over Chronically Failing Public School through 'Parent Trigger' Law, Sends Shock Waves throughout the Nation." *LA Weekly*, December 8, 2011.

Meyer, Michael A. "History: Confronting Crisis." *Reform Judaism* (Fall 2009).

Nathan-Kazis, Josh. "Liberal Denominations Face Crisis as Rabbis Rebel, Numbers Shrink." *Jewish Daily Forward*, February 18, 2011.

Nestor, Kevin. "A Great Trust Betrayed: The Politicization of America's Public Campuses." *Academic Questions* 24 no. 2 (Summer 2011): 194–208.

Neumann, J. "Occupy Wall Street and the Jews." *Commentary*, January 2012.

Oberheim, Eric, and Paul Hoyningen-Huene. "The Incommensurability of Scientific Theories." *Stanford Encyclopedia of Philosophy* (Spring 2009 Edition), archived at http://plato.stanford.edu/archives/fall2010/entries/incommensurability/.

Rosenblatt, G. "Alienation from Israel Hitting Liberal Seminaries" in *Intermountain Jewish News*, May 13, 2011.

Rothman, Stanley, S. Robert Lichter, and Neil Nevitte. "Politics and Professional Advancement among College Faculty." *The Forum*, Vol. 3, Issue 1, Article 2 (Berkeley Electronic Press, 2005), available at http://www.bepress.com/forum.

Sacks, Jonathan. "Reversing the Decay of London Undone," Essay. *Wall Street Journal*, August 20, 2011.

Scruton, Roger. "T. S. Eliot as Conservative Mentor." *Intercollegiate Review* (Fall 2003/Spring 2004): 53.

Spero, Aryeh. "What the Bible Teaches about Capitalism." *Wall Street Journal*, January 30, 2012.

Vincent, C. Paul. "The Voyage of the *St. Louis* Revisited." *Holocaust Genocide Studies* (Fall 2011) 25 (2): 252–89, doi: 10.1093/hgs/dcr038.

Wallison, P. J. "Wall Street's Gullible Occupiers." *Wall Street Journal*, October 12, 2011.

Weidhorn, Peter. "The Chairman's Perspective." *Reform Judaism* (Summer 2011).

Wertheimer, Jack. "What Does Reform Judaism Stand For?" *Commentary* (June 2008), http://www.commentarymagazine.com/article/what-does-reform-judaism-stand-for/.

Wolfe, A. "Israel's Moral Peril." *The Chronicle Review, The Chronicle of Higher Education*, Section B, March 30, 2012.

Wuerl, D., C. Colson, and C. Y. Soloveichik. "United We Stand for Religious Freedom." *Wall Street Journal*, February 10, 2012.

Miscellaneous Publications

Ames, Rachel Aliza. "The Private School Voucher Debate in the Jewish American Community: A Window into a Greater *American* Question." Senior thesis, Barnard College, April 18, 2007, http://history.barnard. edu/sites/default/files/inline/rachelames-thesis.pdf.

"Betrayed—Why Public Education is Failing." betrayed-whyeducationisfailing. blogspot.com.

"France Acknowledges Responsibility for Deportation of Jews during Holocaust." Article in The Jewish Virtual Library, February 16, 2009, http://www.jewishvirtuallibrary.org/jsource/Holocaust/francedeps. html.

"John Adams and the French Debate the American Constitution." *Online Library of Liberty*, Liberty Fund, Inc., Indianapolis, Indiana.

Opinion exchange between Joel Alperson and Rabbi Eric Yoffie published in the *Intermountain Jewish News*, August 5, 2011, 4.

"Treat Antizionist Rabbinic Students Like the Four Sons." *Center Field blog*, Blogs.jpost.com, April 20, 2011.

Union for Reform Judaism. *Cultivating the Future: Long-Range Planning for Congregations* (1999, updated 2006), available at http://urj.org//cong/ finance//?syspage=document&item_id=14861.

————. "What Is Reform Judaism?" As posted at http://urj.org/about/ reform/whatisreform/.

Yoffie, Eric. Address to Union of American Hebrew Congregations, 65th General Assembly, Orlando, Florida, December 1999, available at http:// www.urj.us/orlando/speakers/ysermon.shtml.

Index

German-educated, 39
as leaders, 110
as moderators of dialogues, 109–10
ordained, 109
Orthodox, 104, 165n2
Reform, 104
reformist, 19
role of Reform, 41–42, 71–72, 141
spiritual Jerusalem and, 192–93
RAC. *See* Religious Action Center
Reformed Society of Israelites, 35
Reform Judaism
American, 32–51, 113–29, 226–27
belonging to, 187–88
communication about, 228–29
Dana Kaplan and, 85n7
description of, 2–6
in Europe, 194–95, 225–26
expectations, 212–24
goals of, 153
governance of, 101–12
historic goal of, 5
interpretation of, 212–13
leadership, 102–3
leaders of, 102, 151
as living bearers of, 216
pursuit of happiness and, 187–93
as a religious denomination, 130–45
Zionism and, 194–211
Reform Judaism, 108
Reform Judaism Today, 32
Religion
constitutional status of, 91
definition of, 234
discrimination against, 98–99n1
freedom from, 16, 90
freedom of, 100n7, 130
love versus emotion, 223
religious perception, 72–73n3
rituals and practices, 176–85, 192
separation from state, 87–100, 122
social action and, 130–45
Religious Action Center (RAC), 4, 46–
47, 86n8, 94–95, 117, 137
Response to Modernity (Meyer), 25,
129n13
Rice, Abraham, 35
Richardson, H. H., xiv

Rituals and practices, 176–85, 192. *See
also* Culture
aesthetic enrichment, 181–82
ceremonies, 179–80
dancing, 179
media and, 180
praying, 176
singing, 179
technology and, 178–79
through art, 180–81
written word, 177–78
Roosevelt, Franklin D., 42, 138, 144n9
Rosh Chodesh, 156
Rothschild, Baron, 17
Russia, 17–18

S

Sacks, Rabbi Jonathan, 150–51
Saperstein, Rabbi David, 219–20
Scandinavian welfare model, 46
Science, definition of, 234
Scruton, Roger, 56
The Secret Knowledge (Mamet), 146
Selfish person, 50n28
Shabbat, 156
Shalom, Gershom, 196
Sheikh Jarrah Solidarity Movement,
210n12
Silver, Abba Hillel, 44, 195
Sinai desert, 79–80
Singing, 179
Six Day War of 1967, 47–48, 53,
129n13, 198
Social action, 130–45, 218–19. *See also*
Politics
activism of, 133
origins of, 131–32
riots, 143n2
Socialism, 31n29
during the 1950s, xi
definition of, 234
Israeli, 196–97
Social justice, 146–54, 154n7, 223–
24n5. *See also* Politics
activists of, 149, 152
in economic and cultural terms, 150
meaning of, 146
notion of, 148

CPSIA information can be obtained at www.ICGtesting.com
Printed in the USA
LVOW11*1949110215

426642LV00008B/293/P